APACHE

ED MACY
APACHE

Harper
Press

Harper*Press*
An imprint of HarperCollins*Publishers*
77–85 Fulham Palace Road
Hammersmith, London W6 8JB
www.harpercollins.co.uk

Visit our authors' blog: www.fifthestate.co.uk

First published in Great Britain by Harper*Press* in 2008

Copyright © Ed Macy 2008

1

Ed Macy asserts the moral right to
be identified as the author of this work

A catalogue record for this book
is available from the British Library

HB ISBN 978-0-00-728816-8
TPB ISBN 978-0-00-728818-2

Typeset in Minion

Maps © HarperPress
Drawn by HL Studios

Printed and bound in Great Britain by Clays Ltd, St Ives plc

Mixed Sources
Product group from well-managed
forests and other controlled sources
www.fsc.org Cert no. SW-COC-1806
© 1996 Forest Stewardship Council

FSC

FSC is a non-profit international organisation established to promote the
responsible management of the world's forests. Products carrying the FSC
label are independently certified to assure consumers that they come
from forests that are managed to meet the social, economic and
ecological needs of present or future generations.

Find out more about HarperCollins and the environment at
www.harpercollins.co.uk/green

This is dedicated to
Mathew Christopher Ford.

CONTENTS

LIST OF ILLUSTRATIONS

Photographs not credited below have kindly been supplied by the author. While every effort has been made to trace the owners of copyright material reproduced herein, the publishers would like to apologise for any omissions and will be pleased to incorporate missing acknowledgments in any future editions.

The Apache's CRV-7 Flechette rockets: Image by Corporal Mark
Ballantyne RLC; © Crown Copyright/MOD. Reproduced with
the permission of the Controller of Her Majesty's Stationery
office.

The Apache's M230 30mm underslung chain gun: Image by
Corporal Mark Ballantyne RLC; © Crown Copyright/MOD.
Reproduced with the permission of the Controller of Her
Majesty's Stationery office.

Ed and Trigger with Hambly reconnecting Ugly 51's gun: Si
Hambly.

Hellfire at the back, rockets in the sangar and 30mm HEDP being
loaded by Si: Si Hambly.

The infamous Rocco: Rocco Seffredi.

Page 6 and 7:

A Taliban commander talks on a radio carrying an RPG launcher
and spare rockets: AP Photo/ Zaheerudding Abdullah.

The IRT pair returning from a mission empty: Gerban Van Es.

Arming Teams 3 and 4: Si Hambly.

SECOND PLATE SECTION

Page 1:

Ammo Sgt Kev Blundell paying his respects on Christmas Day:
Sgt Kev Blundell.

A message for the Taliban at Koshtay from arming point 2: Si
Hambly.

Ed and Carl's Hellfire page: SSgt Carl Bird.

Pages 2 and 3:

An Afghan National Policeman overlooking the Lashkar Gah
Green Zone: AFP/ Getty Images.

Rockets fired in quads: © Crown Copyright/MOD. Reproduced with the permission of the Controller of Her Majesty's Stationery Office.

Hellfire fired by Ugly Five One and guided by Ugly Five Zero at Jugroom Fort: © Crown Copyright/MOD. Reproduced with the permission of the Controller of Her Majesty's Stationery Office.

Pages 4 and 5:

Mountains that surround Now Zad and the Green Zone: LCpl Mathew Ford RM.

The rescue team for Jugroom Fort: Sgt Garry Stanton, RAF.

The rescue briefing in the desert: Sgt Garry Stanton, RAF.

Lt Col Rob Magowan MBE RM – the loneliness of command: Sgt Garry Stanton, RAF.

On the wings of the Apache ready to go: Sgt Garry Stanton, RAF.

Ugly Five One with Capt Dave Rigg and Mne Chris Fraser-Perry riding to the Fort: Sgt Garry Stanton, RAF.

Ugly Five Zero with RSM Hearn, filmed by Ugly Five One: © Crown Copyright/MOD. Reproduced with the permission of the Controller of Her Majesty's Stationery Office.

Pages 6 and 7:

A true account of the rescue by the military artist David Rowlands, Ed Macy (with pistol) in front of Mathew Ford: David Rowlands.

The Jugroom Fort before and after January 15th: © Crown Copyright/MOD. Reproduced with the permission of the Controller of Her Majesty's Stationery Office.

Taliban village next to Jugroom Fort before and after January 15th: © Crown Copyright/MOD. Reproduced with the permission of the Controller of Her Majesty's Stationery Office.

Page 8:

3 Flight – Charlotte, Darwin and Nick where the marines strapped onto the Apache during the Jugroom Fort rescue, and FOG: Si Hambly.

Investiture ceremony at Buckingham Palace: Charles Green Photography.

Lance Corporal Mathew Ford, Royal Marines: LCpl Mathew Ford RM.

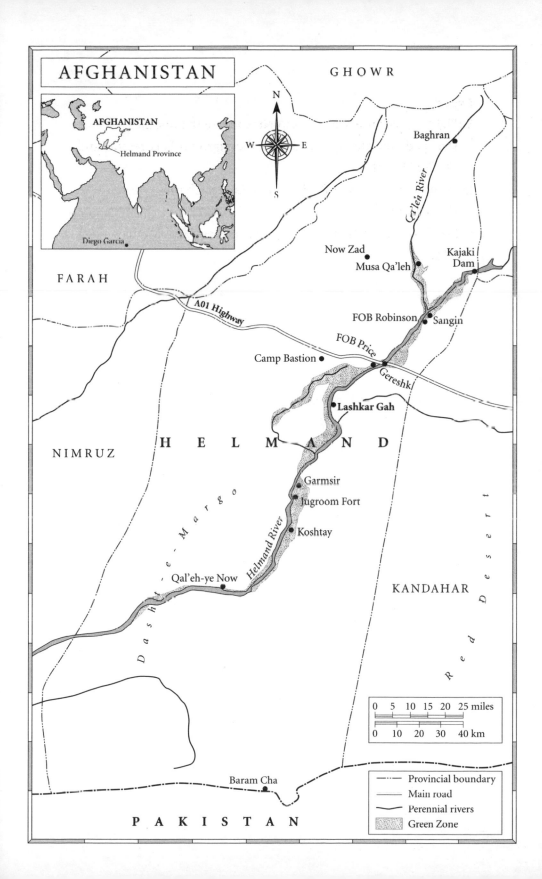

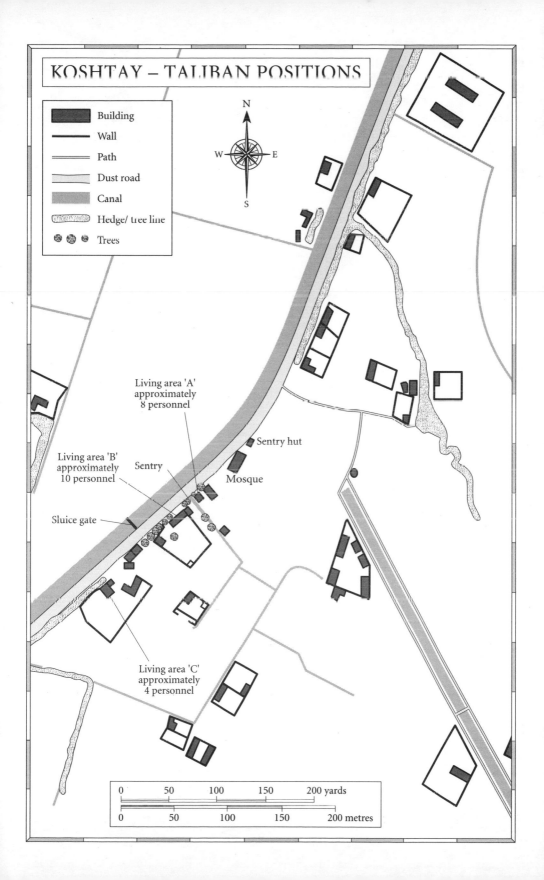

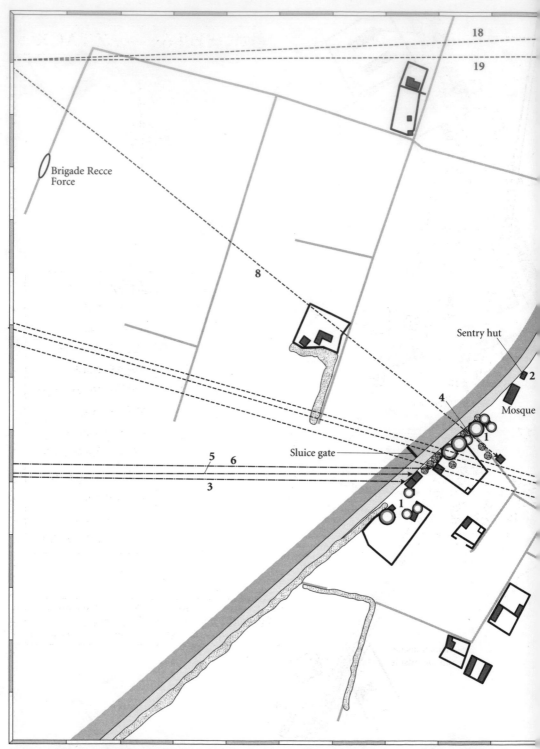

Sequence of events: (1) B1 Lancer bomber drops four 2000 lb and six 500 lb bombs. (2) Ugly Five Zero kill the northern sentry in the sentry hut. (3) Ugly Five One destroys the southern half of a double building. (4) Ugly Five Zero kills the second sentry in his position by the wall. (5 and 6) On the same run Ugly Five One Hellfires the northern half of the double building and then a sentry hut in depth. (7 and 8) Ugly Five Zero kills a leaker escaping from the mosque to the east and then Hellfires the last remaining building on the target. Mission success – the first AAC Deep Raid. (9) Apaches radioed and told of senior Taliban

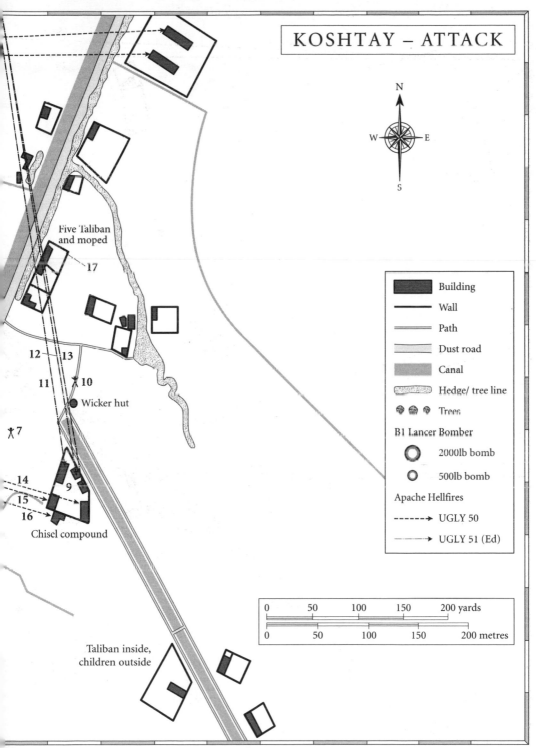

KOSHTAY – ATTACK

N
W — E
S

Legend:

- Building
- Wall
- Path
- Dust road
- Canal
- Hedge/ tree line
- Trees

B1 Lancer Bomber
- 2000lb bomb
- 500lb bomb

Apache Hellfires
- ----→ UGLY 50
- ----→ UGLY 51 (Ed)

Five Taliban and moped

17

12 13
11 10
Wicker hut

7

14
15
16
9
Chisel compound

Taliban inside, children outside

| 0 | 50 | 100 | 150 | 200 yards |
| 0 | 50 | 100 | 150 | 200 metres |

commanders in a chisel compound. (10) Ugly Five One kills a Taliban man running south towards the chisel compound. (11 to 13) Ugly Five One destroys the three northerly buildings at the chisel compound with three remaining Hellfire. (14 to 16) Ugly Five Zero destroys the three southerly buildings at the chisel compound. Mission success – No one escaped – Taliban commanders destroyed. (17) A further radio mission is sent and Ugly Five One kill five Taliban with Flechette rockets. (18 and 19) Ugly Five Zero uses his last two remaining Hellfires on two big sheds northeast up the canal.

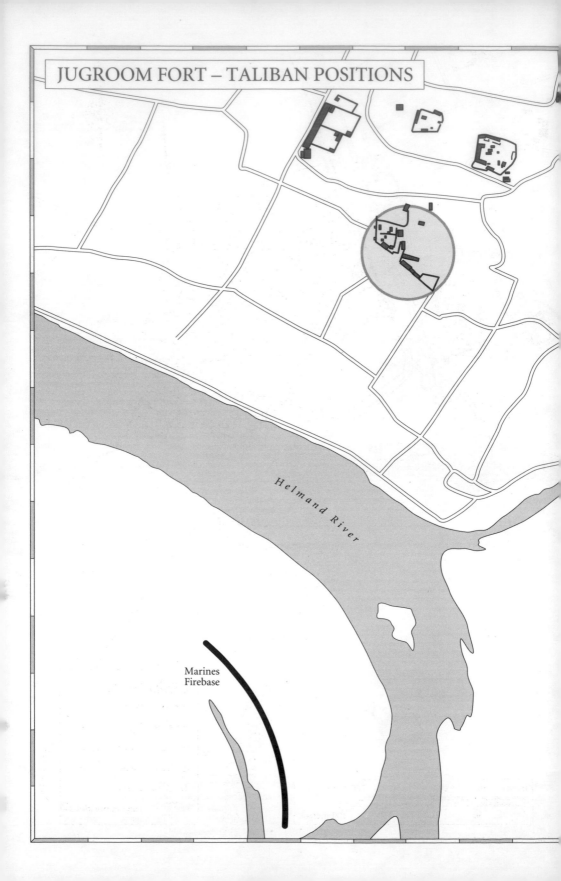

JUGROOM FORT – TALIBAN POSITIONS

Helmand River

Marines
Firebase

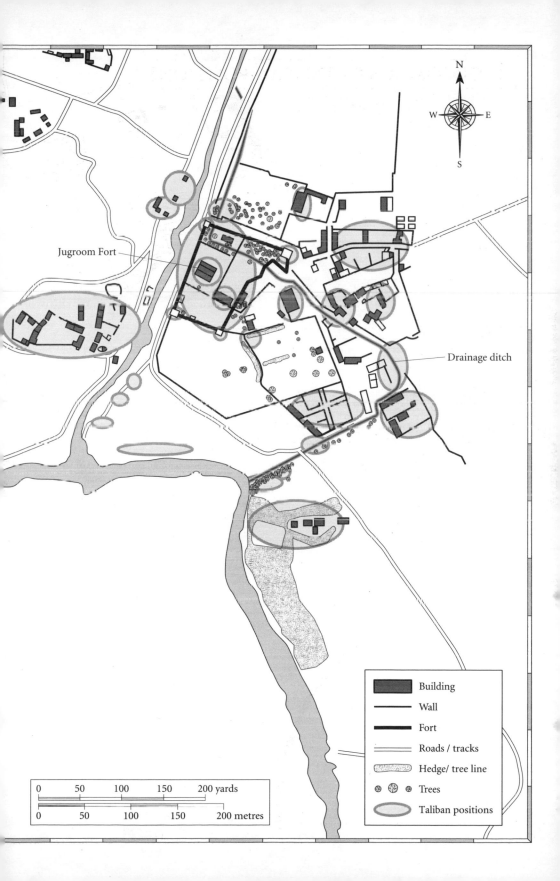

Jugroom Fort

Drainage ditch

	Building
	Wall
	Fort
	Roads / tracks
	Hedge/ tree line
	Trees
	Taliban positions

N
W   E
S

| 0 | 50 | 100 | 150 | 200 yards |
| 0 | 50 | 100 | 150 | 200 metres |

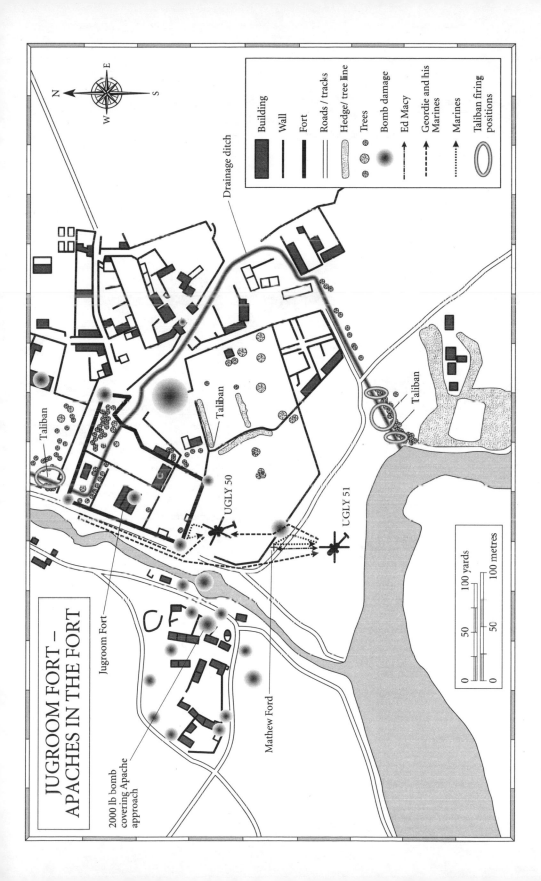

JUGROOM FORT –
APACHES IN THE FORT

Legend:

- Building
- Wall
- Fort
- Roads / tracks
- Hedge/ tree line
- Trees
- Bomb damage
- Ed Macy
- Geordie and his Marines
- Marines
- Taliban firing positions
- Drainage ditch

Jugroom Fort

2000 lb bomb covering Apache approach

Mathew Ford

Taliban

Taliban

Taliban

UGLY 50

UGLY 51

100 yards

100 metres

N
E
S
W

0   50   100 metres
0   50   100 yards

AIRFRAME

130. Left Environmental Control System (ECS) Evaporator
131. Left Main Landing Gear Wire Cutter
132. Main Wheel
133. Left ECS Compressor
134. Left Extended Forward Avionics Bay (EFAB)
135. Window Ejection Miniature Detonating Cord
136. Armoured Co-pilot Gunners Seat
137. Armoured Pilots Seat
138. Upper Wire Cutter
139. Storage Bay with Bin Removed
140. ECS Evaporator Bay Panel
141. Left Wing
142. Main Rotor Gearbox
143. No.1 Engine Nose Gearbox
144. No.1 Engine Bay – ECU Removed
145. Engine Nacelle in Servicing Position
146. Footsteps
147. Stowage Compartment

ROLLS ROYCE/TURBOMECA RTM322 01/12 MK120

Apache AH MK1 Port view

148. Rear Fuselage Footsteps
149. Castoring Tailwheel
150. Moving Horizontal Stabilator
151. Tail Rotor Hub
152. Tail Rotor Hydraulic Servo
153. Tail Rotor Gearbox
154. Intermediate Gearbox and Cooling Fan
155. Tail Drive Shafts
156. Main Rotor Blade
157. Catwalk Access Panel
150. Pre-cooler By-pass Exhaust

159. Catwalk Access Panels
160. Main Rotor Head
161. Integrated De-ice De-rotational Unit
162. MRB Strap Packs
163. Swash Plate Assembly and Scissor Links
164. Static Rotor Mast
165. Left Transmission Air Cooling Intake
166. Pilots and Co-Pilot Gunners Integrated Helmet and Display Sight System
167. Canopy Jettison – Miniature Detonating Cord
168. Pilots Crew Station Access
169. Co-pilot Gunner Crew Station Access Door

ELECTRICAL/AVIONIC
230. Left Aft Missile Warning Sensor
231. Rear Left Laser Warning Receiver
232. Left Flare Dispenser

233. Left Wing Intercommunication Receptacle
234. Left Wing Formation Light
235. Laser Warning Receiver Left Upper
236. CTS Dummy Missile
237. Centre EFAB Electronics Bay
238. Forward EFAB Electronics Bay
239. Left Forward RWR Quadrant Receiver
240. Left Forward MW Sensor
241. TADS Day Sensor Assembly
242. Target Acquisition & Designation Sight (TADS)
243. TADS Night Sensor
244. Pilot Night Vision Senor (PNVS)
245. Embedded GPS Bays (Left and Right)
246. CTS GPS Antenna
247. Outside Air Temperature Probe
248. Static Vent
249. Radar Frequency Interferometer
250. Fire Control Radar (FCR) Mast Mounted Assembly (MMA)

ARMAMENT
301. M230EI 30mm Chain Gun
302. Hellfire Missiles
303. 70mm Rocket Pod
304. Chaff Dispenser

Apache AH MK1 Starboard view

232
231 **230** **229**
125
125
ZJ173
125
124
123
228
227
DANGER
224 **225**
223
226 **221** **122** **121**
220 **219** **218** **216**
ARMY
217 **120**
212

AIRFRAME
101. External Canopy Jettison Handle Access Panel
102. Right Fwd ECS Evaporator
103. Right ECS Compressor
104. Footstep
105. Fire Extinguisher
106. Right Extended Forward Avionics Bay (EFAB)
107. EFAB Stowage Bin (Open)
108. ECS Evaporator Bay Panel
109. Pressure Refuel Control Panel
110. Fwd Gravity Refuel Point
111. Pressure Refuel Manifold Panel
112. Servicing Access Panel
113. Main Gearbox Access Panel
114. Upper Fuselage Fairing
115. No.2 Engine Nacelle Servicing Platform
116. Aft Gravity Refuel Point
117. Battery/Charger and Radar Processor Panel
118. Aft ECS Condenser Bay
119. Auxiliary Fuel Tanks
120. Stowage Compartment
121. No.2 ECU Ducted Exhaust
122. Hydraulic Ground Servicing Supply Panel
123. Aircraft Towing Point

124. Tail Wheel Hyd/Manual Castor Lock
125. Extendable Foot/Hand Holds (Left and Right)

ARMAMENT
300. M230EI 30mm Gun Ammunition Side Loader

ELECTRICAL/AVIONIC
201. Front Right Missile Warning Sensor
202. Front Right RWR Quadrant Receiver
203. EFAB – Forward Right Avionics Bay
204. CTS GPS Antenna
205. Co-Pilot's Low Height Warning Indicator
206. Windscreen Wipers
207. Pilot's Low Height Warning Indicator
208. Ice Detector Sensor
209. IFF Upper Diople

210. Right Pitot Tube
211. Right Wing Formation Light
212. VU1 & FM2 Full Band Antenna
213. Laser Warning Receiver Right Upper
214. Aft Right Avionics Bay with Cooling Grills
215. Nav. Light
216. Anti-Collision Strobe Light
217. Doppler Antenna
218. Right Side Airspeed and Direction Sensor
219. Right Flare Dispenser
220. VU2/UHF Blade Antenna
221. Laser Warning Receiver Right Rear
222. Safety Disarm Unit
223. Rear Right RWR Quadrant Receiver

224. Spine Formation Light
225. Rear Left RWR Quadrant Receiver
226. Right Aft MWS
227. IFF Lower Dipole Antenna
228. CTS UHF Antenna
229. Tail Formation Light
230. GPS Antenna
231. Tail Navigation Light and Bi Directional Radar Warning Receivers
232. VU2 & FM 1 Whip Aerial

© AgustaWestland

The following is an account of operations involving 656 Squadron, Army Air Corps, in Afghanistan over several months in 2006 and 2007. At the time of going to print, some inquests have not yet been held into the deaths of British Army and Royal Marine personnel reported in these pages. The author has, to the best of his knowledge, reported events faithfully and accurately and any insult or injury to any of the parties described or quoted herein or to their families is unintentional. The publishers will be happy to correct any inaccuracies in later editions.

Identities have been obscured in a few cases to protect the individuals and their families.

PROLOGUE

27 June 2006
08.49

I flicked a glance at the digital clock top right on my control panel.
Shit. The Paras had been on the ground for almost thirty minutes
now, and I was starting to sweat. The longer we stayed in one place,
the more time it gave the Taliban to put together an attack.

Maintaining the same gentle pressure on the cyclic stick, I continued our broad right banking turn into the sun. I felt its warmth
on my face through the cockpit's Perspex window. It was going to
be another scorching day.

Two thousand feet below us, the Paras were about to finish
sweeping the first field. It was twice the size of a football pitch. They
had another one as big to do next. Half of them had fanned out
across the length of it, weapons at the ready; the rest provided cover
from the bushes and undergrowth along the southern edge. The
company commander and his signaller followed closely behind the
line, moving from west to east.

A crop had been planted, but not long ago. For once, it wasn't

1

opium. Much of the field's surface was bare, dark earth, making the search easier, but the Paras still had to move painfully slowly, looking for the slightest clue as to the whereabouts of the two missing SBS men. Anything could help – a strip of clothing, spent ammunition shells, dried blood.

We'd seen no sign of the KIA or MIA since our arrival. It didn't bode well.

Our flight had been scrambled at dawn to relieve the pair of Apaches up at Sangin before us. They – the Incident Response Team (IRT) – had been scrambled three hours previously. It had been a long night.

We'd been given a quick update on the ground as we were firing up the aircraft.

In complete secrecy, a small SBS team had lifted four Taliban organisers from a village near the northern Helmand town at 3am. The team were from Force 84, the British contingent of the Joint Special Forces command. They hadn't notified the local Para garrison in Sangin's District Centre about the mission – the usual SF drill to ensure total operational security. They were no different when I used to fly them around the Balkans during the 1990s.

The arrest had gone without a hitch. But on the way home the snatch squad was ambushed by a large and very angry Taliban force who wanted their people back. The team's lead Land Rover was destroyed by the first enemy RPG, kicking off a massive fire-fight and a desperate chase through the fields. The elite SBS team had been pursued by at least seventy Taliban.

They only got out of there three hours later, thanks to a platoon of determined Gurkhas, who fought their way through the Talib lines twice, and close air support from two Apaches, an A10 jet and two Harrier GR7s. The Apaches stuck a Hellfire missile down the throat of their abandoned Land Rover to deny it to the enemy.

In the chaos, the SBS team lost a couple of their prisoners. More importantly, two team members were separated from the main group: SBS Sergeant Paul Bartlett and Captain David Patten, attached from the Special Reconnaissance Regiment. Though their whereabouts were unknown, Patten was seen going down hard while sprinting across a field, and was already presumed Killed in Action.

The battle over, our task was to escort a company of para-troopers carried by two Chinooks into the area and help them locate the KIA and MIA. Somehow we had been given a reasonably precise grid reference for the search.

I was flying, and Simon, my Royal Navy co-pilot and gunner, was in the seat six feet in front of me. While the Paras combed the ground, we scanned the immediate landscape for enemy or hidden IEDs. Simon stared into his Target Acquisition and Designation Sight, constantly probing the treelines, bushes and shadows ahead of the Paras with the 127-times-magnification daytime TV camera lens.

An Apache crew always worked as a team, so while Simon controlled the telescopic view I maintained the overall perspective from the back seat. That meant covering the Paras' rear as well as keeping one eye on the second Apache in our flight. They were responsible for the outer security cordon, keeping their eyes peeled for any new threat coming into the area. Anything already inside the lads' two square kilometre radius was ours.

I had slaved the 30-mm cannon to my right eye. Its rounds would now zero in on any target in the crosshairs of the monocle over my right eye. All I needed to do was look at the target and squeeze the weapons release trigger on the cyclic with my right

3

index finger. It left Simon free to scan. He'd be quick to pull his own trigger too if he spotted anything in the TADS' crosshairs.

We were in close to the Paras on this one, directly overhead. We wanted anyone in the area to know that we were ready to engage in an instant if the Taliban wanted to start something again. It was normally enough to put them off, but not always. They'd stood and fought here once already this morning. That's why I was keen to speed things up.

'The boys are about to cross into the second field. You sure that irrigation ditch is clear?'

'From what I can see it is.'

'Nothing else of note?'

'No, nothing.'

'Okay. I'm just watching the clock a bit, you know?'

'Sure.' Simon paused. 'I'm going deep into the treeline on the far eastern end of the second field now. It's the only place I haven't yet been in detail.'

It wasn't just here. I never felt comfortable anywhere inside the Green Zone. Nobody did, not for a single minute. It should have been called the Red Zone. It was where the Taliban were, and we weren't – a thin strip of well-irrigated land, no more than ten kilometres wide at its broadest point, on each side of the Helmand River. The great waterway snaked its way down the entire length of the province, through vegetation dense enough to make it a guerrilla fighter's paradise.

We preferred the desert which covered the rest of Helmand. There was nowhere to hide there, which was why the Taliban fought the battle in here instead. British forces had first entered Helmand and its Green Zone two months earlier. Only now though were we beginning to realise what a massive tough battle it was going to be.

'I've got something,' Simon said quietly.

I eased the cyclic back a centimetre or so, to reduce our airspeed. That would make it easier for him to hold the image he wanted on the TADS.

'I think I've got a body.'

'Where, buddy?'

'North-east corner of the second field. Just under the trees. No thermal off it, but it's definitely a body. Lasering now for the grid reference.'

I radioed the company commander on the ground, passed on the grid reference and gave him verbal directions as well. It would save them valuable time.

A minute later, Simon spoke again. 'There's something to the north of it.'

I knew what was coming.

'I think I've got a second. Ten metres to the north of the first. Tucked under the trees this time; in a ditch, in the shade. No thermals off this one either.'

My heart sank. Unless the second body was a dead Taliban fighter, one KIA and one MIA now sounded very much like two KIAs. We were too late to do anything for either of them.

I radioed the Paras' commander again. They had begun to protect the area around the first corpse, but one of his men seemed to have spotted the second body already and was moving towards it.

A second crosshair on my monocle told me exactly where Simon was focusing his TADS. He was on the second body, and he hadn't moved for a good thirty seconds. We couldn't afford to concentrate on them; we still needed to look out for the boys. The dead weren't going to be any threat. The threat was elsewhere.

I gave Simon another ten seconds. He still hadn't pulled out.

Now I was seriously twitchy. A body might be the perfect come-on for another ambush, but we were never going to spot anyone like that. He needed to scan beyond the treeline now.

'Si, pull out. You've been on the bodies far too long, mate. Look out for the boys.'

'There's something wrong.'

'There's a lot fucking wrong, mate – they're dead. Just pull out.'

'No Ed, you don't understand. There's something wrong with the bodies.'

I looked down my TADS screen above my right knee for the first time. It replicated Simon's vision completely. It was hard to make out a huge amount of detail from the black and white TV image, but it was immediately obvious that there was no tonal difference on either of the guys' body surfaces. It could only mean one thing. They'd been stripped.

'It's not just their clothes. Look at the way they're lying. Does that look right to you?'

Both men were flat out, arms down by their sides. You don't fall like that if you've been hit in combat. As we continued to circle, Simon's view improved. He zoomed in closer. He was right; there was something wrong with the bodies. A lot wrong. I didn't want to look any more.

'You ... fucking ... *wankers* ...' Simon breathed.

A few seconds later, the Paras' commander made it official. 'Wildman Five One, Widow Seven Four. That's two KIA confirmed. We're bagging them up now.'

The Taliban would have been monitoring their every move, so the Paras made a swift withdrawal to the helicopter landing site with the bodies and the Chinooks came back in to pick them up; again, under our watchful eye.

On the flight back to Camp Bastion, Simon and I tried to figure out what the hell had gone wrong. If only someone had known about the raid. I understood the procedure, but right now it was incredibly frustrating – a real double-edged sword. Within thirty minutes of the shout coming in, we could have had a couple of Apaches giving them some cover. We might even have kept the two guys alive.

A silence fell between us. I knew what Simon was wondering, because I was wondering it too. Was Patten or Bartlett still alive by the time the Taliban got their hands on them? For their sake, I prayed they weren't. If they were, the awful terror they must have experienced in the last desperate minutes of their lives was too unbearable to contemplate.

'You know what, Ed?' Simon said eventually. 'If it was me, I know what I'd do. I wouldn't give those bastards the satisfaction.'

I'd been having exactly the same thought.

That flight back to Camp Bastion was the first time I really understood why aircrew were no longer issued with gold sovereigns. You couldn't buy your way out of trouble in this place. These people weren't interested in our money.

Of course, none of us thought the deployment was going to be a walk in the park. We all knew what the Mujahideen had done to the Soviet helicopter gunship pilots they captured; we'd all heard the horror stories. Yes, our Apaches were as mean and powerful as they looked, but that didn't mean we were untouchable. Our intelligence briefs reminded us daily how determined the Taliban were to take out one of our helicopters. And it was the Apaches they hated the most.

'Praise be to Allah, I want you to bring down a Mosquito,' the Taliban commanders could be overheard in radio intercepts regaling their rank and file. That was their word for us: 'Mosquitoes'. They called the Chinooks 'Cows'.

But up until that day, we'd all kidded ourselves that being the good guys would save us. We were on a reconstruction and security mission, not an invasion. If we were shot down, we presumed that we would just somehow get away with it. A bit of a slapping, maybe, like the Tornado boys got from Saddam in the first Gulf War; a few months in a dingy jail, then a traditional prisoner exchange at Checkpoint Charlie.

Now we knew the truth. Reality had bitten. Our enemy in southern Afghanistan couldn't give a stuff what mandate we'd come under. If they got their hands on us, a quick death would be the very best we could hope for.

I gripped the cyclic resolutely as, then and there, I also decided there was no way those evil bastards were going to get me alive. If I was shot down, I'd keep on running until my heart gave out. If I couldn't run, I'd fight until my second to last bullet was gone. Then I'd use the last one on myself.

We talked for hours back in the crew tents that night as word spread about what had happened. Every pilot came to the same conclusion. I'd be surprised if all the paratroopers out in the district bases hadn't followed suit.

We only found out exactly what had happened to the two SBS guys some days later. Patten had been hit in the chest, the bullet exiting from the side of his neck. A rescue attempt for him was out of the question; the sky was raining lead. Now the SBS team was split in two, most in front of Patten and a few – including Bartlett – behind him.

Bartlett was with another SBS lad who'd taken a bullet in the arm. Bartlett stayed with him and found a hiding place in an irrigation ditch. With Taliban all around them, he then went forward alone, crawling through thick undergrowth to recce a route to safety through the enemy's positions. It was the last anyone saw of him.

Bartlett was a very brave guy and he didn't deserve to die like that. Neither of them did.

That wasn't the worst part. The two men's colleagues back in Force 84's secure Ops Room at Kandahar Airfield were forced to sit and watch the whole ghastly show play out as it happened. Patten and Bartlett's last moments were piped through in real time on a live TV feed from a Predator circling above them. That's why they had been able to tell us exactly where to look.

DÉJÀ VU

7 November 2006
14.35

'Two minutes, fellah ...'

I'd been dozing. The Chinook's loadie woke me with a gentle kick. He had to shout the standard warning to be heard over the deafening din of the helicopter's giant rotor blades.

We were his only passengers on the fifty-minute flight from Kandahar. The rest of the cabin was stuffed full to waist level with every conceivable shape of box and bag you could imagine: cardboard ration packs, steel ammunition boxes, big sealed packages of office equipment, crates of dark oil-like liquid and half a dozen fully packed mailbags. There was nowhere to put our feet, so I'd stretched out on the red canvas seats, slid my helmet underneath my head, and drifted off to a chorus of rhythms and vibrations.

Billy and the Boss were sprawled across the seats along the other side of the Chinook when I came to. Billy had been kipping as well, but he was now sitting up. The Boss was still staring avidly out of a glassless porthole window, his short brown hair flickering in the wind. He'd been doing that when I closed my eyes, fascinated by everything below us. Unlike Billy and me, it was his first time.

I sat up and strapped on my helmet as the sound of the rotor blades changed. Our tactical descent into Camp Bastion had begun.

The Helmand Task Force's HQ – meaning the brigadier and his staff – was in the province's capital, Lashkar Gah. But Camp Bastion was its accommodation and logistics hub – its beating heart. It was home to the vast majority of the 7,800 British soldiers stationed in Helmand, and it was to be our home too.

Billy grinned at me. I shook my head and raised my eyes to the heavens, and that made him laugh. He was really enjoying this moment, the twat.

I couldn't believe I was back. I shouldn't even have been in the army. Civilian life for me was due to have started two months earlier, at the end of 656 Squadron's first three-and-a-half-month tour of southern Afghanistan. After twenty-two years serving Queen and Country, I was getting out. I had been really looking forward to signing off too. I'd told Billy as much on our ride out of Bastion, precisely eighty-three days ago. 'Bad luck buddy.' I'd given him a patronising nudge. 'I'll raise a Guinness to you from the bar of my local the day you fly back to this shit hole, eh?' That's why he was grinning at me now. I was half expecting him to start raising an imaginary pint at me.

My dreams of Civvy Street had been postponed for six months, thanks to the army's shortage of Weapons Officers. Apaches were a brand new business and there had only been time to train up a few of us. Every squadron that deployed had to have one. We were in charge of everything to do with the aircraft's offensive capabilities. The other Weapons Officers were all posted, leaving the Army Air Corps (AAC) a shortlist of one. After a fair bit of arm twisting, and no small amount of emotional blackmail, I had agreed to do one more tour.

Newness was also why the whole squadron was coming back so soon. The Westland WAH64 Apache helicopter gunship had only entered operational service with HM Armed Forces in May that year. It was renamed the Apache AH Mk1. The first Apache unit – 656 Squadron – was only passed fully combat ready six days after we deployed in May. By the summer 664 Squadron had come online. They'd relieved us in August and as the only other available squadron we were now relieving them. The Boss, Billy and I had come out to start the handover.

We heaved our Bergens (army slang for rucksack) over our shoulders just after the aircraft hit the ground. On the loadmaster's thumbs up, the gunner lowered the tail ramp and we clambered out onto the metal runway, flinching as the heat from the Chinook's twin turboshaft engines stung the back of our necks.

Waiting for us fifty metres away was one of the saddest looking army vehicles I had ever seen: a battered old four tonner with the windscreen, canopy, frame and tailgate all entirely missing. A sand-ripped cabin and an empty flatbed was all that was left. It looked like something out of *Mad Max Beyond Thunderdome*.

Standing in front of it, his hands clasped together in excitement, was John – 664 Squadron's Second in Command. He was grinning, too, but for a different reason to Billy. John shook all three of us very firmly by the hand.

'It's great to see you guys – it really is.'

It was obvious he meant it too. Our arrival signalled the green light for his team to start packing their bags.

'Never mind the bullshit, John. What the fuck do you call that?' I pointed my rifle at his Mad Max-mobile.

'It's the missile truck.'

'I know it's the missile truck. But when we left it with you, it actually *looked* like the missile truck. It was in good order. You've totally trashed it.'

John chuckled. He was an old mate of mine. We had been warrant officers together before he'd taken his commission.

'Yeah. We've been a little busy. There's a war on – not that you work-shy slackers would have known much about it when you were here.'

It was the normal banter that rival incoming and outgoing units exchanged. We were actually quietly impressed with the state of the missile truck, but we didn't want to let on to John.

I jumped up on the flatbed and let the warm sun dry the sweat on my brow. Late autumn for Helmand province meant bright sunshine and the temperature in the mid-twenties. It was a great relief after the furnace heat of the previous summer, when we slowly boiled in our own blood. One afternoon the thermometer had hit 54 degrees celsius.

Thankfully, sitting at an altitude of 885 metres above sea level, Camp Bastion was always a lot cooler at night. There was nothing in the surrounding desert to trap the day's heat. It meant we could sleep – or try to anyway – in between outgoing salvoes of artillery fire and emergency call-outs.

'I'll ride in the back with you, Mr Macy,' the Boss said, refusing Billy's offer of the front seat. 'I want to get a proper look at this extraordinary place.'

The Boss was the squadron's new Officer Commanding, Major Christopher James. Chris had the biggest hands I have ever seen. His fingers were like cows' udders. He was built like a prop forward, but his blue eyes, chiselled jaw and swept-back hair were pure Dan

14

Dare. His enthusiasm was infectious, and unlike some OCs he was always keen to muck in with the practical jokes.

Taking over a battle-hardened unit like ours without any combat experience in an Apache was a tough task, but if anyone was up to it, he was. His jumbo pinkies hadn't stopped him from being one of the best shots in the Corps. He was also the first British pilot ever to fly the new American Apache model, the AH64D, as the first candidate on the US Army's initial Longbow Conversion Course. While he was in Arizona he'd won the Top Gun shooting prize, beating all the US Apache pilots. That had really pissed off the Americans, but it must have cheered up the Queen – she gave him an MBE.

A very bright man from a long-standing army family, he always talked *with* everyone under his command rather than *at* them – whether you were the best pilot or the most junior rocket loader. It had taken him only a few weeks to become hugely popular with everyone. His job title nickname was always said with affection.

The Boss marvelled at Camp Bastion as we bumped the 500 metres along a churned up sand track from the flight line to our digs. I wasn't surprised – I'd done the same in May. It was a military camp like none of us had ever seen: two square kilometres of khaki tents, mess halls and vehicle parks in the middle of absolutely nowhere.

It wasn't on any maps, because it had been too dangerous to survey Helmand for decades. But you could find it thirty miles north of Lashkar Gah and two miles south off the A01 highway that links the two ancient Afghan cities of Kandahar, 100 miles to the east of us, and Herat, 300 miles to our north-west.

Surrounding the camp was one of the most inhospitable landscapes in Afghanistan. It was as flat as a billiard table, without so much as a shrub in sight. Only on clear days would the thin outline of the far-off mountain range to the north break up the monotone horizon. The locals called it the Dasht-e-Margo – the Desert of Death.

Hairy-arsed veterans frightened first timers at Bastion by telling them about the three different lethal spiders that inhabited the Dasht-e-Margo, including the Black Widow. There were also nocturnal flesh-eating scorpions that injected an anaesthetic into human skin and then munched away to their heart's content without their victim noticing. And tiny sand flies laid their eggs in any soft tissue within easy reach – that brought on leishmaniasis, a disease that resembled leprosy.

Apart from the cheap real estate, there were good strategic reasons to be in the middle of nowhere. You could see and hear anyone coming for twenty miles, which meant the camp was very hard to attack. That was no bad thing, since the nearest sizeable Coalition garrison was twelve hours' drive away, at Kandahar Airfield.

Bastion was the biggest and most ambitious project the Royal Engineers had attempted since World War Two. Every last spanner and tent pole had had to be driven overland from the Pakistani port of Karachi – a 1,000-mile, three-week journey. Hercules transport planes and Chinooks were too busy flying troops around, and there was no runway for them at that point. The sappers had also had to build a self-generating electricity plant and bore wells for their own water and a waste-disposal system big enough to serve a small town – which was pretty much what it was.

I was struck by how much it had changed in our absence: more tents, more fences, and proper, flattened track roads. The army was clearly planning to be here for some time.

The jalopy pulled up. We were back in the same eight man

accommodation tent, a few hundred metres from the Joint Helicopter Force's forward HQ.

'Jammy bugger,' said Billy, after we'd bundled through the zip door and I beat him to the best dark green army camping cot in the far corner. It was the one I'd had on the first tour. The three boxes of bottled water I'd used as a bedside table were still there too. It was like I'd never been away.

Billy was the squadron's most senior pilot. His official title was the Qualified Helicopter Instructor; unofficially, the Sky Police. Like me he was a WO1, and the only other pilot in the squadron – apart from the Boss and me – qualified to fly in both Apache seats: the gunner's front and the pilot's back.

With his dark, swept-back hair, neat physique and good looks, Billy wouldn't have looked out of place in a Cary Grant movie. A northern lad, he'd come a long way since starting out as a driver in the Royal Corps of Transport. Billy had flown more Apache hours than anyone, training initially on the original US model, the AH64A. He really loved his flying, and being an Apache pilot meant a huge amount to him. His standards were high and he didn't tolerate sloppiness, but he was fair with it.

The other thing that really stood out about Billy was his dress sense, and – war or no war – he was never too far from a splash of aftershave. Whether in combats or a pin-striped suit, his rig was never less than perfect. Every unit badge was Velcroed in exactly the right place; his light blue Army Air Corps beret was always perched immaculately on his bonce.

All in all, Billy was the natural candidate to guide visiting dignitaries around the squadron's base, and he loved nothing more than to oblige. In his time with the squadron, he'd toured the Chief of the General Staff, the Chief of Defence Staff, the

Prime Minister and Prince Charles – not a bad haul.

Billy and I went back a long way and he took my regular abuse rather well. He enjoyed giving it back in spades even more.

We began to settle in. Each bed space measured two metres by three, and came with a portable white canvas cupboard with five small alcoves where you stuck your T-shirts, underwear and spare uniform. That was it for furniture, unless you fancied buying your own camping chair from the NAAFI.

We were in part of a network of ten identical tents, five on each side of a covered corridor. The squadron had a couple of these pods: REME and attached personnel in one, aircrew and ground-crew in the other.

The first tent on the right was a recreational room with a TV and a table covered in sun bleached newspapers and old dog-eared paperbacks. On the left was the ablutions block for the network's fifty or so inhabitants. It contained six showers, six sinks and six toilets – all stainless steel. You were guaranteed the most uncomfortable crap in the world there, and not just because they didn't have any seats. In the winter, the rims were ice cold, and in the summer they were so hot they scalded your arse. Hovering the Apache was a doddle compared to hovering over the tin rim.

There were around a hundred identical pods in Bastion in total, arranged in long rows. A latticework of walkways lined with black mesh grilles connected them, and roads with irrigation ditches to their sides, all walled with identical Hesco Bastion bollards.

Losing your bearings and walking into fifteen different tents before you found your own was all too common – and made you feel like a real tit. But you quickly learned to recognise tiny landmarks, like a flagpole, a regiment's insignia or a different coloured Portaloo.

'John looks knackered, doesn't he,' Billy said as we unpacked.

It was true. John had developed a manic stare, skin stretched over his cheekbones and huge bags under his eyes. We knew that look all too well; three months ago we'd seen it every time we'd stood in front of the shaving mirror.

We'd never have conceded it to anyone in our sister squadron, but the sitreps we'd got back at 9 Regiment's North Yorkshire HQ proved they had been just as busy as we were on our first tour. Perhaps more so. The Helmand Task Force's first six months had been a true baptism of fire.

British forces had first been deployed in April 2006 as part of a dramatic expansion of NATO's role in Afghanistan, to establish a secure environment for reconstruction, development and government. We'd had troops in Kabul since the fall of the Taliban regime in November 2001. But while the capital and its northern surroundings had, as a result, remained relatively secure, the rest of the country had dramatically deteriorated.

In many areas, President Hamid Karzai's government existed only in name – hence his derogatory nickname, the 'Mayor of Kabul'. Warlords and, increasingly, rich opium barons held the real reins of power. With nobody to stop it, the heroin business boomed. The opium poppy crop doubled or tripled every year. Every local official who mattered, even slightly, was in the traffickers' back pockets.

Nowhere was the spiralling anarchy worse than in the south. Huge swathes of the four southern provinces – Helmand, Kandahar, Uruzgan and Nimruz – were run by the drugs tsars as their own lawless fiefdoms.

With attention drifting away from Iraq, Tony Blair and George Bush were adamant that what they had started five years earlier in

Afghanistan should be properly concluded. At their insistence, NATO's International Security Assistance Force's remit was widened to take on the mountainous eastern provinces, then the western flatlands, and finally the barren deserts of the south.

The Dutch deployed to sparsely populated Uruzgan and Nimruz, and the Canadians to Kandahar. The British government volunteered to take on Helmand – the hardest nut of all to crack. It was the biggest province, and produced a staggering 42 per cent of Afghanistan's total raw opium.

In the 1980s, the Soviet Army had failed to control Helmand with a whole motorised rifle division of 12,000 fighting soldiers. Twenty years later, we were going to try it with less than a third of that number. And of the 3,300 the British government initially sent, less than a quarter were fighting troops. The British Army has always relished a challenge. This one was called Operation Herrick.

Not even the most cynical military planners dared to imagine the viciousness and intensity with which the resurgent Taliban would oppose our arrival. Forming an unholy alliance with the drugs lords, the Taliban threw everything they had at the Paras of 16 Air Assault Brigade. Its small infantry force was spread out across five thinly manned and remote outpost bases across the north of the province – known as platoon houses or district centres.

A never-ending supply of holy warriors swarmed over the Pakistan border to fight alongside local guns for hire and launch wave after wave of attacks on the DCs at Sangin, Kajaki, Musa Qa'leh, Gereshk and Now Zad. Day and night, each was pounded with small arms, RPGs, rockets and mortars. Each turned into a mini Alamo.

The army had not seen fighting as sustained and desperate since Korea. It was as bad as anything thrown at either American or

British troops during the occupation of Iraq; and, a lot of the time, it was worse.

NATO's intelligence about enemy strengths before we arrived was poor. They estimated 1,000 Taliban fighters spread across both the Helmand and Kandahar provinces. By August, the estimate for Helmand alone was upped to 10,000.

One of the greatest problems the Task Force faced was the distance it had to cover. At 275 miles long and 100 wide (a total of 23,000 square miles), Helmand is not much smaller than the Republic of Ireland. Ensuring every DC had enough ammunition, food and water was a logistical nightmare. At times some of the guys ran dangerously low; down to their last few hundred rounds and the emergency rations they carried in their webbing.

In September, the brigade reluctantly abandoned the most distant DC at Musa Qa'leh, more than fifty miles from Camp Bastion. It was too dangerous to land Chinooks anywhere near it, and a ground resupply couldn't break through the besieging Taliban's lines without a full on battalion-strength attack.

The guys holding the other four DCs just stuck it out with sheer grit and the odd Apache gunship in support. As the RSM of 3 Para declared with relish, 'We're paratroopers – we're *supposed* to be surrounded.' It was a hell of a feat, especially as so many of the lads were on their first operational tour.

It was all a bit of a far cry from the public aspirations of the man who signed the deployment paperwork, Defence Secretary John Reid. He told the House of Commons that he hoped the troops would come home having 'not fired a single bullet'. He'd also somewhat optimistically termed the mission 'nation building'.

Actually, between June and October 2006, the Paras and their supporting cap badges ended up firing a total of 450,000 bullets,

10,000 artillery shells and 6,500 mortar rounds. In addition, and between May and August 2006 alone, the sixteen Apache pilots of 656 Squadron put down 7,305 cannon rounds, 68 rockets and 11 Hellfire missiles. I don't think it was quite what John Reid had in mind.

Our defiance came at a heavy price. A total of thirty-five servicemen were killed in that first six months: sixteen in combat, fourteen when a Nimrod MR2 spy plane crashed, four in accidents – and one committed suicide. A further 140 were wounded in action, forty-three of them seriously or very seriously. It all meant we didn't have much time for nation building.

And there lay the real problem. It wasn't just kinetic – we were also fighting a war of minds. We could carry on killing Taliban forever. But it wasn't going to win over the local Afghan people in whose name we had come. We had to deliver them a better life, and soon. All we'd achieved so far was to turn their streets, orchards and fields into lethal battle grounds.

Most Helmandis were still perched on the fence, waiting in the time-honoured Afghan way to see which side looked like winning. British soldiers were welcomed wherever they went; there was little love for the Taliban. Yet if our presence made things worse, they'd cosy up to the other side soon enough.

The Taliban knew that too. They understood that reconstruction was pretty bloody hard with a war going on. There's an old Afghan phrase their mullah leaders loved to quote: 'They have the watches, we have the time.' They didn't need a spectacular knockout blow – just a constant, paralysing war of attrition.

The squadron's first foray into Helmand had been quite something. I sat on my cot and wondered what this tour would bring. The Taliban were becoming more successful at killing us as time moved on. They learned lessons quickly from each contact and adapted immediately. By sheer luck we hadn't yet lost a helicopter but it was only a matter of time. They'd been getting better whilst I'd been planning my retirement. I'd be the one playing catch up, not them. I needed to be lucky every second I was in the air; they only needed to be lucky once. There were no two ways about it – for the first time in my whole military career, I was genuinely concerned that I might not come home alive.

'You know what Billy? I've got butterflies.'

'Yeah, right. Probably that Gurkha curry in the Kandahar cookhouse.'

Billy was not in a sympathetic mood. He was too busy hanging up his impossibly well-pressed uniforms.

There was no point letting it gnaw away at me; however I played it, what was for me wouldn't pass me. I couldn't wait to climb back into the cockpit and get stuck in again. I'd always loved being on operations, ever since my first Northern Ireland tour as a young Para.

RIDING THE DRAGON

The sixteen pilots in 656 Squadron could not have come from more diverse backgrounds. My route to the Apache cockpit had been one of the longest of all.

I was born and grew up in a seaside town in the North-East. It was a holiday resort for miners until package holidays were invented and the miners stopped coming. After that, most folk worked for the local steel factory and chemical works.

Dad was an engineering fitter at the chemical works, and Mum brought us up. My brother Greg was only thirteen months younger than me. We did everything together; we were known as the terrible twins. Other kids' parents banned us from playing with them. No surprise really; we nicked our first milk float when we were three and four.

My parents' unhappy marriage finally fell apart when I was eleven, and Mum wouldn't let us live with Dad. Without a father's firm hand, my teenage years descended into chaos. Greg and I ran riot. We always stuck up for each other, no matter what the consequences. One day when I was fourteen, Greg burst into my science class bawling his eyes out. 'Ed, I smacked the RE teacher in the face,' he tried to explain. 'It wasn't on purpose. He was taking the Mickey out of me...'

My science teacher, Mr Hastings, didn't take kindly to his own class being interrupted in this fashion and leaped down the classroom to intervene. There were a few seconds of confusion as Greg clung onto my desk while Mr Hastings tried to heave him to the door. Greg wasn't budging, so Mr Hastings hit Greg's arm with the bottom of his fist to dislodge him. I flipped. I jumped up and launched myself into Mr Hastings's midriff with both arms out-stretched. The teacher went head over heels across another desk, sending children, books and chairs flying. They all landed in a heap on the floor, but Greg and I didn't look back, and sprinted all the way home.

It was the final straw. Both of us were expelled and sent to different schools. We were split up for the first time in our lives.

I missed my brother terribly. My new school was a rough one and when I was goaded I fought back. I spent most of my time there fighting all comers – alone. Six months into it, I started missing lessons. In my last year I rarely went at all.

Mum was too busy running a pub so I wasn't missed at home. I'd often spend weeks away, sleeping wherever I liked. The woods were my favourite place, and I lived by stealing food and poaching fish to sell to local pubs. I was turning wild.

On my sixteenth birthday, I was old enough to choose who I lived with, and Dad was waiting with a big smile on his face. He straightened me out, forced me to use a knife and fork again, to keep myself clean, and eventually got me a metalworker's apprenticeship.

I enjoyed training to be an engineer and wanted to be like Dad, but I hated the job. I was trapped indoors in a routine life I didn't want. At night, I'd drink and fight.

Dad remarried and got the person he always deserved; I got three new brothers as part of the deal. They were great lads and all of them joined the army. I'd found my way out.

Two months after my eighteenth birthday, I enlisted in the Parachute Regiment. I didn't particularly want to be a soldier, and I only asked for the airborne because *The Paras* was on TV at the time. It looked like a good challenge.

'You'll never pass, son. You haven't got what it takes,' my dad said. It was a textbook case of reverse psychology, but I didn't recognise it as such at the time. It gave me all the determination I needed to pass P Company.

I was posted to 2 Para. I got one hell of a kicking as a crow – military slang for a junior paratrooper – but everybody did in those days. It was the 1980s, and the battalion was full of hard men with droopy moustaches who'd fought at Goose Green during the Falklands War.

Once my bust nose, dislocated jaw, three broken ribs and split testicle had healed, I fell in love with life as a paratrooper – surprising everyone, myself the most. After a couple of years and a six-month combat tour to Enniskillen fighting the IRA, I won promotion to lance corporal.

But I was still an angry young man, and getting into too many fights. I never started them, but I always had to be the one to finish them. The red mist would descend and I could never back down. I even once flattened an RMP sergeant who wound me up on a train, and had to do fourteen days in the regimental nick.

After promotion to full corporal and with the promise of sergeant's stripes if I could keep out of trouble, I began to take my military career a little more seriously. I wanted to challenge myself at the highest level, so I began to prepare for SAS selection.

Months of hard, self-imposed training followed, but my

ambitions came to a sudden end one night in Aldershot during a gruelling bicycle ride in the pouring rain. I'd let half the air out of the tyres to make the pedalling twice as hard. A Volvo clipped my handlebars on a main road, sending me careering across the road and under the wheels of an old man's oncoming car. My head hit the bumper and my feet peeled round and went through the windscreen, before the bloke drove over my right arm and shoulder. My heart stopped in the ambulance on the way to hospital.

In the days that followed, I learned the true meaning of pain. During one operation I was handcuffed to a bed and a vice-like clamp was strapped around my haemorrhaging kidneys for half an hour to squeeze the blood out of them.

It was six months before I put on a uniform again and nine before I could run. I was no use to the Paras any more; my bust shoulder, spine, hips, knees and ankles could no longer bear any real weight. My front-line fighting career was at an end, and I was devastated. I had lost my purpose in life and was forced to abandon all my dreams of SAS selection. My gloom deepened as I contemplated my lack of a future — until a mate suggested the Army Air Corps. If I couldn't fight on the front line, perhaps I could fly people to it instead. Perhaps I could even fly for the SAS.

Then came a stroke of luck – my doctor lost all my medical records. Suddenly, and against all expectations, I stood a chance of passing the Army Air Corps' stringent medical with my battered body.

I was accepted, and came top of my class at flying school. I had to – it was my last chance. I loved flying and the freedom it gave me and I relished playing my part in battle formations. But I hated flying routine ass and trash flights, so whenever anything interesting came up, I went for it. It was always about the next challenge – it always has been.

I got a place on a reconnaissance squadron, flying Gazelles. Five years later, I began to fly for the SAS, hunting down war criminals in the Balkans. The work was amazing, the most exciting I'd ever done.

Something else happened in Bosnia. In late 2002, I met Emily. She was a nursing officer in the RAF. After a night out in the local town, I hitched a lift back to base in the back of the same Land Rover. In thick fog, the vehicle left the road, flipped and rolled down a bank into a muddy irrigation ditch. Emily was trapped in the back, under four feet of water. I pulled her out.

I went to see her in hospital the next day. I was single again – I was the proud father of two children by two previous relationships, but neither had worked out. Emily was a pretty blonde Scot, and as sharp as she was funny. She was way out of my league and we both knew it. By the end of the week, I'd decided I wanted to spend the rest of my life with her.

But Emily wasn't convinced. At least she was honest with me.

'Listen Ed, I don't date full stop. If I did date, I certainly wouldn't date a Pongo. And If I did date a Pongo you can bet your life I wouldn't date a *flyboy* Pongo. So why don't you quit with your pride intact?'

'Aha – so that's not a no …'

It took some time, but eventually we became an item and have been together ever since. Emily's forces background was both a good and a bad thing. It meant she knew the pressures of military life, and to expect long periods of separation. It also meant she knew the real risks of military flying, and the chances of me not coming home.

The British Army's much hyped attack helicopter programme had been in the pipeline for years. In 2002, it finally came online.

Of course I had to be on it. It was the closest I could ever get to being in the front line again. I bent every rule in the book to make sure I was posted onto the very first Apache conversion course and Emily didn't try to stop me. Before I got there, I read up everything I could about the amazing new machine.

The Apache AH64A was initially designed by Boeing for the US government in the 1980s for the giant battlefields of the Cold War. The Pentagon wanted something to take out Soviet armour the moment it rolled across the West German border.

Following the US military tradition of new aircraft honouring Indian tribes, the Apache was not just the next generation attack helicopter. It was the hunter-killer supreme for all future wars. Its surveillance capabilities far outstripped anything its predecessor the Bell AH1 'Huey' Cobra had, and its destructive capability was without precedent.

It looked very different to any previous attack helicopter too. The smooth aerodynamic curves and contours of the Sixties and Seventies were replaced with the hard angles and mean edges of the very first anti-radar – or stealth – technology.

It was also larger: 49 ft 1 in. from the tip of its nose to the back of its tail, with its rotor blades reaching a further 8 ft. It stood 17 ft 6 in. tall and 16 ft 4 in. wide, and weighed 23,000 lb fully laden – 10.4 tonnes, or 140 fully grown men.

Its angular shape wasn't the Apache's only stealth quality. It had four rotor blades rather than two, allowing it to turn at half the speed – five revolutions per second – and thus with half the noise to generate the same lift as the traditional two-bladed helicopters like the great thumping Hueys of the Vietnam War. Each blade's high-tech design made the aircraft quieter still. Instead of hammering the air like the Chinook, Apache blades sliced through it, giving the gunship its trademark low-pitched growl.

It also gave off the lowest heat signature of any helicopter built. Though the engine burned fuel at 800 degrees celsius, a powerful cooling system meant you wouldn't even burn your hand if you pressed it against the exhaust. That seriously hindered a heat-seeking missile's ability to track it. To mask more heat, its skin was coated with special paint that reflected less light too.

When incoming fire did hit the Apache, its ingenious design meant it could withstand a remarkable amount of it – including a 23-mm high explosive round. A US Apache in Iraq even once took a direct hit from a shoulder-fired surface-to-air missile, shredding its starboard engine and wing and leaving its rotor blades in tatters. It still managed to return fire, kill its attackers and make it back to base.

What went on inside the aircraft was cleverer still. Thirteen kilometres of electric wiring linked the avionics, engines, visual aids and weapons systems run by a myriad of on-board computers which monitored every tiny electronic pulse.

Most impressive of all the Apache's cutting edge technology was how it found its prey. Its Target Acquisition and Designation Sight system was made up of an array of cameras housed in a double-headed nose cone that looked like a pair of giant insect eyes. Its 127-times-magnification day TV camera could read a car number plate 4.2 kilometres away. At night, the thermal camera was so powerful it could identify a human form from a distance of four kilometres, and spots of blood on the ground from a kilometre up.

Then there was the Apache's punch. The aircraft's three weapons systems struck with varying degrees of power, speed and precision, depending on the desired target. The 30-mm M230 cannon under the Apache's belly was best for individual targets, firing ten High Explosive Dual Purpose rounds a second to an accuracy of within three metres. Their armour-piercing tips made light work of Armoured Personnel Carriers, vehicles and buildings. Their bodies fragmented on impact just like a large grenade, throwing out hundreds of sharp red-hot pieces of metal. But duality came from the incendiary charge; once it had penetrated or fragged the target, it set it alight. The helicopter's magazine packed up to 1,160 of them, fired in bursts of 10, 20, 50, 100 – or all at once.

Rockets were its optimum area weapon for hitting infantry, dismounted or in vehicles. A maximum of seventy-six could be loaded into up to four CRV7 rocket pods on the weapons pylons, hung from the stubby wings either side of the aircraft. There were two types of rockets: the Flechette, an anti-personnel / vehicle weapon, containing eighty five-inch-long Tungsten darts; and the HEISAP for buildings, vehicles or ships. Its kinetic penetrating head drove through up to half an inch of steel, and the body of the projectile contained an explosive zirconium incendiary that stuck to light alloys and combustibles, torching them.

Finally, thick-walled buildings and fast moving armour were taken out with our main anti-tank weapon, the Semi-Active Laser Hellfire II air-to-ground missile. Each Apache could carry up to sixteen of them, mounted on four rails under the wings. Laser guided from the cockpit for pinpoint accuracy, its 20-lb high explosive and dual shaped charge warhead packed a 5 million-lb-per-square-inch punch on impact – defeating all known armour.

The gunship first saw active service with the US Army during Operation Just Cause, the 1989 invasion of Panama, but it was during the first Gulf War that it really won its spurs. At 2:38am Baghdad time on 17 January 1991, eight AH64s fired the opening salvoes of the conflict. They destroyed an Iraqi radar site near the Iraqi–Saudi Arabian border.

The devastation they then wrought at Mutla Ridge reset the height of the bar. A fleet of Apaches – backed up by A10s – destroyed hundreds of Iraqi military vehicles fleeing Kuwait on the Basra road. The endless line of twisted and smouldering metal was nicknamed the Highway of Death. Their final tally for the war was 278 tanks, 180 artillery pieces and 500 Armoured Personnel Carriers.

In 1998, the AH64D came into service. It was even deadlier; 400 per cent more lethal (hitting more targets) and 720 per cent more survivable than its predecessor. The most significant addition was the state of the art Longbow Radar which could operate in all weathers, day or night, simultaneously detect 1,024 potential targets, moving or static, up to eight kilometres away, classify the top 256 and display the sixteen most threatening for destruction – all in three seconds. Twenty-five seconds later, every one of those targets could be destroyed by a single Apache's Hellfires. A squadron of eight AH64Ds working in unison could terminate 128 tanks in twenty-eight seconds – just by raising one Apache Longbow Radar above the tree or ridge line for a few seconds. They christened it 'Fire and Forget'.

Gradually, the US allowed its closest allies to purchase the Apache. Israel were the first, followed by the Netherlands, Saudi Arabia, Singapore, Egypt, Greece, Japan, Kuwait and the United Arab Emirates. In the late 1990s, the British government finally decided it needed them too. As a nation, we didn't have an attack helicopter capability, just a few Lynx squadrons armed with a couple of TOW anti-tank missiles strapped onto the side of each craft.

Despite its cutting edge design and astonishingly powerful Longbow, the AH64D still had a few ongoing shortcomings. They couldn't operate off ships, and they weren't powerful enough to carry a significant amount of ammunition and fuel at the same time. To fly them at low level meant heavy anti-aircraft fire could still bring them down.

Our generals approached the government with an ambitious plan. Why didn't we buy Boeing's Apache shell, keep the good bits and make the rest even better ourselves? The boffins at Westland Helicopters went to work.

The most important change was two Rolls Royce RTM 322 engines. Each churned out more than twice the brake horsepower of a Formula One racing car, giving our model 30 per cent more power than the American AH64D. It allowed us to fly further, higher and fight with more weapons.

The Brits also scoured the globe for the best countermeasures and built them into the world's most sophisticated defensive aide suite. It allowed pilots to take the aircraft above small arms range, which downed 95 per cent of all military helicopters, and into the previously lethal SAM belt – because the British Apache could now defeat surface-to-air missiles.

They also added a folding blade mechanism so we could operate off aircraft carriers in confined space; an automatic de-icer built into the blades so we could fight in the Arctic; Saturn radios so highly encrypted that their transmissions couldn't be decoded by any intercept; new motors for the CRV7 rockets, making them faster and more accurate; and a unique health monitoring system which enabled the aircraft to automatically diagnose any problems through dozens of microscopic sensors.

The UK bought sixty-seven of Westland's finished article for a cool £46 million each – making the Apache AH Mk1 the second most expensive British aircraft ever made, behind the £62-million

Eurofighter Typhoon. The whole Apache project set the MoD back £4.13 billion.

On paper, the British Apache was the most expensive – and best – attack helicopter in aviation history. For once, even the Americans were jealous. All the army needed to do now was find the pilots to fly their new creation. And that was the most challenging part of all.

As the most technically advanced helicopter in the world, the Apache AH Mk1 was also the hardest to fly. Selection for the eighteen-month conversion course was even more competitive than Special Forces Selection. Of the Army Air Corps' 800 pilots, only twenty-four could make it into the Corps' elite, the six serving Apache squadrons, every year – the top 3 per cent of all British Army pilots. There was no shortage of candidates; the instructors would have passed twice as many if they could have. But the bar couldn't be lowered, or pilots would start to hit the deck.

To train each Apache pilot from scratch cost £3 million (each custom-made helmet alone had a price tag of £22,915). It took six months just to learn how to fly the machine, another six to know how to fight in it, and a final six to be passed combat ready. And that was if you were already a fully qualified, combat-trained army helicopter pilot. If you weren't, you'd have to add four months for ground school and learning to fly fixed wing at RAF Barkston Heath, six months learning to fly helicopters at RAF Shawbury, half a year at the School of Army Aviation learning to fly tactically, and a final sixteen-week course in Survival, Evasion and Resistance to Interrogation, courtesy of the Intelligence Corps' most vigorous training staff. Three years in total.

'I bet it's not as tough as you and the Yanks make out,' I said to Billy on Day One. He smiled.

It was the hardest thing I have ever done, or will ever do. Some of the best pilots I've known fell by the wayside during Apache conversion training. Cranchy was an instructor for twelve years. He failed. Paul was the chief instructor for an entire regiment, and he failed. Mac was a display pilot with the Blue Eagles and got an MBE for it. He failed too.

Why was the aircraft so hard to master? In a nutshell: because of the unimaginably demanding need to multi-task. Taking an Apache into battle was like playing an Xbox, a PlayStation and a chess Grand Master simultaneously – whilst riding Disneyworld's biggest roller coaster. US studies found that only a very small percentage of human brains could do everything required simultaneously to operate the aircraft.

Information overload was a major issue. At least ten different new facts had to be registered, processed and acted on every few seconds in the cockpit. We were constantly bombarded with new information – from the flight instruments, four different radio frequencies chattering at the same time, the internal intercom, the weapons computers' targeting, the defensive aid suite's threats and the Longbow Radar.

Then there were the challenges outside the cockpit too. We had to know the position of our wingmen, the whereabouts of other allied jets and helicopters, spot for small arms fire flashes on the ground, remember friendly ground forces' positions and keep a visual lookout for the target.

All this not just for a minute or two, but for three hours without a break. Miss one vital element, and you would kill yourself and your co-pilot in an instant.

US pilots called flying an Apache 'Riding the dragon'. If you got something wrong or irritated the machine, it turned around and bit you. A cool temperament was even more important than a good pair of eyes and ears – the ability not to panic no matter what was being demanded of you.

The second great challenge was physical coordination. Flying an Apache almost always meant both hands and feet doing four different things at once. Even our eyes had to learn how to work independently of each other.

A monocle sat permanently over our right iris. A dozen different instrument readings from around the cockpit were projected into it. At the flick of a button, a range of other images could also be superimposed underneath the green glow of the instrument symbology, replicating the TADS' or PNVS' camera images and the Longbow Radars' targets.

The monocle left the pilot's left eye free to look outside the cockpit, saving him the few seconds that it took to look down at the instruments then up again; seconds that could mean the difference between our death and our enemy's.

New pilots suffered terrible headaches as the left and right eye competed for dominance. They started within minutes, long before take off. If you admitted to them, the instructor grounded you immediately – so none of us ever did. Instead, you had to 'man up' and get on with it.

As the eyes adjusted over the following weeks and months the headaches took longer to set in. It was a year before mine disappeared altogether. A few weeks out of the cockpit though, and they'd be back again on a high concentration sortie – low level, large formation, poor weather, under pylons, hunting and being hunted by the enemy.

It took me two years to learn how to 'see' properly – how to see in Apache World. I once filmed my face during a sortie with a video camera as an experiment. My eyes whirled independently of each other throughout, like a man possessed.

'That's disgusting,' Emily said when I showed her the tape. 'But does it mean you can read two books at once?'

I tried it. I could.

Being a member of the world's most exclusive aviators' club had its personal price. It was also very tough on Emily, the other wives and girlfriends and especially our children. When we started, our American counterparts warned us about AIDS – Apache Induced Divorce Syndrome. Marriage and the Apache didn't sit well together.

To master the machine, we had to eat, sleep and breathe it. It was an obsession, and it had to be. There was never time to stop and relax in the cockpit, the simulator or the classroom. If there was, you were forgetting to do something. 'You can sleep when you're dead,' the instructors loved to say.

It was the same on the squadron once we'd all qualified. Apache pilots were at work for fourteen hours a day, every day, just to keep on track. You had to stay one step ahead of the aircraft at all times. If you didn't, it would turn and bite you.

Unlike any other army units, there were very few 'sirs' used among the aircrew in our squadron. Officers called each other by their first names, and the other ranks did the same with each other. We'd gone through so much together, proved ourselves so many times, the ceremony of official title felt redundant. We were all close friends – and it felt odd to call a good mate 'sir'. Above all, we didn't have the time.

There was one more quality you needed to be an Apache pilot. The best attack pilots had the soul of an infantryman. Army Air Corps personnel had always been known as flying soldiers rather than pilots. It's why we preferred to wear combat fatigues and not flying suits – with the exception of Billy, of course. The founding ethos of the Corps, since the first time soldiers took to the air to artillery spot from their nineteenth-century balloons, was to help the blokes on the ground win the fight – and that wouldn't ever change.

'We're going through the wood,' the ground commander might have said to us as we provided top cover in a Gazelle or a Lynx.

'Roger,' we'd reply. 'Move slowly and we'll cover the treeline and the high ground.'

You could teach a monkey how to fly; Soviet scientists proved that during the Cold War by attaching electrodes to a cyclic stick. But you couldn't teach a monkey how to fix a bayonet and charge. To fight an Apache, it wasn't enough to be a gifted pilot and a geeky tech-head. That would only get you to where you needed to be at the right time. The real challenge was what happened next.

In the months before we were first sent to Afghanistan, some of the top brass were quite sensitive about classifying the Apache as a killing machine. They didn't really like us to talk about it, despite the fact we were walking around with a big fuck-off attack helicopter badge on our arms. God knew what they thought we were going to do when we got there.

To me it was breathtakingly simple. Attack pilots didn't deliver soup. We didn't help old ladies across the road, and we didn't shoot out lollipops. Our main battle function was to close with the enemy and kill them.

Snipers and Apache pilots were the only two combatants to get a detailed look at the face of the man they were about to kill. Nine times out of ten, we'd watch them in close-up on a five-inch-square screen before we pulled the trigger. It was no different to a sniper fixing his quarry in the sights of his bolt action rifle until the optimum moment to engage. We shared the same mindset: the mindset of a professional assassin.

The first sixteen of us qualified in October 2004, allowing 656 Squadron to be declared an Initial Operating Capability – a viable strike force, but unable to sustain prolonged operations. On 5 May 2006, the squadron deployed to Afghanistan, and we were finally declared ready to fight as a battlegroup – six days *into* the deployment.

The Apache force arrived a month after the rest of the brigade, and none of the ground commanders really knew what to do with us at first. Years late and way over budget, the Apache programme had been derided as a white elephant by everyone in the military – an overpriced Cold War glamour machine of little practical worth in a twenty-first-century close combat counter-insurgency. They sent us out on missions anyway, because we were there. Then we were called to our first firefight – and we showed what we could do.

Within a few weeks, they were converted. So much so that 3 Para's Commanding Officer often refused to allow his men out of their platoon houses unless they had an Apache above them.

We proved the aircraft was phenomenally good at close – sometimes very close – air support, swiftly overtaking the Harrier as the troops' aircraft of choice. We were the Paras' big brother; we turned up and immediately turned the tables on the bullies picking on them. Soon, the lads on the ground began to refer to us as 'the muscle'. 'Things were looking pretty shitty until the muscle turned up,' was a regular refrain in the cookhouse.

For us, the mad summer was one constant rush between one under fire platoon house to another besieged district centre. At times, the job felt like playing the Whack-A-Mole game at the fair;

the one where you never know which of the multiple holes the little bugger will pop out of first. You have to thump it quick with a mallet, but as soon as you have, another pops up from another hole. If you don't keep on smashing them hard, you lose.

On a few occasions we almost did lose. I was on the phone home when we got the Broken Arrow call from Now Zad. Broken Arrow is an emergency call for assistance from any available aircraft. It meant the platoon house was in the process of being overrun. We got up there to find the company of Royal Fusiliers in a grenade fight with the Taliban at their walls.

Our major weakness was a limited play time. Our fuel and weapons load would always run out eventually, and then we had to go back to base or get relieved by another Apache pair.

Sometimes all we had to do was turn up. The enemy had learned to fear us. 'When the Mosquitoes come, stay underground,' Taliban commanders were overheard telling their men. But most of the time they fought on regardless.

I must have been in twenty different battles on that first tour; some a few minutes long, others lasting for hours. Yet despite all of that, there I was, sitting on my cot at the start of the second tour pondering my destiny.

It wasn't that I was afraid of dying. After twenty-two and a half years of close scrapes all over the world, I'd come close to rolling a number seven several times – not least in Aldershot. And I'd believed for a long time that if your number was up, it was up – there was no point in fussing about it. What I was really bothered about was dying *now*.

I'd got away with the first tour, and that was supposed to be it for me. I just couldn't help thinking that it would be a crying shame if

I checked out now, minutes before I was about to leave. I'd been a bad boy in my past, and got away with all of that too. Maybe it was my turn next: fate, karma, Sod's Law, Murphy's Law; or just plain old tough shit – call it what you will. All I knew was that one bloke only gets a certain amount of luck in any one life, and my lucky bag should have been nigh on empty.

I didn't tell Emily about any of this. Instead, I quietly upped my life insurance to the maximum, updated my will and ensured everything was in order for her and my kids if I didn't come back.

But Emily had her own worries. Not long before I left for the second tour, we'd agreed to start a family together. We'd been together for years, she was thirty-four and the time felt right. I hadn't realised how much the decision had affected her.

On my last night, Emily made me promise not to do anything stupid. It was a promise that I told her I had every intention of keeping – and I meant it. Then she gave me a tiny little good luck charm, a silver angel the size of a postage stamp.

'Have it on you always, it'll keep you safe,' she said.

I burst out laughing. She burst into tears.

So I carried it in my top right breast pocket which was double sealed with buttons and Velcro. It went everywhere I went – as much from guilt as superstition … to start with, anyway.

HANDOVER

There was an awful lot to be done in the five days before 664 Squadron left. Our handover had to be seamless. It was vital that the quality of Apache support to the guys on the ground wasn't affected. There were lessons to be learned from their tour; we had to adapt to all the procedural changes and familiarise ourselves with any aircraft issues that might have cropped up after three more months of hard combat.

There were some nervous people in London. An awful lot of money had been spent on the Apache and the last thing they wanted was for us to break one in less than a year of ops. Because it was so new, the procurement pencil-necks back at the MoD watched us like hawks.

The MoD had given us an encyclopaedic document known as the Release to Service which told us what we were and were not allowed to do with the aircraft. If any pilot broke any of the RTS rules – in the air or on the ground – he would be investigated. If he was found to have broken them deliberately, he would be removed from flying duties – permanently.

As Mr Sky Cop, the flying regs were poor old Billy's bag. I didn't envy him the responsibility, but it was good wind-up material.

'I take it looping the Apache is still out this tour is it, Billy?'

'Don't even think about it. You're only an average pilot, remember.' Then, under his breath but loud enough for us to hear: 'Unlike me.'

'I suppose a barrel roll or two is out the question too?'

While Billy exchanged notes with 664's QHI, I ironed out the weapons systems' nuances with their Weapons Officer. I also signed for the gun tape laptop, on which recordings of all our weapons releases were stored. The gun tape laptop was kept in a special safe in the Joint Helicopter Force Forward office. A lot of the material on it was highly classified. 'Kill TV' could be really damaging to us if it fell into the wrong hands. Something stuck on *YouTube* under a provocative headline could make us look like war criminals.

You only needed to look at the infamous gun tape of the US Apache slaughtering the 'Iraqi farmers'. US intelligence intercepted a plan to bring down an aircraft with a surface-to-air missile. The Apache was launched and dispatched every member of the insurgent team. The tape was leaked, cut and restructured to show the brutal servants of the Great Satan routinely wiping out innocent Iraqi farmers. It didn't show the SAM being drawn from its bag and put in position.

The JHF was the squadron's nerve centre, right next door to the Joint Operations Cell – a central Ops Room from where the three battlegroups based at Bastion (42 Commando, 45 Commando and the Information Exploitation Battlegroup) were managed.

The JHF and JOC compound consisted of as many tents, flags, masts and antennae as you could cram into fifty square metres. It was encircled by razor wire, and Minimi machine-gun-toting guards manned the only entrance twenty-four hours a day. It was the most secure area in the camp, and everyone who went in and out had to state their official purpose. Traffic was frequent between the JHF and JOC – each had to know what the other was up to at all times if operations were to be smoothly dovetailed.

The JHF was a large air-conditioned and sound-insulated khaki tent, five metres wide and fifteen long. A huge map table stood at its centre, with desks for the Boss, squadron ops officers, watchkeepers and signallers lining the four sides. We and the Chinook pilots planned our missions, gave briefings and ran the sorties from here.

There were eight CH47 Chinooks in theatre by then, upped from the original six in an emergency reinforcement over the summer. There were only ever two emergency response choppers in Bastion at any one time, with the rest of the CH47 force at the Coalition's giant southern air hub, Kandahar Airfield.

The Chinook's five-man crews – two pilots and three load-masters – usually only came into the JHF for briefs. If we needed to make detailed plans with them before they left Kandahar, we'd generally do it over a conference call. Kandahar housed our rear echelon elements as well, and it was where we'd take the Apaches for heavy maintenance or repair. There was neither the spare equipment nor the capacity at Bastion. Thankfully, this handover only involved a changeover of personnel. All the equipment and airframes were staying where they were.

The Apache was a very hungry beast: it chomped through ammunition, fuel and spare parts at an alarming rate. A squadron of eight aircraft needed a massive logistics footprint to support it in the field: eighteen four-ton trucks for parts and ammunition, seven articulated lorries, five fuel tankers, three forklift trucks, two motorcycles, five technician vans, one eight-ton engineers' lorry and a fire engine.

The machine was hugely labour intensive at the best of times, and Afghanistan was the cruellest place on earth to operate helicopters. It cost £20,000 for every hour in the air and needed thirty-two man hours of maintenance on the ground for every hour flown – and that wasn't just a couple of hairy-arsed blokes in boiler suits sharing a wrench. Our Apaches needed REME avionics and airframe technicians, armourers, arming and loading teams, drivers, refuellers, signallers, IT specialists, Intelligence officers, clerks and storemen – ninety-eight people in total; more than six of them to every one pilot, and every one of them an expert.

The REME split into two tribal groups, depending on their role. There were the Greenies: the brainboxes, the technicians who worked on the avionics (from the TADS to the defensive aide suite). And there were the Blackies: the grease monkeys, who worked on the airframe – blades, rotors, gearboxes and engines. Each camp considered itself the most vital for the machine, so Greenies and Blackies lived in a state of permanent mutual abuse. 'What's the definition of a Blackie?' was the Greenie refrain. 'A Greenie, with his brains knocked out.' In response, the Blackies watched the Greenies crouched in front of their computers, and dismissed them as work-shy, tea-glugging, muscle-dodging skivers.

The truth was, each had a healthy respect for the other and they always worked side by side on the airframes in two mixed shifts. They were an excellent and close-knit team, and they needed to be: the aircraft's maximum flying hours had been upped again, so our second tour was going to be a whole lot harder than the first. We could now spend eleven and a half hours in the air per day; at the start of our first tour, it had only been six. The Chinook and Lynx's flying hours had also been extended. As an equally limited resource, the pressure on them was also intense.

I only had one question when Billy told me: 'So who's agreed to pay for that?'

Aircraft flying hours is a money thing. The more time we spent in the air, the more replacement parts we'd need, and the more our deployment would cost the MoD. And they'd already forked out £4 billion.

'There's no new money. They're cannibalising the aircraft stored at Shawbury for the spares.'

Now it made sense. 'Excellent.' I raised an imaginary glass. 'Here's to our glorious future.'

'Tell me about it. The bet is that combat will have decreased in a few years until the spares chain kicks in.'

'I think I'll stick with the horses …'

'What do you care, anyway?' he grinned. 'You'll be raising a real one of those in your local while I'm pulling up the floorboards for rotor blades. Or maybe not …'

Very funny.

It took all five days of the handover to get everyone in and out on the air bridge from Kandahar and Kabul, where the RAF's Tristars came in from Brize Norton.

The squadron was divided into four flights – 1, 2, 3 and HQ – with two Apaches in each. On Day Three, happy day, Carl caught up with us. He, Billy, the Boss and I made up HQ Flight. A staff sergeant, Carl was the unit's Electronic Warfare Officer – the resident expert on the aircraft's self-defence suite.

'Bloody Tristar broke down, so there was a two-hour delay at Brize. Then I had to wait ages for my Bergen and weapon, then no one came to meet me … And every CrabAir trolley dolly had a spray-on desert flying suit and a spare in her wardrobe, but I can't get one for love nor money …'

'Nice to see you too, Carl.'

Carl was an excellent pilot, a very safe pair of hands, and knew the aircraft's systems better than anyone, but he didn't half like a moan. He was always bleating on about something or other, and got a fair bit of stick for it. But when it came to how unfair it was that he'd been passed over for promotion – which had happened a few times – I had every sympathy. His front-seater on the last tour had got an MiD whilst Carl got nothing, despite being the Aircraft Captain. He really was Mr Unlucky.

Carl arrived with the four members of 3 Flight, so half our pilots were in and 664's first two flights could head for home. The Boss shook hands with the outgoing OC on 11 November, Armistice Day, and the handover was complete.

One of the reasons Chris was so popular was his enthusiasm for team bonding. He wanted the squadron to be one big happy family, and did everything he could to make it so.

For starters, he got permission for us to choose our own call-signs. It was what the Americans did, and their aircrew came up with some real screamers: 'Steel Rain' and 'Thumper' were amongst my favourites, both fittingly employed by AC130 Spectre gunships.

For some reason that I've never understood, the British military was far more reserved. Most units took the shockingly dull callsigns they were given, randomly generated by some NATO computer. 'Opal' and 'Torsion' were two of the worst I'd worked with in Afghanistan.

The Boss put it to the floor. Up until then, the Apaches had been working under the callsign 'Wildman' – which wasn't bad, but a bit of a mouthful if you were in a hurry. After hours of spirited debate over several days, someone came up with 'Ugly'. It summed up the machine perfectly – how it looked and what it did. From then on, we'd be known as Ugly Five Zero, Ugly Five One, Ugly Five Two, and so on. We'd announce ourselves at contacts over the net with fresh pride.

'Who are you?'

'We're Ugly.'

'Funny guys; who are you?'

'We really are Ugly. We're the Apache boys.'

We weren't the only troops to be changing over in Helmand. After one hell of a tour, the Paras and airborne gunners of 16 Air Assault Brigade were being replaced by Britain's other elite infantry formation, the Royal Marines of 3 Commando Brigade.

The commandos did their best to keep things quiet for their first few weeks, to find their footing. That worked well for us too, allowing us to ease the squadron's new pilots gently into the scene. As well as the Boss, there were four more new faces on this tour, and there was a vast amount for the three men – and one woman – to take on board.

Every pilot did an initial familiarisation flight. It was important to learn about – or reacquaint ourselves with – the key locations and the general lie of the land over which we were expected to fight. I flew with the Boss (as Ugly Five One), with Carl flying Billy on our wing (Ugly Five Zero). Apache crews nearly always flew in pairs so they could watch out for each other in the air and share the workload on the ground. Double the birds meant double the fire power for the boys beneath us, though we didn't always get the option. We were due to lift at 1500, so we got changed straight after lunch.

Strict rules dictated every shred of clothing we wore while flying – right down to our underwear: a pair of special socks, long johns and a long-sleeved T-shirt, all fire retardant. One Apache pilot I knew even used to wear a Formula 1 driver's facemask. Surrounded by 3,000 lb of aircraft fuel, every one of us knew that we were flying a potential fireball.

Over our underwear went a desert camouflage shirt and trousers. Our uniforms were designed to look just like normal army Disruptive Pattern Material (DPM), but were also fire retardant. The pockets were double-sealing, so nothing would fall out of them and foul the flying controls in flight.

Flying suits were a big no-no, whatever Billy thought. They were fine for training in the UK, but if we got shot down we wanted to look like regular infantry. Our uniforms carried no unit markings, and I didn't even wear rank slides. The Taliban would have given their eye teeth to get their hands on a 'mosquito' pilot.

We wore fire-retardant shammy leather gloves – in white, green or black thin enough to give you a good feel of the controls, and flying combat boots with a special sole that didn't pick up debris on our walk to the aircraft. Anything loose in the cockpit could jam the controls and cause the helicopter to crash

Over our shirts, we wore a Life Support Jacket – a camouflage canvas survival waistcoat packed with the kit we might need to evade capture and keep us alive if we went down. The survival LSJ was tailor-made; it had to fit tightly enough to hold in our innards and help preserve circulating body fluid if we got shot. A few more minutes of consciousness might make the difference between getting to the ground safely and dropping out of the sky.

Clipped to the survival jacket was a triangular-shaped bullet-proof Kevlar breastplate that would stop a 7.62-mm round at point-blank range. We tucked it up inside the jacket to cover our heart but called it the Ball Cruncher because if you grabbed your kit in a hurry and threw it over your shoulder as you ran, the plate would coming winging down between your legs.

My 9-mm Browning and a couple of ammunition clips – thirteen rounds in each – were strapped to my right thigh in a black holster with Velcro fastening. Every pilot kept his second personal weapon – an SA80 carbine – in a bracket inside the cockpit. It looked like the normal full length assault rifle but had a very short barrel and an additional grip at the front.

Strapped to my left leg was my Black Brain – a filofax-like note-pad, knee board and pencil for any crucial information I needed to jot down for or during the sortie. That meant the day's codewords, the JTAC callsigns we needed to hook up with on the ground, or grids we were heading for.

I also kept a crib sheet in it containing any detail I might have needed to know about the myriad other offensive coalition aircraft that were working around us. There was quite an array: the UK's Harrier GR7s, the US's F16s, A10 Thunderbolts, EA6B Prowlers, B1B Lancer bombers, B52 bombers, AC130 Spectre gunships and AH64 Apaches, the Netherlands' F16s and AH64s, France's Mirage 2000s, and Belgium and Norway's F16s. We needed to recognise all the aircraft callsigns the moment they came on the net, their national Rules of Engagement restrictions, what weapons they carried, and the safety distances we needed to hold to avoid catching any of their impact.

'Ramit Three Seven, launching a GBU38 in three zero seconds, Ugly Five One acknowledge?' If the shout came in there was no time to play Twenty Questions; we had to know who Ramit was and what he meant by a 38. A few seconds to discover that a Dutch F16 was about to launch a 500-lb JDAM bomb was usually enough for us to skedaddle to the safe distance.

Each pilot also had their own grab bag, a canvas satchel wedged beside their seats. If we went down, we'd grab them and go. What went in them was entirely down to personal preference. Some of the guys put ammo and rations in theirs; others stuffed them with bottles of water too. Apart from my field dressing and spare morphine vial, mine was crammed full of ammunition. I'd asked our storeman for everything he could spare.

As an ex-infantryman, I knew all about ground fighting. The way I saw it, the more bullets I had, the longer I'd stay alive. I've never needed to drink very much and I could kip when I was safe. In my ammo-bag I put four additional magazines of 9-mm, four thirty-round magazines of 5.56-mm for the SA80 carbine, and an extra bandolier of 120 5.56-mm rounds – as much as I could carry.

I'd also slipped in two L2 fragmentation grenades I'd stashed from the first tour and two smoke grenades – one green smoke, one red. Grenades were strictly forbidden inside the aircraft in case they went off, but I knew my weapons and was happy to carry them.

We stowed our fighting gear and 'go-bags' in the boot of the Apache, just forward of the tail section. Go-bags contained luxury items for long-term evasion in case we went down in the mountains or had a malfunction and needed to land at a distant firebase: sleeping bags, wash kit, warm clothing, waterproofs, a bivvie, spare food, water and the like. I'd also decided to add a full set of army webbing, body armour and a proper combat helmet. It was a lot to run with, but I didn't want to leave the one item that could save my life.

The flight line was at the most easterly point of Camp Bastion. There were two north–south runways; ours, a 200-metre length of metallic matting surrounded by rocks to suppress the dust, and a kilometre-long dirt strip for the C130 transporters.

Three hangars ran alongside the western edge of our runway:

one for aircraft, a second for the technicians' workshop, and a third for personnel, shared by pilots and Groundies. Our hangar contained a row of weapons crates, camping cots for the on-duty Groundie shift (they worked in twenty-four hour stints), a basketball hoop and a row of lockers. Each of us had our own, where we'd dump anything in our pockets before walking out to the aircraft.

We never went up with any personal possessions on us; that meant no wallet, no family pictures, no wedding rings and certainly no US dollars – the currency used around camp – which would ID you in an instant. It was imperative to sanitise yourself entirely so as not to give the enemy any ammunition to break you during interrogation. A small crack was all they needed, and they'd prise it open until it was as wide as a house.

'So you're married are you, soldier? Kids too, I see from the picture in your wallet. You want to see them again? Maybe we'll pay them a visit. I'll call my friend at Leeds University to pick them up from school for you. Maybe we'll slice them up in front of you like fucking salami – unless of course you want to talk to us ...'

I carried Emily's angel everywhere. I thought I might buy time proclaiming my belief in another world beyond our own. No religion at all was scorned by the Taliban. They weren't to know that it was my family album and every letter I'd received. It was also a symbol of hope that I'd get back alive.

All we carried in the air was an official ID card with the 'Big Four' pieces of information that the Geneva Convention obliged us to reveal – name, rank, army number and date of birth. Our dog tags repeated the Big Four; we hung them around our neck alongside a vial of morphine which we could self-inject.

I kept a photo of Emily and my son and daughter in my locker, along with some spare batteries, a softie jacket, a pair of gloves, a cloth, a bottle of glass cleaner, my flying helmet, night vision goggles, survival jacket and a sleeping bag.

As we left the hangar on the fifty-metre walk to the rearming bays where the Apaches were ready to go, two aircraft were landing – 3 Flight completing their familiarisation.

It's hard to forget your first sight of an Apache in the flesh. It still made me stop and stare. Its huge menacing shape, bristling with weapons and silhouetted against the deep blue sky, growing ever bigger as it closed on us. No single feature of the machine, from its angular and callus-like front profile to its chunky stabilator tail wing, was designed to please the eye. It was lean, purposeful and businesslike. Nothing was superfluous: every single bolt added to its killing power. Ugly, sure; but to me, a picture of perfection. Beauty and the beast wrapped into one.

'Hey, Boss … Just because you've got the front seat today doesn't mean you're going to get it on every sortie.'

'You're obviously confusing your position as the Weapons Officer with my position as Boss,' Chris said. 'Get in and drive.'

It made sense for him to be in the front today so he could concentrate on what was below us while I gave him the guided tour.

Corporal Hambly, the Arming and Loading Point Commander, was waiting for us. He was in charge of the aircraft on the ground. He supervised an eight-man team whose sole job was to get us airborne. Simon Hambly stood by a wing, with an intercom plugged into it so he could speak to us in the cockpit when we started up. Whilst he was plugged in, he owned the Apache – not the Weapons Officer, or even his boss.

'A Load Charlie for you, isn't it sir?'

'Yes thanks, mate. Just sightseeing today.'

Load Alpha was just Hellfire, Load Bravo only rockets. Load

Charlie was our default load – a split weapons load on the pylons: two out of the four on the wings held Hellfire rails, the other two rocket pods. What you took depended on the mission. We weren't going to put any rounds down today, but we never left base without a full complement just in case.

I did a quick walk around to double check that the protective covers had been removed from the weapons, intakes and exhausts.

'All okay with the aircraft?'

'She's gleaming, sir. Cryptos loaded; be nice to her.'

I clambered up the right side of the Apache's alloy skin, using the grab bars, and lifted up the back-seater's heavy canopy door. It clicked open and hung there as I contorted myself onto the high, firm, flat seat. The Boss was already in.

Thirty minutes to takeoff.

The rear seat of an Apache was like a throne, high above the worker bees buzzing around below. Unfortunately, it wasn't as comfortable. The foam pads on the seat and back were really tasty when we first got the Apaches, but after three years of heavily laden arses they had completely flattened. Anything more than a few hours in the cockpit these days and it felt like you were perched on a bag of golf balls. That was when the arse dance began, moving from one cheek to the other to try to alleviate the pain. Some of the guys resorted to half inflated therma-rest pillows.

The cockpit was like a sauna. The Afghan sun had beaten down on it all morning. Beads of sweat swelled up on my brow. A bank of controls and instruments faced me: buttons, switches and knobs of every shape and size – 227 in total, and every one designed to feel different so you could recognise them in the dark. Most of them were dual- or triple-purpose, which gave them a total of 443 different positions. Every action could require a combination of button pushes, so the number of potential combinations ran into the thousands.

One five-inch-square Multi Purpose Display screen sat each side of the control bank. We could bring up anything we liked on them, from the TV images filmed by the TADS lenses, to the digital script and diagrams of whatever we asked of the on-board computers. There were well over 1,500 different pages – engine pages, fuel pages, comms pages, weapons pages and radar pages. To the far left of the control bank was an alphabetical keyboard for typing data into the computers, or texting messages between Apaches.

A pioneering helicopter pilot of the 1930s would still have rec-ognised the pedals, cyclic stick between my legs (controlling speed and direction – gripped by my right hand) and the collective lever below my left elbow (for height and power – gripped by my left). But that would be about it. He'd be mighty confused by the myriad triggers and buttons on both.

Because there were so many systems to test and configurations to set, achieving takeoff from cold required more than 1,000 button pushes. It took thirty minutes without any snags, fifteen at a mad push. Any quicker and we'd be switching things on in mid-air without knowing if they were going to work.

I inserted a key into the master ignition switch on a panel to the left of the collective then twisted the switch from 'Off' to 'Battery'. A few seconds' pause as the battery leaked life into the beast, then the distinctive 'click-click' of the relays. The Up Front Display (UFD) – a panel top right of the controls showing critical infor-mation and faults digitally – lit up. The machine was stirring.

I closed the canopy door and flipped my helmet onto my head, making sure that my ears didn't fold inside it (that would be agony in half an hour) and tightened the chinstrap. I plugged in the communication cord and the ongoing conversations of four different VHF / UHF and FM radio channels burst into life inside my helmet. The four channels were: the Joint Terminal Attack Controller's net for us to communicate with the guys on the ground who needed us; the Coalition air net in Helmand so we could talk to other aircraft; the net back to the JHF; and the intra-Apache net to talk or send data to our wingmen and other Apaches in the squadron. In addition, there was a permanently open internal intercom for the two pilots to speak to each other. The Boss's was the fifth voice in my ear. The sixth and seventh voices boomed through.

'This is right wing; how do you read, sir?'

'Nice and clear, Si. What about me?'

'Clear as a bell, sir. Left wing check in.'

'Loud and clear, Corporal Hambly.'

'You got him, sir.'

'I hear the left wing, Si. Let's rock and roll.'

Luckily, everyone didn't always speak at once – though they could. A volume control allowed me to turn up the net most relevant to me at any particular moment.

'Pylons, stabilator, Auxiliary Power Unit; clear, Si?'

'Pylons, stab and APU all clear. Clear to start, sir.'

I pressed the APU button below the ignition switch. A loud whine as the APU engine turned over, then the distinctive ticking of the igniters. The APU burst into life followed by a rush of air from the four gaspers positioned around the cockpit. The air was hot; no air con yet.

I grabbed the cyclic stick and yelped. I'd taken my gloves off to pull on my helmet and forgotten the stick had been sunbathing all morning. A quick glance confirmed the beginnings of a pale white blister between my thumb and forefinger. *Shit*; I'd have to fly the whole sortie with pressure against it.

My rage made me think of my daughter; she'd be laughing her head off if she saw me now. My daughter thought it was hilarious when I hurt myself because I was normally such a hard bugger. Me in pain, face contorted, fighting the urge to curse, made her sides split. That's daughters for you.

It was an even numbered day today.

'Starting number two, Si?'

We always matched the engine starting sequence to odd and even days. It meant one never worked harder than the other in the long run.

'Clear to start number two, sir.'

The heat in the cockpit was close to unbearable. All the hot wiring, glues, resins, metals and rubber cosseted inside my glass cocoon exuded their own distinctive scent. I was still sweating like a pig.

I pushed the right hand Engine Power Lever forward to 'Idle' and the starboard engine fired up. Then a slow, smooth push on the EPL, fully for-ward. As the engine pitch grew the tail rotor started up thirty-five feet behind me and the four main rotors begun to move above my head, slowly at first, and then ever faster, thudding rhythmically as the blades started to catch the air.

My eyes began to sting as the first droplets off sweat trickled into them from my brow. I wished the air con would hurry up.

'Starting number one.'

'Clear to start number one, sir.'

Ten seconds later the thuds were too quick to count and the rotors began a deafening hum.

Twenty-two minutes to takeoff.

I attached my monocle and bore-sighted my helmet. It allowed me to snap shoot at any target on the ground simply by looking at it and pulling the trigger. Tiny infrared sensors positioned around the cockpit detected the exact position of the crosshairs at the centre of my monocle and the computer directed the cannon accordingly. The Apache didn't even need to be facing the target. It was a neat trick.

The sweat finally began to cool on my brow as the air con won its battle with the sun's rays. I started testing the systems.

Fifteen minutes to takeoff.

My hands and eyes swept around the cockpit. The Boss and I kept up a constant dialogue as we worked. Our rotor blades thundered menacingly above the five man arming team. Three … two … one … ten minutes to lift.

'Ugly Five One on one.' I flicked to the second radio. 'On two.' Flicked to the third. 'On three.' Flicked to the last, our data radio, and sent our digital position.

Billy replied, 'Ugly Five Zero on one … on two … on three.' An icon appeared on the MPD showing the position of his Apache.

'Good Data. Ready.' All four radios and data were working.

Billy replied with a 'click-click' over the radio, shorthand for affirmative.

Pushing the APU button again switched it off. 'APU off; pins, cords and chocks please, Simon.'

His team prepared the aircraft for moving and I opened my door to receive the arming pin. The flares and weapons were now armed and we were ready to go.

'Have a good trip, sirs.' Simon disconnected from the right wing and his team moved to the missile and rocket racks. For the first time since we'd arrived, we owned the Apache.

'Your lead, Billy.'

Another double click.

Two minutes and thirty seconds to takeoff.

My left hand moved down the collective to the flying grip. Looking straight ahead as my right eye focused on the flight symbology projected into the monocle, I gave the flying grip a single twist to the right, removing the collective's friction lock. The torque – the measurement of engine power output in helicopter flight – indicated 21 per cent. That was the norm while stationary on the ground, rotor blades flat – the minimum angle of pitch.

My feet pressed on the very top of both directional foot pedals at the same time until I heard a light thud.

'Parking brake off? Tail wheel locked?'

The final two questions on the Boss's checklist. I did my visual check. 'The parking brake is off, the handle is in, tail wheel is locked and the light is out.'

My right eye focused on the torque and my left watched Billy and Carl's aircraft pull out of the loading bay beside us and taxi away. My left hand was poised to pull up the collective, my right wrapped firmly around the cyclic, ready to push forward.

Thirty seconds to takeoff.

With fifty metres between us and Billy, I lifted the collective and depressed my left pedal to increase power to the tail rotor and balance us up against the increased force of the turning rotor blades. Left unchecked, the main blades would try to turn our nose to the right, leaning the Apache dangerously over to one side. The torque climbed to 35 per cent.

With a gentle push of the cyclic control stick away from my body the main blades tipped and pulled the machine slowly forward. A touch on the toe brakes at the top of the pedals to test the brakes then we taxied onto our miniature runway for a running takeoff.

Heat and altitude both reduced the amount of power a helicopter engine could generate. Camp Bastion was long on both. We
could lift vertically, but it was a major struggle if we carried a full
load of ammunition and fuel. Taking a run at it gave us translational lift, the kind fixed-wing aircraft used.

Fifteen seconds to takeoff.

I pointed our nose straight down the runway, with Billy and Carl
still fifty metres ahead of us, and pulled a little more pitch. The
machine picked up pace nicely. Once the torque hit 65 per cent, I
pushed the trim button to hold the collective and cyclic in place. It
was sufficient power to get us up. The speed symbol in my right eye
hit twenty knots and continued to climb.

Six seconds to takeoff.

Eighty metres down the runway, the tail wheel lifted off it. At
thirty-five knots she wanted to fly, but I held her down with a tiny
reduction of power and shift off the cyclic. It wasn't time yet.

Two seconds to takeoff.

I was watching Carl's disc intently … Now … It tipped forward
and I raised the collective again and the main wheels left the
ground. We lifted in perfect unison. Good. I was pleased I'd got it
spot on. If you set the right tone at the start of a mission you'd
remain accurate throughout.

'Your ASE, Boss.'

The Boss armed the aircraft's Aircraft Survival Equipment (ASE)
to protect us against SAMs.

'Okay, countermeasures set; ASE is on semi-automatic.'

'Zero Charlie this is Ugly Five Zero and Ugly Five One. Wheels
off at your location as fragged, over.'

'Zero Charlie, Roger. Out.'

I pulled up the navigation page on the left hand MPD and

selected the pre-planned route heading for Sangin, the first stop on our tour. A glance through the monocle confirmed: 'Eighteen minutes to arrival.'

We were seventy-five feet above the desert floor and heading north-east, the camp's perimeter fence two hundred metres behind us. A quick trim with the right thumb and we accelerated to a cruising speed of 120 knots. The Boss selected automatic on the ASE. The Apache would, we hoped, keep us safe from surface-to-air missiles. SAMs were the greatest threat to us at the heights we operated.

Billy and Carl were a safe distance in front of us to avoid collision. Billy came on the radio.

'Ugly Five One, this is Ugly Five Zero. High-high, five-five and six-zero.'

'High-high, five-five, six-zero copied.'

Billy wanted us to climb high. Him to 5,500 feet and us to 6,000 feet – always a small difference in height too, for safety. The Boss glanced up through the canopy's bulletproof window.

'Clear above.'

'Copied. Climbing.'

I pulled back on the cyclic and hard on the collective while depressing my left pedal. We lost our stomachs and soared.

Despite its gargantuan combat weight, the Apache's mighty Rolls Royce engines made it just as agile and manoeuvrable as any chopper the army had ever had. Turning at up to 38,300 rpm, they pumped out an incredible 2,240 shaft horse power – making the Apache twenty-two times more powerful than a Porsche 911.

The Apache could climb in excess of 5,000 feet a minute, including a one-off, ninety-degree, nose-up vertical climb of 1,000 feet. And it could do a 360-degree loop, barrel roll or a wing over nose dive – every stunt manoeuvre in the book. Not moves I've ever carried out, of course; heaven forbid – especially with Sky Cop as my wingman.

Sixty seconds or so later, we were at Billy's nominated cruising altitude. It was a terrific feeling to be up there again, over that menacingly beautiful landscape, and in that extraordinary machine. Ten minutes into the flight, I felt as confident at the controls as I had on the day I left in August. I was right back in the zone again.

Despite the years of training, it had still taken me a good six weeks of hard fighting on the first tour before I really felt the exhilaration of being at one with the machine.

When you drive a new car, you're slow and cautious. You need to think about every action, from where the indicators are to how far you are from the gatepost. After you've driven it for a while, you don't have to think; you just end up at home without having thought of driving once.

It was the same with the Apache, but on a grander scale. Halfway through the first tour, whatever I wanted to do in the aircraft, I did. From that moment onwards I didn't need to think how to fly and shoot because my fingers, arms and legs were already working in perfect harmony with my mind. I was no longer strapped to the Apache; the Apache was strapped to me.

Almost all of the pilots were there by the end of the tour. But none of that meant that we had lost respect for the daunting reality of having so much firepower at our finger tips. Not for one moment, then or since. Nobody in that war had more potential to do as much damage to human life. With that power came an equal amount of responsibility. We were fearful of being seen as gung-ho; US Apache pilots had that reputation and we didn't want to follow suit. Every single round we put down we put down with good reason; killing someone was a serious business.

As we flew, I watched the Boss's head dart from side to side as he fought to take everything in. 'Amazing ...' he'd murmur every now and then. Occasionally, a swift question. 'Jeez. What the hell do you call that?'

There were no more inspiring places to fly than in southern Afghanistan. It was unlike anywhere I had ever seen before and I was still captivated by it too. The landscape was both epic and primeval; everything about it was extreme. When it was flat, it was flat as a pancake. When it was hot, it was unbearably so. The rivers were never babbling streams but vast raging torrents, and the mountains climbed straight up to the heavens, often from a standing start.

The plan was to do an anticlockwise circuit of the four northern platoon houses where we'd spent most of the first tour: Sangin first, then Kajaki in the far north-east, Now Zad in the far north-west, and finally Gereshk, twenty kilometres shy of Camp Bastion, on the way back.

We stuck to the safety of the desert on the way up, keeping the Green Zone to our right. Immensely fertile before the Soviet invasion in 1978–79, Helmand province had been known as Afghanistan's breadbasket. A decade of bitter fighting against the Red Army ended that. Russian bombers smashed much of Helmand's irrigation system to smithereens. Yet the year-round supply of melted snow off the Hindu Kush was sufficient to keep the river valley's fields and orchards lush enough for two full crops of opium poppies a year.

The vast majority of the province's intensely conservative, desperately impoverished, million-strong, largely Pashtun, population were farmers – or worked the farmers' land. The majority lived in single-storey houses fashioned from adobe and stone, often without electricity or piped water. It was an existence that hadn't changed in a millennium.

The Green Zone only amounted to a tiny central slice of the province. It was bordered by two great deserts. To its west was the Desert of Death and Camp Bastion.

'Dasht-e-Margo ...' The Boss practised his fledgling Pashton.

'Yeah. But aircrew generally call it the GAFA, Boss.'

'GAFA?'

'The Great Afghan Fuck All.'

The GAFA was an ancient, rocky seabed with a thick covering of sand as fine as dust. Nomads set up temporary shelters on it in the winter so their goats and camels could feed on the odd bush. In the summer it remained the exclusive preserve of the drug traffickers. They criss-crossed it south to Pakistan, or west to Iran, moving raw opium or freshly processed heroin to their consumers in the Middle East or Europe, leaving an endless mesh of tyre tracks behind them. It was so barren that you couldn't tell if you were at 100 feet or 10,000.

'What do you call the desert on the east side of the Green Zone, then?'

'The Red Desert.'

'Why?'

'Because it looks red from up here.'

The Boss peered at our right horizon. 'It's actually worse. Makes the GAFA look like Kent.'

The Red Desert stretched all the way to Kandahar: 10,000 square miles of thin, Arabian-style sand, whipped by the wind over thousands of years into an endless succession of dunes. From 5,000 feet up, its surface looked like a sea of rippling red waves. Except by two well-known routes, the Red Desert was completely impassable, even by tracked vehicles. If you went in there, you didn't come out again. That's why nobody ever did. Not even the nomads.

As we moved further north and nearer to Sangin the topography ahead of us began to change. We could see the outlines of great ridges of rock rising from steep valleys to form the foothills of the Hindu Kush. Their peaks were as sharp as knife-blades and coloured seams cut through them as they climbed, indicating the different eras of their evolution. The mountains stretched all the way to Kabul, 300 miles to the north-east. They were almost impassable in the winter snows and boasted only one road flat enough for most vehicles to make the arduous journey during the rest of the year.

Many of the foothills had been tunnelled into, originally for protection from the wind and sandstorms and somewhere to store crops, but then, in the last few thousand years, for war. They provided an excellent defence against invaders since the time of Alexander the Great, and most recently, a haven to Osama bin Laden and al Qaeda.

Conventional British forces tried to stay out of the mountains. Our lesson had been learned 164 years before we got there, when General Elphinstone's 16,000-man garrison was wiped out during the retreat from Kabul in 1842.

'That's Sangin ahead of us now, Boss.'

Sangin sat at the confluence of three green zones, and the District Centre was sited at the point the Helmand was joined by another river flowing from the northern hills. The Taliban had three different covered approaches from which to attack it.

It was no coincidence that the SBS team had got so badly whacked here. The town was the scene of the most intense fighting of our first tour and accounted for half of 16 Air Assault Brigade's body bags. For years it had been a centre of Taliban activity, as well as the market town where all of the opium grown in the north of the province was traded. The traffickers hadn't been too happy about the Paras' arrival either. We dropped down to get a better look.

'Wheel,' Billy called. 'We'll start east, you start west.'

A wheel was a regular Apache combat manoeuvre over a target. We'd circle on the same axis but at different heights, one clockwise, one anticlockwise. It gave the flight 360-degree visibility at all times. We liked to keep between 1,000 and 4,000 metres away from the target, out of small arms range but well within engagement range of our weapons, and close enough for us to see whatever we needed through our optics.

As I slipped us into the gentle circle, I pointed out areas of interest for the Boss to zoom into with the Day TV TADS camera and examine on his screen. It had three fields of view – narrow, wide and zoom. Zoom offered 127-times magnification. If you looked at a guy in the zoom field while standing off at 2,000 metres, you could tell how many fillings he had. The camera was housed in the nose pod, so we could see up to sixty degrees downwards; as if we were looking straight through the Kevlar shell beneath our feet.

Sangin was a maze of mainly single-storey brown and beige buildings connected by dust tracks. I centred my monocle cross-hairs on the wadi.

'My line of sight. The wadi.'

'Looking.' The Boss zoomed in.

The second set of crosshairs in his monocle told him where I was focusing. All he needed to do was line up his with mine and slave the TADS to his eye.

'Seen.'

'Come due east from it and the first building is the District Centre.'

'Okay. Hang on a minute, let me have a look at the map. Yup, I've got it.'

I glanced down at my right-hand MPD, which I'd set on the TADS image, relaying everything the Boss was seeing.

'Bloody hell, they've built the place up a bit.'

The three-storey adobe-clad structure had been vigorously reinforced. A massive Hesco Bastion wall now ran all the way around the building, and the Paras had added wooden planks, sandbags and junk – anything they could lay their hands on – to the rooftop defences. A 300- by 200-metre field alongside it had also been ringed by Hesco Bastion, giving them a permanently protected helicopter landing site. It was a proper fort now, and a fine feat of engineering.

'How they managed to stay alive long enough to build that, I've no idea ...'

I'd heard the dit from 664 Squadron. The DC's complement of Royal Engineers had affectionately renamed it Sangin Built Under Fire. Every man, bar one, had fired his weapon on the job; the only engineer who hadn't was their sergeant major, who'd been too busy lobbing ammunition to the rest of the guys.

'My line of sight – that's the market place.'

The *souk* was 700 metres east of the DC. On the TADS screen, I could see broken wooden frames hanging off its stalls and shredded curtains flapping in the wind. It had been heavily shot up over the summer, but never stopped being a hive of activity. There was money to be made in the opium business.

Old rice sacks were piled high outside several stalls – the favoured receptacle for opium poppy sap – and dozens of locals crowded around them under the watchful gaze of the marines in the DC. Busting the drugs industry wasn't their job. We'd get to that later, once the Taliban had been defeated. Otherwise, we'd be banging up 80 per cent of the local population.

'My line of sight now – that's Wombat Wood.' I was looking a kilometre north of the DC. 'The Taliban use it regularly to shell the guys.'

A wombat was a Weapon Of Magnesium Battalion Anti Tank; the generic slang the army gave to recoilless rifles. They were around eight feet long and fired shells up to a diameter of 120 mm. Nasty.

'Wombats aren't the only sinister things lurking in that wood, Boss. They fire 107-millimetre Chinese rockets from there too.'

A 107-mm Chinese rocket had killed two signallers in a block-house that covered the stairwell to the roof of the Sangin DC in July. Corporal Peter Thorpe died alongside his comrade Jabron Hashmi – the first British Army Muslim killed fighting the Taliban.

'Okay, let's show you Macy House.'

A few months before, I'd found a building 200 metres to the south which the Taliban had occupied, giving them good arcs of fire onto the DC. They'd knocked a series of firing ports into its walls. The Apache crews had named it after me as a way of identifying it to each other. I searched for it in vain.

'Forget it, it's gone.'

Where Macy House once stood, there was now nothing. It had obviously been bombed to oblivion while we'd been away. I looked at the clock.

'We'd better be moving on, Boss.'

We wanted to get in all four DCs, so we only had time for a whistle stop tour. Four minutes in Sangin was enough.

'Okay. Billy, let's move on to Kajaki.'

'Copied, Boss.'

We broke out of the wheel, slipped east of the Green Zone and pointed our noses north-east again. Kajaki was thirty-eight kilometres further up the Green Zone. My monocle said we'd be there in ten minutes.

Two minutes into the flight, an urgent message was broadcast over the JTAC net for Widow TOC – the JTACs' central hub in Camp Bastion's JOC Ops Room.

'Stand by.' The Boss cut across my chat with Billy about the fate of Macy House.

'Widow TOC, this is Widow Eight Four. We are north-east of Gereshk; we have come under sniper and mortar fire. Requesting immediate air support. Repeat, requesting *immediate* air support.'

Gereshk was only forty klicks south-west of us. The Boss stepped on the pressel by his left foot to fire up his radio mike.

'Widow TOC, Widow TOC; this is Ugly Five One. We are two Apaches; we have just left Sangin on a familiarisation flight and we've got plenty of gas. We're available for tasking if required.'

I pushed the cyclic forward and right, throwing the Apache into a tight bank.

'Ugly Five One, Widow TOC. Copied. Stand by.'

Widow TOC needed a senior officer's authority from the JHF to deploy us.

'Wait Widow TOC, I am Zero Alpha of all Ugly callsigns. I am authorising if you want us to do it.'

'Widow TOC, Roger. It's yours.'

'Eight minutes, Boss.'

'Ugly Five One, affirm. Widow Eight Four, we'll be with you in eight minutes; stand by.'

BACK IN THE HOT SEAT

The familiarisation flight was out of the window.

We were tanking it down to Gereshk at maximum speed, 120 knots per hour; we were heavy. It would take forty minutes for the Apache pair on standby at Camp Bastion to launch and get to the marines. We'd be there in a quarter of the time. It was a no-brainer.

I needed to get as much juice out of Ugly Five One as I could; cyclic forward to push the nose down and pick up speed, topping up the collective to keep our height. Cyclic with collective, again and again – my eye constantly on the torque. It edged past 95 per cent.

The Boss got back on the net to talk to the marines directly.

'Widow Eight Four, this is Ugly Five One. Send sitrep.'

'Ugly Five One, Widow Eight Four; we are pinned down on the north-western edge of the Green Zone, at grid 41R PQ 5506 2603.'

The boss read back the grid.

'They're hitting us with mortars. Rounds are landing in and around us as I speak.'

'Copied all. Do you have a grid for the mortar team?'

'Negative. They're firing from the Green Zone, approximately

70

200 to 300 metres east-south-east, but we're struggling to find them at the moment.'

'Roger. I'll call in the overhead.'

Our brains crunched the JTAC's information as we tried to build up a picture of what we could expect. We had to find that mortar team before they put a shell right on top of our guys, but Objective Number One was always to locate the friendlies or we simply couldn't engage. The last thing we needed was a blue-on-blue, the military term for soldiers killed or wounded by friendly fire.

The Boss tapped the marines' grid reference into the keyboard and the TADS swivelled in their direction.

'Okay Mr M, I'm starting to see some thin puffs of smoke on the ridgeline, my line of sight. Confirm you can see them.'

The mortar rounds' point of impact.

'Negative, Boss. We're still eight klicks off.' I couldn't see them with my naked eye. 'I've got the smoke on my MPD though.'

'Okay, keep an eye out for them; I'm going into the Green Zone to see if I can get a bead on the mortar team.'

We were 3,000 feet higher than the rapidly approaching Green Zone, with Billy and Carl 500 feet beneath us, to the left and slightly back. We were leading now because the Boss was back in command.

I pushed the weapons button under my right thumb between 'M' for missile and 'R' for rocket up to 'G' for gun and the cockpit juddered beneath my feet as the cannon followed my line of sight. I flicked up the guard and rested my forefinger lightly on the trigger. The Boss could fire far more accurately with his TADS image, but if I needed to take a snap shot, I was ready.

'My gun, Boss.'

I thought about what lay ahead. My grip on the controls tightened, my heartbeat quickened; I just adored the sensation of flying into combat. I could taste metal. I did so before every fight, as far back as my dust-ups in the school playground. The taste of adrenalin; my body was physically, chemically and mentally preparing itself for battle.

Four kilometres off I shuffled my arse into a more comfortable position, checked my harness was tight and the extendable bullet-catching Kevlar shield by my right shoulder was completely forward.

Exhilaration coursed through my veins. I could see the smoke plumes with my naked left eye now, just to the right of the Green Zone. They were rising out of a gully that led down into the trees. As we closed on the gully, I saw an empty compound on either side of it, then a couple of camouflage-painted vehicles sheltering behind the nearside compound's back wall. A Pinzgauer and a WMIK Land Rover. The marines. Two more vehicles stood at the back of the far compound. Eight or nine puffs of smoke spiralled upwards before being carried away by the wind.

Carl set up a circuit over the Green Zone. I headed towards the marines.

'Got the friendlies in the wadi, Boss. It's 42 Commando.'

'Copied. Let me know if they move.'

I wanted the Taliban to know that Big Brother had turned up to help out Little Brother.

The marines' JTAC came back with a grid for the enemy mortar position: a compound 200 metres in, behind some trees. At the edge of the Green Zone was another line of trees, hiding anyone inside it completely. A good place for an ambush. But it was a false lead.

'We've just been over that compound,' Billy reported. 'Couldn't see anyone in it.'

It wasn't the mortar tube we needed to find first anyway. They'd have no direct line of sight onto the marines. We needed to find their controller. Take him out, and the tube men would be firing blind.

The Taliban's spotters often positioned themselves in trees and reported the necessary corrections back to the tube via walkie-talkie. The Boss searched along the outer treeline, flicking constantly between the Day TV camera and the Forward Looking Infrared (FLIR) thermal camera.

Billy beat him to it. 'I've got a man hiding.'

'Where?'

'From the marines' wadi, follow the treeline to its most southerly end.' He paused to let the Boss follow his talk-on.

'On the ground, under trees, lone man … Don't think there are any weapons on him. Looking for a radio.'

A scruffy bloke with a beard, dressed from head to toe in black, walked out into the field, flapping his dishdash as he went to show us he wasn't armed and didn't have a single walkie-talkie stuffed down his trousers. With two gunships overhead, cannons pointing directly at him, he'd got the message we were onto him. Cunning sod. He knew we couldn't engage him. He moved slowly in the direction of Gereshk, still looking up at us and flapping away. I didn't see his face, but I knew he'd have a grin plastered right across it.

'Ugly callsigns, Widow Eight Four. We've just seen two puffs of smoke east of the previous target grid.'

Were they still engaging? There was no chance of hearing the mortars launch inside our sealed cockpits. But we did hear the first round impacting through the JTAC's open mike. The rounds were now landing alarmingly close to the marines, fired onto coordinates supplied by the smart arse spotter just before he came out to give us the dishdash dance.

Not all the Taliban were running. The carefully hidden mortar tube team were fighting on with the full knowledge we were swarming above them. That did take brass. We'd surely find them now.

Carl and I tracked east, deeper into the Green Zone from the empty compound. Thirty seconds later, Billy spoke up again. Skill fade from the break in Blighty was firmly behind Billy as he got to grips with the sights. He was having a good afternoon.

'I've got 'em. Three hundred metres east of the compound is a triangular-shaped copse. Men moving inside it.'

'Request laser spot.'

Billy pointed his crosshairs at the copse and squeezed his trigger. The Boss flicked his TADS onto Laser Spot Tracker mode, and the lens jumped towards the spot where Billy was aiming his laser energy.

'Where are they in there?'

'Under the trees. At least three of them on my FLIR, and this lot *have* got weapons on them.'

The copse was only fifty metres long but its foliage provided dense cover. We were 2,000 metres south-east of it, and all we could see was forty-foot trees. Billy had gone round the opposite side where, for a few metres, the trees were shorter and the bushes less thick; he'd picked up moving bodies through their heat signatures in his FLIR lens. I banked right to circle the northern edge too. To engage, we needed to be sure. The Boss got a perfect view through the window.

'Look at this heat source, Mr M.'

I looked down to the MPD above my right knee displaying the TADS image in FLIR mode. A long thin rectangle, ten inches wide, chest height and angled in the direction of the marines was practically burning a hole in the camera lens.

'Yup. That's definitely a mortar barrel in there.'

It was a good spot by Billy. And he wasn't going to let them get away.

'Confirmed as Taliban. Engaging with thirty Mike Mike.'

Mike Mike was military air slang for millimetre. Flame licked out of Billy's cannon as it spat HEDP rounds at a rate of 600 per minute and an initial muzzle velocity of 805 metres per second from his stand-off position 1,500 metres from the copse. Less than two seconds later, their shaped charge heads exploded with a blinding flash. Then the incendiary charges inside the 87-mm-long projectiles threw out jets of flame large enough to torch a car, igniting everything within a two-metre radius, and the fragment charges blasted out thousands of red hot shards of metal casing. Billy had set his gun to bursts of twenty. Three or four more of those, and the copse would be neutralised. But he'd only pumped off fifteen.

'Gun jam, gun jam! Your target. Pulling off.'

Our orbit had taken us past the marines again to watch for any leakers while he prosecuted the target. I brought our Apache round to face the copse as another two mortar rounds shot straight out of it. This time I caught a glimpse of their shock wave as they penetrated the treetops. They still weren't running.

'Necky little bastards.'

'These guys are insane,' the Boss said.

I didn't disagree. To carry on engaging us after tasting our firepower was suicidal.

The Boss knew exactly what to do. 'Let's go in with Flechettes.'

'Copied. Perfect.'

Cannon was great if you were on top of the target. But we had the distance now to set up for a rocket run.

Nothing beats a Flechette for multiple personnel out in the open. It was designed to burst open 860 metres into its flight, freeing its cargo of eighty five-inch-long Tungsten darts. An explosive charge powered them onto the ground at speeds well over Mach 2 – 2,460 mph – shredding everything within a fifty-metre spread. Each dart's intense supersonic speed created a huge vacuum behind it. If it hit a man in the chest, that vacuum would suck away everything in its path, and was powerful enough to tear flesh and muscle from a human target if it passed within four inches of one.

The copse was a textbook Flechette target: no civilians anywhere near it. But we had to be quick. 'Stay in the overhead Billy, and keep them fixed. We're coming in for a Flechette shoot.'

They'd be unlikely to do a runner with Billy sitting right on top of them.

We needed a four-kilometre run-in for a rocket shoot, so I banked hard right, pulling us away from the target, and thrust the cyclic forward to gain the extra 1,000 metres.

'Co-op shoot Flechettes. Two rockets.'

'Copied, Boss.'

Front and back seat worked together on a co-operative shoot. 'CRKT' popped up in my monocle; the Boss had just actioned the rockets. I flicked the cyclic's weapon select button to 'R'. A vertical letter 'I' appeared on the left edge of my monocle; the Boss's targeting symbol. I had to match my crosshairs onto the Boss's 'I bar' for the rockets to land on target, and then pull the trigger. I was flying the Apache, so I was the only one who could successfully line up a launch. He aimed, I matched, I fired.

'Coming round hard …' I slammed the cyclic stick into my left leg at the same time as pulling a huge chunk of power from the collective. The machine flipped onto its left side as we spun on a sixpence. I shot my head back to look at the copse behind us through the canopy roof. All ten tonnes of the fully laden Apache, the Boss and I were rotating 180 degrees around my eyeballs. The G-force pulled down on every sinew in my body, doubling the weight of my helmet, monocle, tight straps, heavy chicken plate and survival jacket. The rotor blades thumped furiously and the engines groaned.

As we rolled out of the turn, I gradually moved the cyclic back to the cockpit's centre. We were flying a direct charge to the copse. The Boss began to aim his TADS where he wanted the Flechettes to go, fixing his crosshairs bang in the centre of the wood. Three thousand five hundred metres to the target. We were gassing it, flat out at 125 knots, and needed to fire in 1,000 metres time. I had to get Billy well out of the way.

'Five One running in from the south. Confirm direction, Billy.'

'Breaking east, breaking east.'

I saw his Apache's nose dip as it powered off to the right.

At 3,000 metres, the Boss was ready.

'Match and shoot!'

Now the rest was down to me. The Boss would watch the 'I bar' come to meet the crosshairs on his TADS screen. I focused on the 'I bar'. The problem was, I had no 'I bar'. There was nothing. The monocle in my right eye was completely pink. My mirror had vibrated away from the centre of my pupil during the violent turn. I pushed it back into place. It immediately vibrated away again. *Fuck.* The screw had come loose. I could still do the shoot from my MPD. The 'I bar' would be there too. But the sun was shining into the cockpit from directly behind us, making the MPD impossible to read.

'Match and shoot, Mr M.'

'I'm trying …'

I snapped my head from one side to the other to escape the glare on the screen. I unlocked the seat straps so I could lean as far forward as possible. I kept the cyclic forward, the collective up and the foot pedals balanced, and my face just six inches from the screen.

'Two point five klicks to target.'

I can do this. I took up the pressure on the trigger as I eased the cyclic left, right, left, and then right again. Every time I aligned the 'I bar' with the crosshairs it passed straight through to the other side.

'Two klicks to target. Are you going to shoot today?'

Fuck it. I'd just have to take a snatch at it. As they came together for the third time, I pulled the trigger and my 'I' shot off. A rocket tore away from each side of the aircraft. I yanked my head up fast; I knew immediately that I'd arsed it up.

For a second they were two black dots trailing wisps of vapour smoke. Then their cradles exploded and two torrents of Flechette darts impacted into the ground, kicking up 160 pinpricks of dust – all between fifty and 100 metres left of the copse.

'What was *that?*'

The Boss was horrified. So was I.

'Match and shoot again. We're running out of distance.'

I looked down. Miraculously, the crosshairs were superimposed over the 'I bar' so I pulled the trigger immediately. Two more bright orange glows either side of me as the rockets shot away. The first few darts erupted twenty metres short but the vast majority cracked straight into the copse, slicing through branches and vaporising leaves before burying themselves deep into whatever walked or crawled on the ground below them. Anything in there would have been immobilised now, if not by a dart then by falling branches or splintered timber. Thank God for that.

'Good set, sir.'

'That time anyway,' the Boss said drily.

I was the squadron's Weapons Officer. I taught people how to shoot these things for a living, for Christ's sake. And I'd missed the target by close on 100 metres. The reason didn't matter. I was livid with myself.

'Breaking left into an orbit.' I pulled the cyclic back, lowered the collective and banked left, decelerating swiftly.

The Boss was keen to finish off any survivors.

'My gun.'

We circled the copse's western edge.

'I can't see any movement.'

Ten seconds later, we'd reached its northern window.

'I've got something.'

I looked down on the MPD. The Boss was right. There was a flat-shaped heat source moving extremely slowly towards the northern edge of the copse.

'It's somebody crawling towards the tube. Engaging.' The Boss squeezed off a burst of twenty.

An Apache pilot always announced when he was opening up so his co-pilot knew they weren't taking rounds. An M230 cannon firing less than a metre from your feet sounded and felt like a sledgehammer banging away on the aircraft's exterior. It bounced the balls of your feet and shook you in your seat.

The cannon pointed down and eighty degrees to the right, and was powerful enough to throw the Apache a few metres to the left as it engaged. The on-board computer compensated for the change in direction.

The cannon ramped itself backwards as the first three rounds flew from the barrel. Now in its optimum position, the remaining seventeen HEDP rounds streaked towards the target. By the time the nineteenth and twentieth rounds were away, the first were tearing through the trees. When the smoke cleared, the heat source had split into two smaller heat sources. But the Boss wasn't satisfied.

'There's got to be a few of them in there. Is that another heat source further back or just the mortar barrel? Better make sure.'

He gave it another burst, then a third and a fourth.

The whole of the copse's floor glowed red on the FLIR screen. The Boss still kept hammering away, only stopping when we'd reached its southern edge again. The soles of my feet were tingling.

He'd pumped seven bursts into the place, 140 rounds in total, leaving a great smoking pile of scorched earth, ripped foliage and charred branches. And enough lead to start a pencil factory. We continued to circle.

'Do you think there's anyone left alive in there?'

I laughed. 'Not a hope in hell, Boss.'

So this was how the OC had won Top Gun in the States. The man was merciless.

'Widow Eight Four, this is Ugly Five One. Target destroyed. Do you have any further targets for us?'

'Negative. We're pulling back into the desert.'

'Copied. We'll cover you into it.'

'Ugly Five One, Ugly Five Zero. My suggestion, we go back to Camp Bastion. You need to rearm and refuel, and I need a new aircraft.'

The engagement had lasted twenty minutes, leaving us with only an hour's combat gas left. And with a broken gun we wouldn't be going anywhere near Kajaki or Now Zad. The rest of the famil could wait.

'Copied, Billy. That is an affirmative. I've got a conference call with the CO (Commanding Officer) in Kandahar at 1800, so we'll finish the famil tomorrow.'

Everyone's spirits were sky high on the flight home. One sortie down, one-nil to us. We'd just been expecting a routine turn around the houses. The action was a bonus.

Killing the enemy didn't make me punch the air or whoop with joy. At the same time, I never got beardy about it or started to ponder the meaning of life. We'd helped out the guys on the ground, and some Taliban had gone to meet their maker. Ah well. They shouldn't have shot at us first. Next target please.

'Boss, do you fancy doing some flying on the way back?'

'Thanks, Mr M. Much appreciated.'

I wanted to give him the controls so I could text Billy. And I hoped that if he had something to do he might forget about my shocking performance with the rockets.

U SEE HOW MANY RNDS BOSS STUCK IN THAT PLACE

AWESOME ... LIKES A BIT OF 30 MIL ACTION DOESNT HE ...

HE'LL FIT IN WELL

IS THAT HIS 1ST KILL

NO EYED DEER

ASK HIM

'Er, Boss, was that you popping your cherry then?'

'Sorry?'

'First successful engagement with a real enemy, sir?'

He was sheepish. 'Yes. Yes, I suppose it was.'

'Congratulations.'

YES … FIRST BLOOD

'That mortar team needed their heads examining, Mr M. Quite unreal. It was almost as if they were asking for it.'

'Probably so smacked out they wouldn't have cared either way, Boss.'

It wasn't the first time I'd witnessed a pointless last stand in Helmand. The Taliban weren't like any other enemy the modern British Army had come across. Much of their senior leadership was still made up of the people who controlled Afghanistan between 1996 and 2001. Their 'Emir', the one-eyed Mullah Omar, was still believed to be top of the pile. He'd started the whole Taliban movement (Taliban meant 'God's Students') in a small village near Kandahar as a reactionary counter to the corruption of the war-lords. In those days Mullah Omar had preached simple but strict Islamic ideals. He knew little of the rest of the world, and cared less.

By 2006 the Taliban we were fighting was a very different beast. Its leadership had been infected and taken over by international Islamic extremists. Now it espoused global Islamic domination too.

It was led from Quetta, the hot-blooded Pakistani city sixty miles south-east of Kandahar province, by no more than a dozen ageing men. They sent their senior commanders, all hardbitten ideologues, over the border to do their bidding.

These field commanders were Tier One Taliban; the first of three very diverse groupings, each of which had motives as different as their backgrounds. It was rare to take any Tier One Taliban alive. Many never left home without their suicide belts. Mostly Afghan by blood, the commanders worked closely with the Baluchi drug lords across the Pakistan border, protecting their opium smuggling columns in exchange for money and arms. The Taliban leadership didn't necessarily approve of the drugs barons, but they shared a common goal – to oust Western troops so they could carry on as before.

Tier Two were the foreign jihadis: central Asians, Arabs, and especially Pakistanis – young idealists, from their early teens to their mid-twenties, products of the madrasas, the strict religious schools of northern and western Pakistan. Many of these madrasas were set up during the 1980s and funded by wealthy Saudis, anxious to be seen to be doing their bit in the war against the godless Soviets. Since then they had taken on a life of their own. Their students came not just from militant hotspots such as Waziristan and Swat, but also from the Punjab, a rich agricultural province, as well as the big cities: Karachi, Lahore and Islamabad.

Others came from as far afield as Bosnia, Brooklyn and Bradford (though no British Taliban were actually caught in my time). For these radically indoctrinated young men, war was a religious obligation. It was an honour to fight and die for Allah. The chosen few, or the most brainwashed, were hand-picked for martyrdom and became suicide bombers. The madrasas exported their brand of fanaticism not just over the Afghan border, but to the Middle East, Europe and London.

Tier Two fighters seldom ran. 'This is our moment,' they announced over their radios before they went to their deaths. 'This is the moment Allah has chosen for us. Allahu Akbar.' 'God is the greatest.'

Tier Three were at the other end of the food chain, and often had no belief in the cause at all. They were the local Afghan guns for hire, the 'Ten Dollar Taliban'. They were not emotionally committed to fighting the Great Satan, unless a brother or their father was killed by the Coalition and they wanted to finish a blood feud. Ten dollars was good money in a land where few jobs existed. In the poppy growing season from November to May, they were labourers – busy planting, watering and then harvesting the poppy fields. When summer arrived, they fought for cash. It didn't matter *who* they fought for, as long as they got paid. Life was cheap, but alternatives were in short supply.

Most of them adopted the Taliban's trademark black clothing and turban, which made them tough for us to spot in shadow on our black and white Day TV cameras.

Only a few had access to anything heavier than RPGs and AK47s, but we still came up against everything from the mortars we'd seen that morning to Soviet-made DShK heavy machine guns and even surface-to-air missile launchers – so they were not an enemy to be underestimated.

They were physically fit, they knew the landscape, and they knew how to exploit it. Some of their more senior guys had been fighting in Helmand and Kandahar provinces all their lives. Soviet soldiers in the 1980s used to call them the *dhuki* – the ghosts. They'd arrive without warning, strike hard, and disappear into thin air.

Their tactics were as militarily adept as they were audacious. They were always up for a close-quarter battle; they were a world away from the 'shoot and scoot' insurgents of Iraq. Encirclement was their favourite tactic, even when they were outnumbered; they'd trap their enemy in a killing zone and then do their best to wipe them out. They wouldn't withdraw unless it was absolutely obvious they were beaten – and sometimes not even then.

If you shot a Taliban warrior, one 5.56-mm bullet wouldn't do. You'd have to put two or three in him. A lot of them were so smacked out they didn't even feel the rounds. Their commanders kept them well supplied. And they didn't do helicopter evacuations or trauma theatres on twenty-four-hour standby; they barely did first aid. If their men got shot, they died – so they just kept on coming.

APACHE TRIV … US 1ST … YEAH

'What's that, Mr Macy?'

'Apache Trivia, sir. Their aircraft asks ours a question. You ask them one in return. The first crew to get an answer wrong makes the brews in the JHF.'

The rows over whose turn it was to make the brews had been horrendous before Apache Triv. It had become a bit of a tradition on our homebound flights. We always routed back to Bastion over the desert, where there was no threat to worry about. We could relax a little during the forty-five kilometres from Gereshk.

Carl went first. As the aircraft know-all, it was his favourite game. I always asked the weaponeering questions and Billy generally kept to flying questions, but Carl didn't limit himself to the defensive aide suite. It was his Apache Triv downfall.

You were allowed to find the answer in your Flight Reference Cards, but the trick was to come up with a question they didn't cover.

Carl adopted his smuggest tone. 'Check Data.'

WHATS THE MAX OIL TEMP FOR THE NOSE GEARBOX … CARL

'Hang on Boss, don't say a word …' I knew that one was in the Cards. Carl had screwed up, or was trying to be kind to the Boss. I grabbed them from the dashboard alcove.

134 DEGREES … ED

'Check Data.'

DEGREES … WHAT …

CENTIGRADE … P**S BOY

CORRECT … JAMMY BUGGER

Our turn.

FLECHETTES … WHAT DISTANCE THEY COME OUT … +/–50M … ED

The reply was instantaneous.

900M … CARL

Bollocks.

860M ACTUALLY … IN THE BRACKET … ED

Billy asked their second. It was immediate elimination now.

WHAT IS UNDER PANEL L330 … BILLY

'*What?* Tell me that's an in-house joke …'

'Nope. That's Billy for you, Boss. All I know is "L" means left-hand side.'

'I had to learn this crap in the States. Whatever it is, it's 330 inches back from the nose.'

It must have been a panel opening about halfway back.

'That stinks.' The Boss was indignant. 'I bet he looked under some random panel before the sortie just so he could ask a bone question like that.'

It was exactly what Billy did. Regularly. It would be so obscure we'd never guess it.

'You have control, I know what's under it, Mr M.'

The Boss pounded his keyboard with his sausage fingers.

UNDER L330 IT SAYS … SCISSORS … PAPER … RANK … YOU LOSE … BOSS

WRONG … WRONG … WRONG … U2R THE P**S BOYS

'I'll make the brews Mr M, don't worry. I'm the new boy.'

We were five minutes off from Camp Bastion.

'Five Zero, Five One, we will lead you in.'

'Copied.'

We crossed the A01 Highway at 3,000 feet.

'Descending.'

Every descent was tactical. We never knew who was watching us or with what. I pushed the cyclic hard forward and lowered the collective, sinking the aircraft to the ground nose first. We dropped like a brick. With 500 feet to go, I pulled the cyclic back hard to throw the nose up against the wind, slamming a massive brake on the aircraft's speed.

The runway was a thousand metres directly ahead. Camp Bastion stretched away to our right. I pulled up the Aircraft Page on the MPD; the wind was from the south. We could come straight in. We landed into the wind as it gave more lift, so more control.

I flared the aircraft a fraction to take us down to forty knots then lowered it again, timing our gradual descent with the approaching runway: 400 feet, 200, 100, 50 … I stuck the nose forward as we crossed the lip at thirty-five knots and all three wheels hit the metal grids simultaneously. A perfect three-point running landing. It was all about timing.

It was a short taxi past the Chinooks' parking area and the Apaches' arming bays. Behind them were the hangars, and behind the hangars stretched the rest of Camp Bastion.

First stop was always the refuelling bay, fifty metres down the taxi lane and left again another fifty. A Groundie directed us into Point One and Billy and Carl joined us in Point Two thirty seconds later. Number Two engine first. Pouring nearly 3,000 lb of fuel into an empty set of tanks took six minutes. We began the lengthy process of closing the aircraft down. Off went the PNVS, the TADS, the FCR – the full start-up checklist in reverse.

The second and final stop was the arming bay, where we would shut down completely once the fresh rounds, rockets and missiles had been loaded. Power needed to be running through the aircraft to load the cannon, and only aircrew could do that.

Rearming was a tricky business. It took thirty minutes on average, longer if there was a lot to slap on. A team of eight guys buzzed around below us.

The cannon's electrics had to be disconnected first, and then the chain disengaged. The side loader equipment had to be attached and the rounds fed through the chain; and so on. In the meantime, there was always some fine tuning to be done. That afternoon, the technicians needed to sort out Billy's jam.

We tried as hard as we could to look busy, but there was nothing we could do to escape the attention of Sergeant Kev Blundell. Kev was the squadron's Ammunition Sergeant. The arming bays and everything that went into them were his kingdom; and he ruled over it like Idi Amin.

King Kev was a giant of a man, as broad as he was tall, and he ate all visiting pilots for breakfast. A gruff Yorkshireman, he took no shit from anyone – up or down the entire chain of command. He had a sinister frown and the demeanour of the world's most sardonic policeman, and as far as he was concerned, everyone could 'just fook off'.

As the Weapons Officer, I was the pilot who worked closest with him; which meant I copped the very worst of his abuse.

While his guys beavered away, Kev would zero in on the Apache. He'd do a slow walk round the aircraft, arms folded, head shaking. Finally, he'd plug into the wing.

'Fired fook all again, I see. You're supposed to be fooking attack pilots.'

Kev's greatest hatred in life – and he had many to choose from – was having to box up out-of-date weaponry and send it back to the UK. Hellfires and rockets could only take so much vibration on the wing before they became unstable, and all of them had a limited flight life. Backloading them all the way for inspection and maintenance was a bureaucratic nightmare, so any ammunition that came back from a sortie guaranteed us a mouthful.

'Fooking useless, like normal.'

'What do you mean? It's not that bad, Kev. We were only supposed to be on a famil, and we still got 160 rounds off, plus four Flechettes.'

'But no fooking Hellfire. You big jessies. Mind you, could be worse. You could be Mr Fly-Boy-Sky-Cop-Tom-fooking-Cruise in Point Two next to you. He only managed fifteen cannon rounds before he went and broke his gun! Makes you wonder why we fooking bother ...'

'What a twat ... You won't believe this Boss.'

I let him drag his webbing and fighting helmet from the boot and closed the panel securely. Stencilling across the door hatch in black was *I.330.* Billy grinned down at us from ear to ear.

The Boss and I managed to escape in twenty-five minutes. Billy's broken gun meant he had Kev breathing down his neck for almost an hour. We dumped our flight clobber in the lockers and picked up our wallets.

We'd often shoot a quick basket in the JHF. It was a handy way of resolving any residual disputes about the winner of Apache Triv and confirming that sortie's Piss Boy. 'Double or quits,' Billy would offer if he'd lost. But there was no dispute that afternoon. Billy's deviousness had triumphed again. Carl and I signed the aircraft back in with the crew chief and returned the start-up keys. Then the four of us trooped up to the JHF.

The Boss had forgotten his generous offer, so I ended up making the brews.

'Hey Piss Boy, one coffee Whoopie Goldberg and Carl would like a tea Julie Andrews.' Army slang: black nun and white nun.

We filed into the briefing room. Every engagement was debriefed thoroughly for fresh enemy intelligence and to learn lessons from our own combat skills. We played the relevant moment from the gun tapes from each Apache that opened fire.

The Boss, the Chief of Staff or the Operations Officer sat in on every debrief to confirm each kill was lawful. Every round we put down was recorded. We could never get away with a cover-up so we had to be super sure about what we were doing. It also provided closure on the sortie for the crew if it had been a bloody one.

Nobody else was normally allowed into the debriefs because we didn't do Kill TV. Occasionally we'd invite the Groundies up to view some non-gory sequences as a morale booster. It really worked. 'Yes!' one of them would call out gleefully. 'I loaded that Hellfire!'

Later on, I would watch the gun tapes on the computer to analyse shooting standards and the weapons' performances. We reached the point the Boss and I began our rocket run-in on the copse. I was dreading what came next.

'Just one second – pause it there …'

The Boss ducked out of the room. Twenty seconds later, he burst back in, followed by every single member of the squadron he could find in the JHF or the JOC – about twenty-three of them in total.

'Right. The Weapons Officer would like to show you exactly how to fire a pair of Flechette rockets. Play the tape please.'

There was no point in trying to explain. None of them would have believed me. I tried diversion tactics. 'What about the Boss? He went through 160 cannon rounds to get his target!'

It was too late. The room erupted with laughter. None of them listened to a word I said.

'Play Mr Macy's rockets again, play Mr Macy's rockets again,' they hollered.

Excruciating. I just had to man up and take it on the chin.

ALICE, TRIGGER, FOG AND ROCCO

The next morning, our intelligence officer gave the squadron pilots her warts and all situational brief. It lasted ninety minutes, and it brought us right up to date on Operation Herrick.

Everyone listened to intelligence briefs in absolute silence; we couldn't afford not to. Especially when they were given by Alice. She was not a woman to cross. We all made sure we were in the JHF tent in good time before she started.

Alice was attached to us as an RAF reservist, and she was a big hit. Like Kev Blundell, she took no shit from anyone. Unlike Kev, she was tall and auburn-haired, and, if the occasion demanded, had the temperament to go with it. She was a consummate professional and knew her int inside out.

Alice was loaded; her father owned a plantation somewhere, and she was always chomping on bags of walnuts he'd sent out to her. She'd crack them with her bare hands. She was also immensely clever and highly educated, with at least three different degrees. Alice didn't need to be in a war zone for a single second. She could have been back at home making a fortune in her civvy job, selling microwave technology to the military. Instead, she'd volunteered for the tour because she wanted to 'do something interesting'.

Alice won me over the very first day we'd met in the JHF during the handover. She'd listened in respectful silence to the Boss's long and slightly lugubrious speech – designed entirely to impress her – about the feats he'd achieved inside the Apache cockpit. The Boss's finale was his Top Gun triumph. He waited for the inevitable oohs and aahhs.

Alice just smiled politely and said: 'That's all very good, sir. But I bet you can't lick your own nipples. I can.' She'd cracked another walnut and walked away.

Alice had a lot of news for us. As the Helmand campaign had gradually evolved, the enemy were evolving too. The Task Force's footholds in the north were becoming more substantial. Troops were just beginning to move out, albeit gingerly, on exploratory patrols from the district centres and platoon houses in which they had been holed up all summer. But they were paying for it in blood. A total of twenty-four British servicemen had been killed since we'd left – fourteen of them in the Nimrod air crash near Kandahar. And two-thirds of the province – the far north and its entire southern half – had yet to be touched.

'Everyone now accepts that it's going to be a very, very long fight.'

The most substantial strategic change was the establishment of a new district centre in the town of Garmsir, taking the tally back up to five. Fifty-five kilometres from Helmand's capital Lashkar Gah, Garmsir was the most southerly point of the province that British troops had penetrated. Everything below it was uncharted territory.

'Literally uncharted,' Alice said. 'No maps have ever been drawn of the 120-mile sweep down to the Pakistan border. Not even the Afghan police go there. They used to, but they had a nasty habit of coming back without their heads.'

The Paras had pushed a few exploratory patrols down to Garmsir in September. Each time they were met by fierce opposition, and had to vacate the town after only a few days.

Garmsir was strategically important for both sides. It was the gateway into and out of the province for the Taliban as well as the opium trade. It was a geographical choke point where the Green Zone was at its thinnest. Everything that didn't want to get picked off by Coalition air power in the desert had to pass through the place.

If we were ever to make progress in the south, we needed a permanent footprint in Garmsir. So the marines launched Operation Anthracite at the start of October 2006, to set up a DC in an old military barracks in the town. Alice revealed that the man given the job of expanding influence in the south was Lieutenant Colonel Rob Magowan, who commanded a 500-strong assortment of ISTAR units, known as the I X Battlegroup.

'The what?' someone asked.

'Information eXploitation, a new unit; they gather and exploit Taliban int.'

But Garmsir wasn't going well. The Taliban were enraged by the new arrivals, and were doing all they could to oust them. The DC's occupying force, a company of 120 Royal Marines, had been pinned down there ever since they'd arrived. Under attack day and night, barely able to step outside the decaying base, they stood no chance of dominating the ground around them.

'Like the worst days of Sangin,' Alice said.

It was siege warfare, the marines prisoners in their own castle.

'Now here's the good news.' Alice handed out a photocopied stack of lengthy crib sheets. 'The specific instructions on when you can open fire have been changed. You'll be pleased to see you've got a lot more leeway. Have a good read of this.'

I scanned Alice's crib. It was welcome news indeed. The powers that be had finally dispensed with the myth that Helmand was a tree-hugging mission.

When we'd first arrived the instructions were as strict as they'd been in Northern Ireland: rounds had to be practically coming in on the Paras before we could engage. Once it had all kicked off at the district centres, we were allowed to attack first on a few occasions as long as it was to save life. But that still left one hand tied behind our back.

Now both hands had been untied – we could shoot pretty much at our own discretion as long as we were comfortable we were killing people that we knew had been up to no good. They didn't even need to be armed any more.

The Boss whispered, '*That's* more like it.'

His ever more infamous trigger finger was obviously itching again. I nodded; I didn't want Alice to catch us talking.

The new instructions would make life a lot easier for us all. It wasn't quite like war fighting as yet, but the gloves were certainly off. But Alice had more for us. We learned why the generals had taken these steps.

'This is not the enemy you were fighting in the summer. They are shrewder and meaner. They've learned good lessons from the pounding the Apaches have given them. As the days pass they are attempting fewer and fewer full-on assaults. They're moving to more cunning asymmetric attacks.'

We looked blank.

'Asymmetric. It's the new buzz word in the int world. Means suicide bombers, roadside bombs, that sort of thing. Less manpower for greater effect.'

I remembered the suicide bombing just a couple of days before we'd arrived. I'd seen it on the news. It was the first successfully launched on us in Helmand, and it had killed a young commando, Marine Gary Wright. The bomber had rushed up to his Snatch Land Rover as it drove through Lashkar Gah. He was top cover. He wouldn't have known anything about it.

'For you guys in the air, it means the enemy have become a lot harder to locate. They use more cover from view and they're pretending to be locals all the time.

'The Taliban's make-up is also changing – which has helped increase their competence, we think. It's the poppy season now, so there are fewer Tier Three locals but more Tier Two jihadi foreigners. One estimate I saw out of Kandahar the other day put the Tier Twos at 60 per cent of the Taliban's total manpower. These guys are smarter, mostly better trained and, as some of you have already seen, definitely more committed.'

The mortar team up at Gereshk must have been Tier Two.

'Also, be aware that their desire to take out an attack helicopter is still very high. Regular intercepts confirm that. They really hate you. But it's more than that; they know it would do a huge amount for their recruiting to show that the thing that does them most damage is defeatable.'

A thoughtful silence hung over the room. A total of eight US Apaches had gone down in Iraq from hostile action in the four years the Americans had been fighting there. The most recent had been hit the day we got on the plane at Brize Norton – a stark and timely reminder that we weren't invincible. An AH64D had crashed north of Baghdad, killing both crew.

Helicopters were vulnerable in every theatre of war; they always have been. They were big old targets to aim at, and full of highly flammable materials. A British Lynx had been shot down over Basra by an Iranian-supplied SAM in May, killing all five people on board, including a talented young female RAF officer not unlike Alice. Taliban and al Qaeda fighters had managed to bring down American Chinooks, Black Hawks and even two US Apaches in Afghanistan in the five years since the post-9 / 11 invasion. None of us wanted to be the first Brit on the list.

'Unfortunately, one thing hasn't changed – there is still no shortage of them.'

Alice leaned over the bird table to make her final point.

'Only speed and cunning will allow you to catch them with their pants down now. And before they catch you.'

Alice's prognosis was sobering, but it didn't dent the squadron's upbeat mood during the early days of the tour. Despite our uncomfortably swift return, there was a buzz of anticipation. The new pilots were excited, and that rubbed off on all of us. None of the rookies caused more of a stir than Charlotte. She was the talk of Camp Bastion.

A young captain with long blonde hair, Charlotte had come straight out of Sandhurst to be streamlined onto the Apache programme. This was her first tour of duty. She was the first woman ever to fly a British Apache, and now the first to do so on operations. A few days into the tour, she became the first British woman to kill in an Apache. Getting to where she had done was no mean feat, and had taken a huge amount of grit and hard work.

A lot of the old hands didn't think a woman would be up to fighting an Apache, and I was one of them. We didn't think she'd be able to take the immense physical pressure in the cockpit. She proved us completely wrong. She was a great pilot and had no problems with pulling the trigger; so much so, the instructors qualified her as a front-seater.

Remarkably, she hadn't sacrificed one ounce of femininity in the process. She was warm-hearted, high cheek boned and fitted her combats more appealingly than I've ever managed to. She was also engaged to a fast jet jock, and wore his huge rock on her finger – largely to keep the rats away.

You'd often see marines wistfully pointing out Charlotte in the cookhouse. A good-looking blonde, AND she flew the world's meanest killing machine. For a spunky young commando, she was too good to be true.

All in all, our lone female flier was a great addition to the team. But I put most of the good squadron vibe down to the Boss's management style. By the end of the first week, he had introduced two more initiatives that made morale soar.

Every evening brief, the crew chief technician read out each airframe's serviceability and the number of flying hours it had left. 'XZ172: serviceable, fifteen hours clear. XZ179: ten hours clear but will be pulled offline at 7am. XZ193: twelve hours clear, and it's your spare for tonight. XZ196 …' and so on.

It made for dull listening. One of the techs came up with the idea of giving the aircraft names, as the RAF had in World War Two. The Boss put it to the floor. A Groundie suggested famous Porn Stars – a suitable tribute to the lifeblood of deployed armies. It was passed unanimously.

Out went letters and numbers; in came Heather Brook, Tabitha Cash, Lolo Ferrari, Jenna Jameson, Tera Patrick, Taylor Rain and Sylvia Saint. Utterly childish, but it gave us endless hours of banter with the techs as we climbed out of the aircraft on the flight line to announce: 'I've just spent three hours inside Lolo Ferrari, and she goes like a belt-fed Wombat.'

Just to show the Army Air Corps wasn't sexist, Apache XZ204

was renamed Ron Jeremy (the fastest dick in Hollywood). We didn't want the female Groundies to feel left out. It opened up a hundred more elbow-nudging double entendres.

The second of the Boss's morale boosters was the ordination of every pilot's tactical callsign. We used the Ugly callsign to talk to each other over a secure military net when we were airborne. To summon each other around the camp, we had insecure personal walkie-talkies. Broadcasting our real names over them was a massive no no, as anyone with a cheap Motorola radio could be listening in.

On the first tour, we just used the acronyms of our official job titles: OC, EWO, QHI, etc. The Boss decided to have some fun. He called a meeting of all the pilots to come up with more amusing tactical callsigns.

It took place one night in the Tactical Planning Facility, a soundproof metal Portakabin round the back of the JHF tent where we went if we needed to discuss something securely. A five-foot-square screen was rigged up in it for viewing the gun tapes during the sortie debriefs. The only problem with the place was temperature control: like our thunderbox rims, its metal shell turned it into a sauna in the summer and a freezer in the winter. But in November it was great.

There were five or six comfy chairs in the TPF – not enough for sixteen bums. There was always a race to get them whenever a pilots' briefing was called. If you were too slow, you had to sit on a hard chair or just perch. We all made a brew and sat round in a big circle.

'Right,' the Boss announced, playing master of ceremonies. 'These are the rules: the name has to be relevant to something you've done or are famous for. It has to be funny, but it can't be offensive because we can't go around shouting obscenities over the radio. Most importantly, it has to sound reasonably polite – so I can explain it away to a visiting VIP. I can't have the general staff thinking we're all twats. Okay Billy, you're first. Out you go.'

The pilot being named wasn't allowed to play any part in the process. Billy's was quite quick. As soon as someone opened up with the *A-Team* theme tune – 'Dur, da, dur, duuurrr, dur duuuuurrr' – we all got it.

The Boss called Billy back in. 'Okay Billy. You are "The Face". Can you work it out?'

Billy just looked puzzled, so Carl helped him out.

'You're The Face for two reasons. First, because you always get the face time with the visiting big cheeses.'

'No, that's not always true.'

'Yes it bloody well is,' the Boss retorted. 'Do you want me to give you a list?'

Billy grinned. 'Well, you've either got it or you haven't.'

'Well said. That's the polite reason. The real one is because *only you* think you're a pretty boy.'

Billy had kippered himself. Carl was ejected next. Billy slipped into the comfy chair he had just vacated, blocking two other pilots. 'Too slow, gentlemen.'

Carl took longer. Unfortunately for him, there were quite a few suggestions.

'I've got one, but I can't remember his name,' the Boss said. 'Borat's producer from his Kazakhstan film. You know, the great fat bloke who puts his horrible hairy arse in Borat's face?' Despite raucous laughter, it was rejected as too cruel.

'Okay, what about Cartman from *South Park* then?' suggested Geordie, a member of 1 Flight and the squadron's Combat Search and Rescue Officer. He adopted a cod American accent: *'Why the fuck not? Fuck, fuckety, fuck, fuck, fuck.'*

But Tony had had a bolt of inspiration. He was a back-seater on 3 Flight, the team with whom we worked closest. We sometimes doubled up on missions, and our tents were next door to each other.

'I've got it! Ewok out of *Star Wars*. He's small, strange and hairy, and he's the EWO – the Electronic Warfare Officer.'

It was perfect. Then it was Nick's turn.

Nick was another very talented young captain, like Charlotte. They were close friends, having gone to university together, and they flew alongside each other as the two front-seaters on 3 Flight.

Devilishly good looking, with blond hair and blue eyes and a mouth full of Hollywood teeth, the Army Air Corps had never had more of a pin-up than Captain Nick. He'd won the Sword of Honour at Sandhurst, went on to become the first pilot ever to go through training directly onto the Apache, and won the Corps' own highly coveted Sword of Excellence while he was at it. Not a bad CV. He'd become a general one day, if he stayed in the army. He had the talent. More importantly, he had the luck.

Women melted in front of Nick's charm and old-fashioned chivalry. He left a string of them utterly broken-hearted wherever he went. He was always good humoured, never swore, and didn't like pornography.

I liked Nick a lot. It was hard not to. We trained on the Apache together – he was another of the sixteen originals and we'd been through the first tour together too. As a newish pilot, Nick was always bursting with enthusiasm and bounding around the place like an overexcited spaniel. He'd take the odd risk in his constant drive to better himself – which landed him in a few scrapes – but he always got away with it.

'Rover?'

'Lassie?'

'How about Bonnie?' Charlotte piped up. 'As in Bonnie Tyler. Remember *I Need a Hero*?'

During the first tour, Nick just happened to be the first pilot that visiting *Sun* journalist Tom Newton Dunn collared for an interview. An article and photo duly appeared in the next day's paper under the headline 'Hero Nick'. He'd got a shed-load of abuse for that. We made sure it lasted weeks, but it didn't faze Nick for a second.

'You know, Mr M,' he told me one day. 'Some of us have got the looks, and some haven't. I didn't see *The Sun* chasing you too hard ...'

Nick became Bonnie. Charlotte came next.

There had always been a strong suspicion that some of the blondeness came out of a bottle.

'This might be a bit close to the bone,' one of the other pilots began. 'But what about Cuffs?'

There was a baffled silence.

'Come on you lot. First because she's, you know ... Posh.'

'Very clever. And?'

'Well, it's just possible that her collar doesn't match them ...'

That brought the house down. The Boss plumped for Posh, but she was always Cuffs to the rest of us.

Geordie was Vidal, on account of the fact that he had always driven hairdressers' cars, a convertible Saab or an Audi TT – and that he was also slightly thinning on top.

Geordie was an honorary member of HQ Flight really. He often filled in for the Boss when he was called away to meetings. Everybody liked him. He was a typical Newcastle lad with a quick

ABOVE: The Apache AH Mk1.

LEFT: Ed's home for 7 months.

BELOW: A sandstorm squall moves fast and without warning.

LEFT: The coveted Apache badge worn on the right arm of an Attack Pilot's flying suit after qualifying (656 Sqn AAC have a modified version to denote the first Combat Ready Attack Squadron in the British Army).

LEFT: The monocle. 656 Sqn motto:
Volans et Vidans – Flying and Seeing.

BELOW: 656 Sqn Apache Pilots. Top row, left to right:
Dusty, Spoons, Vidal, Shermanator, Trigger, Stone,
Bonnie and Dom. Front row left to right: Face, Elton,
Whitney, Ewok, Cuffs, Darwin, Del and FOG.

TOP: The Camp Bastion Apache flight line.
ABOVE: Apache Gunner's Cockpit.

BELOW: Ed Macy.
BELOW LEFT: Ed in the bag.

ABOVE: Cockpit pilot's view.

LEFT: The cannon spitting out 10 rounds a second.

BELOW LEFT: The Apache's CRV-7 Flechette rockets – 80 darts in each rocket.

BELOW: The Apache's M230 30mm underslung chain gun.

ABOVE: The technicians work 24/7 to keep the Apaches airborne in temperatures as high as 54°C.

RIGHT: Ed and Trigger with Hambly reconnecting Ugly 51's gun.

BELOW RIGHT: Hellfire at the back, rockets in the sangar and 30mm HEDP being loaded by Si.

BELOW: The infamous Rocco.

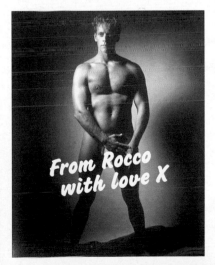

From Rocco with love X

ABOVE: A Taliban commander talks on a radio. He is carrying an RPG launcher and spare rockets.

ABOVE: 30mm High Explosive Dual Purpose (HEDP) being loaded by Cpl Bennett, the ALPC.

MAIN PICTURE: A pair of rockets streak into the Afghan sky.

LEFT: The IRT pair returning from a mission empty.

ABOVE: Arming Teams 3 and 4. The unsung heroes.

OVERLEAF: Ed and Carl are Ugly Five One.

wit and a razor-sharp tongue. All of his sentences ended with 'like', and as far as Geordie was concerned, everyone was a 'canny lad, like'.

Despite being a staff sergeant and well into his thirties, his lifestyle hadn't changed since he was nineteen. Commitment wasn't his bag – he never had a girlfriend for more than five minutes. He loved nothing more than pissing it up with his mates and pulling birds in the Toon on a Saturday night. And he'd cane it up the motorway to Newcastle in his soft top every weekend to do exactly that, music blaring and his thinning blond hair blowing in the wind. He was one of life's perennial good blokes and we'd been mates for ever.

In the air, though, Geordie was as serious as they came, and one of the very best pilots in the Army Air Corps – his long-held place on the Blue Eagles Display Team testified to that.

Geordie's sidekick was Tony. They were close buddies and spent every spare minute shooting out wisecracks as a double act. A cheeky chappie cockney, Tony was just as quick-witted as Geordie, and a staff sergeant too. He was also the shortest pilot on the squadron and had big ears, closely cropped dark hair and a small forehead. Not even Tony would deny that he looked uncannily like a chimp. It wasn't hard to crack his callsign.

'Spank, as in Spank the Monkey,' someone suggested.

The OC rejected it as too crude, so he was renamed Darwin, because he was the missing link.

The final member of 3 Flight was Jim, a WO1 well into his forties. He was the granddad of the squadron. He'd also flown for the SAS, and was a quiet and unassuming man who often kept his own company. Out of work, he had two obsessions. The first was eating healthily and regularly. If Jim missed a meal, he'd go man down. It was that serious. When he checked in to order up a rearm on a sortie, he was often heard to say, 'One Hellfire, 60 thirty Mike Mike, and *five* late meals with fruit please,' so he could have an extra one for himself.

He was also the Grand Master of the Internet – to the point that it would send people mad because they could never get on the terminal. God knows what he did online for so long, but he loved it.

'How about FOG?' Tony said. 'Food or Google. If he's not doing one, he's doing the other.'

'And?'

'Well he's a Fucking Old Guy isn't he?'

Billy and I came up with 'Trigger' for the Boss. He was the fastest in the squadron and had the MBE to prove it. He was also completely incompetent when it came to texting. His replies always carried half of the original message – possibly because his fingers were too big for the keyboard. But we knew he hadn't found the 'Clear Text' button and that made him as thick as Trigger from *Only Fools and Horses*.

They christened me Elton. 'Rocket Man', after my disaster at Gereshk – I was never going to be allowed to live that down.

The tactical callsigns were so good that some became immediate nicknames. From that night onwards, Trigger, Darwin and FOG were seldom known as anything else.

By week two, our period of grace was over. While the Garmsir skirmishes continued, 3 Commando Brigade began to ramp up their operations all over the province and we were back into the hard routine. It was gruelling and rewarding work in equal measure. Every day followed a similar pattern.

My alarm clock went off at 6.45am – unless we'd had to fly a mission overnight and were already up and about. I'm a good riser, but Billy's shaggy arse was not a sight I looked forward to at any time of day. One particularly gruesome morning I was greeted by one of his bollocks wedged between the backs of his legs. It could put a man off his food.

A trip to the cookhouse followed a shit, shower and shave, but Billy and I never fancied breakfast, so instead we strolled the 200 metres from the accommodation tents down to the JHF together for the 7.30am brief.

On the way down, we played the temperature game.

'Okay, I reckon its 24.5 degrees celsius today.'

'It's warmer than that buddy. I'm going for 26.'

On arrival, we checked the digital thermometer on the weather terminal. Whoever was furthest away made a fresh pot of filter coffee. It was usually me.

After the Boss's morning brief we got stuck into whatever our shift pattern dictated. The squadron's four flights took it in turns to do the four tasks required of the Apache force. Each shift lasted three days. The cycle began with 'Duty Ops'. We became four extra pairs of hands in the JHF, helping the Ops Officer and his team run the show from the ground. The pilots often did flight following: tracking the progress of ongoing missions over the radios. Being on Duty Ops also gave us time to read up thoroughly on the minutiae of the operational landscape. If it was quiet, we got a chance to plan the next shift, 'Deliberate Tasking'.

Deliberate Tasking comprised any pre-planned sortie, from escorting a Chinook on an 'ass and trash' flight to prosecuting a deliberate attack. Most ops were planned days in advance, but some came as fastballs, giving us only a few hours to prepare.

As attack pilots, we lived for these moments. Creeping up on the enemy and smacking them hard was exactly what the Apache was built to do and why most of us wanted to fly it. Our resources were scarce, so sadly they were rare. Most of the time, the deliberate taskings were mundane. We spent long hours shadowing Chinooks around Helmand while they collected and dropped off bombs, beans, bullets and bayonets. The Green Zone was considered too dangerous for a highly vulnerable Chinook to land in – or even fly over – without us providing top cover.

The third shift was 'IRT / HRF' – the emergency scramble – the most important of the four, and the biggest adrenalin rush. Two Apaches were under starter's orders 24 / 7, to lift immediately for any location in the province. We scrambled to bail out troops in a contact, cover reinforcements, or protect a medivac Chinook flight. It was proper seat-of-your-pants, World-War-Two-fighter-pilot stuff that always involved a mad dash to the flight line. We had thirty minutes to be off the ground once the call came in during daylight hours and sixty at night to wake up properly and allow our eyes to adjust to night vision.

There were two types of scramble. If we were going to a location that wasn't under fire, a vehicle accident in the desert perhaps, only one aircraft – the Incident Response Team – would escort the Chinook. Two Apaches – the Helmand Reaction Force – would lift for medivacs in the Green Zone and other dangerous locations, and in support of troops in contact.

After three days of flying deliberate taskings and three more on IRT / HRF call-outs we were ball-bagged, so the fourth shift, 'Testing and Maintenance', provided a welcome break.

We had a total of eight aircraft in theatre. Four had to be fully serviceable in Camp Bastion at all times. That wasn't easy. The technicians needed pilots to make sure that the parts they had replaced or repaired functioned correctly.

Aircraft were flown back to Kandahar for repairs or routine servicing. Only minor servicing was conducted at Bastion – so much of the shift was spent yo-yoing between the two bases. We'd test fly them around Kandahar Airfield and the makeshift shooting range next to it, returning the serviceable ones to Bastion.

An average three-hour sortie in the cockpit meant never less than six hours' hard work on the ground: an hour's planning and preparation, a twenty-minute crew brief, thirty minutes to start-up and taxi, forty minutes to refuel, rearm and shutdown, thirty to complete the aircraft paperwork and post-mission report, and a three-hour debrief – both gun tapes had to be viewed in their entirety and the average time at the pointy end was ninety minutes.

If you knew the time between sorties was going to be less than two hours, it was more efficient to keep the aircraft powered up, so we had to stay in the cockpit. We couldn't even get out for a pee. Early in the first tour Nick had to fly three sorties in one day, one after the other. He was in the cockpit for fifteen hours on the trot, then each sortie had to be fully debriefed, adding a further nine. By the end of the summer we'd all been there.

In training, we found that our reactions started to slip after more than six or seven hours a day in the air. The aircraft sapped concentration levels and shredded energy reserves. Man simply couldn't keep up with machine.

To avert disaster in Afghanistan, a strict eight-hour daily flying limit was imposed for each pilot. It didn't include time spent preparing or even taxiing – just wheels off the ground. In emergencies, this could be extended to ten hours, but only with the signed permission of the CO of the aviation regiment.

Each pilot had to get eight hours' undisturbed rest a day, of which six had to be sleep. In a squadron of workaholics, the Boss enforced the Crew Rest Periods as best he could.

'Mr Macy, I know what time you were up this morning. Off you go to bed, please.'

'Boss, I've got to finish this report –'

'Bed, Macy. Now.'

I'd sneak the work out of the JHF and finish it on my cot with the aid of a head torch.

The odd half-hour of free time was catered for by the TV room at the tents (showing a couple of British Forces Broadcasting Service channels, Sky News and MTV via satellite), a NAAFI where you could get a really bad cup of coffee, and a Spar shop that sold cigarettes, toiletries and a few motoring magazines. The Groundies had also built their own makeshift gym.

If I fancied shooting the breeze, I headed to the ten foot by twelve communal area we'd partitioned off at the end of the JHF tent. It was a less formal place for pilots to work in, with brew making facilities, Sky News showing 24 / 7 on a TV in the corner and an Internet terminal with a time sheet divided into twenty-minute slots. FOG booked about seven of them a day, and he'd stand over us tapping his watch a full five minutes before his next stint was due to begin.

I spent much of my Crew Rest Periods tapping away on my laptop, keeping up with weapons reports, or I phoned home. We got thirty minutes' call time a week free, but I always paid out for more.

'Are you okay, sweetie?' Emily would always begin. 'You're taking care aren't you? Have you still got my angel?'

Some of us called home all the time; others used to do it as little as possible – not because they didn't love their wives or children, but because they hated not being able to tell them anything about what we were up to. Sometimes it was better not to talk at all.

Even the Boss had to take rest periods, chivvied out of the JHF by his second in command. He'd plug his headphones into his computer and lie on his cot to watch the first season of *24*. He'd never get more than a few minutes into the first episode before falling asleep. He must have played that opening sequence twenty times over.

The official day ended at around 9pm, after the evening brief. It kicked off after dinner, following the same agenda as the one in the morning. We always started with the weather, the temperature, sunset, sunrise, moon state and light levels. Then came the permanently disappointed Kev Blundell's ammo report, the fuel stocks, the callsigns and codewords for the radios the next day, the porn star airframe's service standards, and Alice's intelligence brief.

The Ops Officer spoke about that day's missions and firefights, the next day's tasks, which crews were on what shifts, and what the ground troops were up to. Billy might then say something about flight safety, I'd do a little on weapons and Carl would give an update on the aircraft's self-defence. Trigger (aka the Boss/Major Christopher James) wrapped it up with a few last points of his own.

It was during Carl's brief in the second week that Rocco made his first appearance of the tour. Rocco was the longest-serving member of the squadron, and in more ways than one, judging by his picture. He'd been around for years – since the mid-Eighties, by the look of him. So long, in fact, that nobody knew where he'd originally come from. He had more Apache flying hours than Billy and FOG put together.

Rocco was an Italian porn star, with perfectly tousled fair hair, giant pecs and a cock that would have been the envy of a king rhinoceros. FOG looked him up on the Internet once. Rocco had starred in more than 340 hardcore porn films over his twenty-year career, directed and produced another 200, and written fifty more. That was an awful lot of shagging. Among his back catalogue were the truly classic *Fantastica Moana* (1987), *A Pussy Called Wanda* (1992), *Intercourse with the Vampire* (1994), and *Buttman & Rocco's Brazilian Butt Fest Carnival* (1999).

For us, though, Rocco existed only in photographic form – a page torn out of a long lost magazine, glued onto a piece of cardboard and laminated for his own protection. He stood on a bed, stark bollock naked and posing manfully, with his right eyebrow suggestively raised, 007-style. His flexed left arm met his right where his hand covered his pubic thatch, but did little to conceal the launch pad of his very own disconcertingly potent Hellfire missile. The picture bore the dedication, 'From Rocco, With Love. x.'

Rocco might not be seen for weeks, then make a dramatic reappearance when he was least expected, like Monty Python's Spanish Inquisition.

Carl had been talking about a new upgrade to the Defensive Aide Suite. 'Ewok,' Geordie piped up, 'Alice told us yesterday that the Taliban might have a ZU23 anti-aircraft gun in the Garmsir region.'

'Yes, that's right.' He should have seen it coming.

'Well I was just wondering what the ZU23's effective range is, like? Is it a threat, like?'

'Yes, it's a threat. Hang on, I've got it here. I'll look it up.'

Geordie knew it was a statistic Carl couldn't have known off the top of his head. Darwin had already doubled up, red in the face, desperately trying to suppress his giggles. But, holding the floor now, Carl was feeling too important to spot him. He reached for his Black Brain and turned to face the packed room. He ripped back the Velcro fastener and flicked it open.

There he was. *From Rocco, With Love. x.*

Carl blushed to the roots of his hair, and the JHF erupted.

'Very f … funny … *VIDAL*.'

'Ahaa! You've been Roccoed!' Geordie was beside himself with glee.

You could get Roccoed at any time, day or night, in the air or on the ground. Then it would be your turn to Rocco someone else. Rocco didn't discriminate between rich or poor, giant or dwarf. Everyone was fair game. We even got our old CO once in the simulator at Dishforth, as he flicked his Black Brain bang in the middle of a particularly challenging Hellfire sortie.

Now he was out and about, there would be a frenzy of Rocco activity for a couple of days. Then, just as quickly, he'd go undercover again.

The Boss stepped forward as the laughter subsided.

'Okay guys, very funny. I said all I wanted this morning, so nothing from me tonight. Any other points from the floor before we close? Alice?'

Alice had slipped in late. She'd taken a quick call from the brigade's int cell in Lashkar Gah. She looked uncomfortable.

'Sorry, not very good timing, but there's something that's probably worth mentioning. I've just been briefed on an enemy intercept.'

The room fell silent.

'The Taliban have a new plan for what they'll do if they capture a Coalition soldier.'

I realised I'd stopped breathing. The TADS image of the two SBS boys filled my head.

'They intend to set up a webcam for a live Internet broadcast, and then skin him – or her – alive.'

ARNHEM CALLING

The Taliban kept up a permanent bombardment of the new Garmsir DC. The marines had put the boot into their lovingly kept hornets' nest, and they weren't going to let them forget it.

But their focus on the four other northern district centres now seemed to ebb and flow. For a week or two, they'd have a concerted crack at Sangin and its defenders would be back at the ramparts. Then, without any apparent reason, they'd tire of Sangin and turn their attention to Now Zad or one of the others.

During the first few weeks of our second tour, they threw all they had against Kajaki, the furthest outpost, ninety-five kilometres north-east of Camp Bastion, right at the top of the Helmand Green Zone. The town itself was not much to shout about – it was barely more than a village. But control of the giant Kajaki Dam was something else again; it stood 100 metres high and 270 metres wide, in front of the biggest lake in Afghanistan.

It had been a Cold War playground, constructed by the Soviets in 1953 as a gesture of comradeship. Then along came the Americans in 1975, wanting to spread their share of love and influence, and built a thirty-three megawatt hydroelectric power station beside it. By the time we arrived, the dam irrigated the entire province, neighbouring Nimruz and a sizeable chunk of Iran, and also provided Helmand with almost all of its electricity.

Hold the dam, and you controlled the livelihoods of half a million Helmandis. To lose it would have been a strategic disaster. If the Taliban destroyed it, they'd wreak havoc, plunge the province into darkness – and blame the atrocity on a US bombing raid.

A 3,000-metre-long ridgeline towered over the south-eastern side of the dam. The tallest of its three peaks had been fortified by the Paras and was occupied by a troop of thirty marines. It was an excellent vantage point from which to spot any approach. It was given the codename Arnhem.

The marines were skirmishing daily as the Taliban probed towards the hydroelectric dam. The marines held them off, but the Taliban had them surrounded – and took out their frustrations by giving them a fair kicking.

HQ Flight took over the IRT / HRF role from 2 Flight at the height of the Taliban's Kajaki-thon; 2 Flight had gone up there twice. It was a racing certainty we'd follow suit.

'Ten quid says we'll have to go all the way up to bleeding Kajaki and back every day of the shift,' Carl grumbled. The longer flight meant a greater chance of him missing a meal, which alarmed him almost as much as it did FOG. But none of us took his bet.

The IRT / HRF handover always took place after the morning brief. Since the task was all about getting airborne as fast as we could, every aspect of our existence for those three days was tailored to that objective. Two aircraft were on permanent standby to scramble at all times, their pilots' kit out of the lockers and ours already in them. To ensure someone was always ready to power up, we even went down to the flight line with 2 Flight. While they took their stuff out of the Apaches, we put ours in.

My ammo-bag went beside my seat and my other running clobber went in the boot with my go-bag as usual. Perched on the seat was my helmet, leads plugged in. I left my Flight Reference Cards and gloves on the dash, stowed my carbine in its bracket and hooked my survival vest on top of it – open and ready to slip into.

Carl and I – the two back-seaters again – signed out our aircraft.

'A very saucy little Lolo Ferrari for you today, Mr Macy, and the one and only Taylor Rain for you, Staff.' The crew chief just loved his new fleet of sex goddesses. 'Lolo's sucking beautifully today – fuel, that is.'

There was no time to load up a specific weapons load on an emergency shout. So the IRT / HRF aircraft were given a routine Load Charlie. Each Apache normally went out with 300 cannon rounds, twenty-four rockets and two Hellfires. We used the rest of the takeoff weight allowance on extra fuel in a specially fitted second tank. It gave us between ninety minutes and two hours more time over the target, depending on where we went.

For the duration of the shift, the flight moved out of our normal accommodation tents and into one set aside for the IRT / HRF by the JOC compound. The emergency Chinook crews slept in another alongside it.

We would be summoned for a call-out on insecure radios we carried everywhere. For the same reason we had tactical callsigns, emergency shouts came to us in code. We didn't always want the Taliban to know that Big Brother was on his way. The codewords had a theme – pop stars, football teams, literary classics, whatever the Ops officer fancied – and they changed every few weeks.

The IRT / HRF tried to stay together as much as possible during the shift. We ate together, washed together and worked together.

There were only two radios, so if one of us had to go for a dump, we'd do so as a pair.

We didn't lift on every scramble, only on half the shouts that came in. Our commanders were reluctant to throw us up unless they were sure it was necessary. They might need our limited pilot and aircraft hours later. It was a tricky balance.

I once sat in a powered-up Apache cockpit for four hours on the flight line while Sangin took a pummelling. They didn't want us to go up there and risk running out of combat gas only for the real assault on the DC to kick off.

'You're our ace card,' the brigadier had told us. 'It's a game of poker with these bastards. And a good poker player hangs on to his aces as long as he can.'

The order for us to launch always came from the brigade air cell at Lashkar Gah. Only they had full sight of the whole battle space, and knew best how to allocate their paper-thin resources. The truth was, they desperately needed more aces. To help them, our Ops Officer listened in to the ground net to get us the earliest heads up he could. He'd often scramble us down to the flight line before the brigade's call arrived. When it did, all we had to do was pull up the collective.

Sure enough, we didn't have to wait long for our first Kajaki shout – five hours and forty-three minutes after the handover, to be precise. We had just eaten lunch. Billy had agreed to stay on in the cookhouse with Carl and one of the radios, so Carl could have a slice of strawberry cheesecake – his favourite. Trigger had gone back into the JHF, and I had popped back to the IRT / HRF tent with the second radio. I wanted to write a quick bluey to my son. Emails and phone calls were great, but nothing beat the post. It was more intimate; the connection between you more tangible. I began to write. In the quiet of the tent, the voice over the radio made me jump.

'BART, HOMER, SPRINGFIELD, PIZZA.'

It was *The Simpsons* theme week. The IRT, Trigger and I, were Bart, and Homer was the HRF; all four of us, to the Ops Room, fast.

I grabbed the radio to acknowledge. 'Bart, Springfield, Pizza.'

Something nasty had obviously kicked off in the Green Zone. Leaving my son's bluey on my cot, I sprinted out of the tent and up the forty-five degree wooden ladder specially built for us over the waist-high Hesco Bastion wall. My feet stung as I landed on the dust road in front of the JOC. 'Aircrew,' I hollered as I nipped past the sentries and into the JHF tent.

The watchkeeper looked up from his radio set. 'Kajaki is under attack. The Boss is already next door.'

'Roger.'

I grabbed my Black Brain from the secure steel box as Billy and Carl burst into the tent. The cookhouse was a good 700 metres away. Billy and Carl had taken the IRT Land Rover to lunch, but they were still red in the face from the rush. Not ideal for strawberry cheesecake digestion.

'It's Kajaki, guys. Billy, go next door. Come on Carl.'

On a fastball, the front-seaters always popped into the JOC for a quick low-down on the ongoing incident from the ground ops officers, while the back-seaters made a beeline for the aircraft to start firing them up.

Carl wheel-spun the Land Rover away from the JOC compound, turned sharp left down a 200-metre dirt track then left again. The suspension clanked as we sped across the metal bridge over the irrigation ditch and swung right towards the hangar. We drew up hard with a squeal of brakes and ran the last seventy-five metres to the arming bays. Our two Apaches were crawling with Groundies.

Ten minutes later, Trigger and Billy popped up over the berm. They'd taken the off-road route between the JOC and the flight line. I pushed the throttle forward to start the rotors turning the second the Boss slammed his door shut. We were off the deck in twenty-two minutes. Once we'd hit 3,000 feet Trigger caught his breath and gave me the fill.

'It's Arnhem. They're taking heavy incoming from three different firing points: north, north-west and west. Heavy calibre stuff, rockets and a whole load of RPGs. A lad's already taken a 7.62 to the head – good job he was wearing his helmet. Looks like the Taliban might be trying to take the position.'

'Copied.'

'Five Zero, Five One – Buster.' Buster was the call to press the pedal to the metal.

It was the worst attack on Arnhem yet. And my monocle told me we were still twenty-eight minutes away. I was pulling so much power, the torque was bouncing on and off 100 per cent. The second it dropped into the 90s, it was nose down and collective up again. We were tanking it; a straight line, max chat.

There was no time to test the weapons on the ground during an IRT fastball. So we did them on the way.

'My gun.'

I looked full left, full right, hard up and straight down. The gun followed my every move. 'Your gun.'

Trigger did the same.

'Coming up rockets.'

Actioning the rockets, he made sure their steering cursor came up on his TADS screen and the correct quantity of each showed up on his weapons page.

'Come co-op.'

I followed the Boss's 'I bar' around my monocle as he moved his TADS.

'Good movement; co-op confirmed, Boss.'

'Good. My missiles.'

'CMSL' popped up in my monocle.

'Missile locked onto the laser, Mr M. Your missiles.'

I looked down and left; the Hellfire's seeker followed my eye movement.

I tried to picture the scene up in Kajaki; how we were going to prosecute the targets. The enemy's favourite hangout was a loaf-shaped hill between two wadis, about two and a half klicks north-west of Arnhem. It was known as the Shrine because some mullah had been buried up there years ago. The site was covered in tatty green, red and white flags; a typical Afghan grave.

The Taliban's drill was always the same. They set up their weapons, gave our boys on the mountain a good pounding, and escaped like rats up a drainpipe into three or four old tunnels on its western edge as soon as we turned up.

I hoped the marines were getting it from the Shrine because it was safer ground for us to attack: no buildings, so no collateral damage. If the Taliban were on Falcon, too, it would be trickier.

Falcon was our codename for the peak immediately west of Arnhem, less than 400 metres along the same ridgeline. The enemy used to climb its blind side and our guys would only know they were there when the rounds started tearing up the ground beneath their feet. Unless we got our munitions spot on when engaging Falcon, they'd overshoot and spill onto Arnhem, especially if we were firing from the west.

From the brief sitrep Trigger had received, it sounded like the enemy were on the Shrine *and* Falcon. It sounded like they were everywhere.

'Widow Seven Eight, this is Ugly Five One. How do you read me?' As the mission commander for the sortie, the Boss got on the net to the JTAC at Arnhem.

'Ugly, Widow Seven Eight. Lima Charlie. You me?'

'Lima Charlie also. We are two Apaches carrying 600 thirty Mike Mike, forty-eight rockets and four Hellfire. Callsigns Ugly Five Zero, Ugly Five One. Requesting update.'

'Copied Ugly Five One. We're taking machine-gun and RPG fire from Falcon. They're massing there and trying to move across to assault our location. We think they're going to try to over-run us. Confirm you know that location.'

'Affirm.' I'd taken the Boss up to Kajaki on our second attempt at a familiarisation flight.

'Also, Ugly Five One, be aware I've got a Harrier GR7 on station: callsign Topman …'

Good. The marines were getting the heavy artillery as well as the cavalry.

'He is going to drop a 500-lb bomb on the top of Falcon. I'd like Ugly callsigns to follow up and kill any leakers after Topman drops.'

'Ugly Five One, copied all. Have you any other further targets for us?'

'Widow Seven Eight, affirm. Are you familiar with the area of the Shrine?'

'We are.'

'The enemy are shooting rockets at us from somewhere near the top of the Shrine. Firing position as yet unidentified. Can you locate and prosecute Taliban there too please?'

'Affirm.'

'Roger. One more thing, Ugly: can you give me your time on target?'

A loud burst from a heavy machine gun echoed across the JTAC's radio microphone and we could also hear curt instructions being issued in the background. Our JTAC was very calm for a man about to be overrun by a highly trained guerrilla force. But they nearly always were. It was a testament to their training, professionalism and, above all, courage.

'Ugly Five Zero, we'll be with you in figures eight minutes.'

We divided up the workload.

'I've spent ages up at the Shrine, Boss. If we take that, Billy and Carl can go for Falcon.'

Trigger detailed the tasks to our wingmen.

'Copied all. Happy with that.'

All we needed to know now was when the Harrier's bomb would impact. I hoped for the marines' sake it would be soon.

'Ugly Five One, Widow Seven Eight. Confirm time on target for Topman.'

Topman replied himself. He was a Brit – RAF – even better news.

'Time on target … six minutes …' I could hear him demand oxygen from his facemask every few words. He sounded like a public school version of Darth Vader. We'd be there only a minute or two behind them. Less, if Carl and I could squeeze any more power out of our beasts.

The Boss tapped in the Shrine's coordinates, and our lenses shot towards it. Billy did the same for Falcon. From that distance we could already make out the shape of the loaf, but we were too far off to see heat sources. Not long now though; maybe only a couple of minutes. Then we'd be amongst it. Bring it on.

'Topman … Impact one minute …'

Now we were heading north over the Green Zone, with four klicks to run. I could see the Falcon and Arnhem ridgeline clearly now in our one o'clock, as jagged as a dinosaur's back.

My right eye flicked back and forth from the ridgeline to the clock, keeping count of the seconds. Carl and I had bought us some time. The other Apache was right in behind us, 500 feet lower and to our right. At four klicks a minute we'd be coming level with Falcon almost as the bomb went off. If we got too close we might catch a bit of the blast.

'Ease up a touch, Carl. Drop to 100 knots – that should do it.'

'Copied mate. Just what I was thinking.'

The Harrier came on one final time.

'Topman's pickled the load ... Impact in Two Zero seconds.'

'I better have a look at this.' The Boss slewed his TADS across to Falcon. He didn't want to miss the fireworks, and the Shrine was still some way off.

White light erupted on Falcon's pinnacle and a crown of orange flame curled up around its epicentre, enveloped a second later by a vast dust cloud that mushroomed high into the sky. At 2,000 metres off, we had a grandstand view.

'Okay, moving the TADS back to ... Wait; hang on, I've got a runner ...'

I glanced down at my right MPD screen. A Taliban fighter was shifting it down the western side of Falcon, right out in the open, around 150 metres below the crest. He was going like the clappers, leaping from one rock to the next. If Trigger didn't get him, the hail of stone splinters from the explosion would.

'I've got him in my crosshairs ... engaging with cannon.'

Trigger was preparing to go into Top Gun mode. Two bursts, angled seventy-five degrees right of our nose, from no more than

1,500 metres. The runner disappeared in a cloud of dust and flame. The air cleared and he was nowhere to be seen.

'Wow. Good shooting, Boss.'

'Tally one dead fighter,' Billy said. 'I was lined up ready to engage.'

Too professional to say so overtly, he was clearly pissed off.

'Topman … Negative playtime remaining … Top shooting, Ugly …' With that, Darth broke station for Kandahar.

It was Billy's target, no question. But we were a few hundred metres ahead of our wingmen and there was no escaping Trigger. Now he wanted to pay his respects at the Shrine too.

'FLIR should pick up the residual heat from the rocket motors. Come on Elton, where are these tunnels I've heard so much about? Let's nail them before they bolt.'

Tracking the Boss's FLIR image on my MPD, I talked him onto the tunnel entrances at the western edge of the Shrine. One large heat source appeared to the right of the screen – where the rockets must have been launched – then two more melted away down a blowhole nearby.

'See those heat sources, Boss?'

'Yeah, visual.'

'Widow Seven Eight, I have two men at the top of the Shrine, western end, dropping down a shaft. Is that where you were taking fire from?'

'Affirm. You are cleared to engage.'

Only a weapon with pinpoint accuracy could do the job.

'Copied. Engaging with Hellfire.'

The AGM-114K SAL Hellfire II missile landed precisely where we pointed the laser beam projected from the TADS on the Apache's nose. A Hellfire climbed after leaving its rail whilst a seeker in its head searched for the coded laser energy. Once found, it locked on, lined itself up and screamed down onto the painted target at 475 metres a second. The missile was so accurate we could post it through a letterbox.

But the shaft entrance was still going to be a hell of a shot. Every Hellfire we had was programmed to hit the target from above because that's how tank armour was best penetrated. We were 1,500 metres south of the Shrine and 3,000 feet above it. If the Boss banged the Hellfire in from here it would explode on the lip of the shaft, blowing the Taliban's ear drums and showering them with rock splinters — but if they'd got ten metres or so down from the surface, it probably wouldn't kill them. The missile's forte was penetration; its 12.5-lb warhead propelled a molten slug at thirty times the speed of sound through up to three feet of solid steel. It wasn't the explosion that did the killing, but the pressure wave that followed.

The Taliban were already inside the shaft, and would be burrowing deeper with every passing second.

'Don't fire until I say, Boss. We'll ram it right down the vent.'

I reduced our speed but maintained the height. The closer we got, the lower the TADS was pointing. The only way we'd get the Hellfire into the shaft was to fire it at a sharp angle from the shaft's entrance so it wouldn't have time to track down to its normal impact angle.

'Trust me, Boss. One thousand metres.' I wanted vertical and didn't have time to explain. 'Lase the target now, *but hold fire.*'

Five hundred metres from the target would do it. But we only had ten more seconds before our quarry would be out of harm's way. The bottom right-hand corner of my MPD told me that the dog had seen the rabbit – our missile had locked onto the laser. The

Boss's crosshairs were still on the shaft but the TADS could move no further.

'Mr M, I'm about to break lock – and they're about to escape.'

'Seven hundred and fifty metres. Stand by to fire.'

I dumped the collective and thrust the cyclic forward in one fast, smooth movement.

The Apache's nose dropped and its tail shot up. Within a second it was pointing straight down and hurtling towards the Shrine at 100 knots.

'Okay, fire Bo –'

'Firing.'

The Hellfire's propellant ignited with a bright yellow flash as it slid off its rail and blasted straight towards the target. The cockpit window was filling up with Shrine, and fast – 125 knots … I couldn't pull up because the Boss would lose lock.

The Boss hunched over his screen, keeping the TADS crosshairs over the shaft entrance and his laser trigger tight. A fraction over two seconds after it left us, the missile followed the beam straight into the blowhole and impacted five metres down the tunnel with five million pounds of pressure upon every square inch of rock it hit. *Yes* …

One hundred and fifty knots … I pulled back hard on the cyclic. Dust and debris shot from the top of the shaft, 100 feet into the air. We were under 1,000 feet. I'd sworn I'd *never* get this low. At 750 feet, still fighting the inertia, I punched off eight flares as the nose came up, just in case a missile decided to lock onto the heat from our now vertical engines.

'Widow Seven Eight, Ugly. That is a Delta Hotel. Repeat, Delta Hotel!'

Direct hit. We could hear whoops of delight over the JTAC's

mike. We skirted around the back of the Shrine to look for runners while Billy scoured Falcon. Both were as dead as a whore-house on a Sunday morning.

'I want that Hellfire method taught to everyone, Mr M … *after you've explained it to me …*'

Between us and the Harrier, every threat had been removed in under two minutes. Alice would have been proud of us.

The Boss was delighted with his sharp-shooting. 'I think that's what you call catching the enemy with their pants down, isn't it?'

'Kind of. They'd barely unbuckled their belts.'

'Widow Seven Eight, Ugly Five One. We have no more targets. Do you have anything else for us?'

'Negative. But they'll probably be back the moment you go.'

'Boss, we've got plenty of combat gas,' Billy said. 'Let's pull a trick.'

'Affirm. Good idea.'

Trigger flipped onto an insecure frequency and told the JTAC we were heading back to Camp Bastion. Instead, we pulled south ten kilometres into the desert, and waited.

It was a ruse we'd used a few times with success. We listened to the Taliban's radios; they listened to our insecure nets. Each side heard the other loud and clear. But neither knew for certain whether they were being bluffed.

We circled at endurance speed – seventy knots – while the sun dipped over the foothills of the Hindu Kush, painting the sky blood red. There was not a trace of humanity as far as the eye could see; the scene was so primeval that Billy and Carl's brutally uncompromising helicopter gunship beneath us looked strangely at home.

After twenty minutes, it was still all quiet at Arnhem. The Taliban were either all dead or had decided against stepping back into the ring for Round Two, so the JTAC released us.

'Drop us some fish and chips the next time you're passing,' Widow Seven Eight added. 'The lads are sick to death of ration packs.'

We landed back at base at dusk. The arming teams threw on the same Load Charlie for our next call-out.

'Stand by, you two,' Carl warned from the next door arming bay. 'Kev is on his way over.'

Kev circled the aircraft, his belly leading the way. He peered into our rocket pod tubes and under the Hellfire rails. He plugged into the wing with the inevitable slow shake of his head. 'Absolutely fooking typical.' We'd launched one of his precious Hellfires – what more did he want? 'You launched one all right. But you launched the wrong fooking one, didn't you?'

Kev pointed to the Hellfire on our right-hand rail. 'See that? Its serial number's out of date next week. You were supposed to have fired the fookin' right 'un, not the left. That one was good for another couple of months. I'll have to backload her now. Un-fooking-believable.' He unplugged and stomped off.

As we turned in that night, the four of us popped into the JOC one last time to check on the situation at Kajaki. The District Centre and Arnhem had taken the odd pot shot since we'd left, but on the whole it had remained quiet.

I got into my sleeping bag and hoped we didn't get an overnight call-out. I didn't mind them normally, but the whole squadron had to be up early the next morning. The Prime Minister was on his way.

A MATTER OF TIME

Prime Minister Tony Blair's clandestine visit was the worst kept secret in Camp Bastion. Everyone had known about it for days.

'Listen, I know you all know who's coming out,' the Boss said one night at an evening brief. 'But from now on, *please* stop talking about it. It's supposed to be classified.'

Darwin gave Trigger's knickers an extra twist. 'Can we ask the PM to sign Rocco, sir?'

'No we bloody can't! And please don't Rocco anyone while they're talking to him. Seriously guys, I'll get sacked. In fact, who's got Rocco? Can you hand him over, please?'

Thirty blank faces stared back at him; twenty-nine genuinely, one not so. Rocco wasn't coming out that easily. Trigger looked at Carl. His eyes narrowed.

'I swear I don't have him, Boss.'

The official order had gone out for maximum attendance at a 'VVIP visit' twenty-four hours before. They wanted everyone in the camp apart from those on essential duties to line up for him on the Hercules's landing strip. He was due to land, have a walkabout and a how-do-you-do and then leave an hour later without even going into the camp proper. It was fine by us. If we needed to scramble, we were in the right place. And it would give him a good show.

We all had to get up at 6am to be down there by seven for his arrival at eight. It was the military's usual hurry-up-and-wait scenario – and it put Carl on supermoan mode.

'Blooming typical. The one night we don't get an IRT shout, we have to get up at sparrow's fart anyway.'

There was a frisson around the camp that morning – not because anyone was particularly excited to meet the man, but because it was something different. A welcome break from the daily grind.

We were told he was going to make a speech, which was why I hadn't dreamt up an essential task for myself instead. I was curious to hear what he was going to say. Maybe he had an announcement to make; perhaps he'd tell us how long we'd be there, or where else we were headed. Whatever it was, I wanted to hear it first-hand.

Blair was on a two-day trip to the region according to a Sky News report I'd caught a glimpse of in the JHF. He'd already met Pakistan's president Pervez Musharraf in Lahore. After us, he was going up to Kabul to meet Afghan president Hamid Karzai.

The Leader of the Opposition, David Cameron, had already beaten his rival to it; he'd come out to see us in July. Helmand had been a new and sexy war at the time, so the new and sexy politicians were all over it like a rash. They didn't go to Iraq any more; can't think why. True to form, Billy had elbowed his way into giving Cameron a tour of the Apache's cockpit. He'd even strapped on his flying suit especially for the occasion, badges, sidearm and all.

Tragically for the Face, there was no chance of a one-on-one bore-athon with this bigwig. Tony Blair would say a quick hello to all of us and that would be it. Each of the brigade's sub-units had been instructed to stand in semicircles down one long line, with samples of our kit on display to give the press photographers a nice backdrop. For most of the boys that just meant rustling up a WMIK Land Rover, a Viking tracked armoured vehicle, an ambulance or a row of sniper rifles. For our unlucky Groundies, it meant having to get up even earlier than us to push an Apache 200 metres from our runway to the Hercules strip. Then they'd have to push it all the way back again.

It was a really nippy morning – overcast, with just the odd ray of sunshine bursting momentarily through the cloud to give us some warmth. Without the sun, first thing in the morning and at that altitude, Bastion wasn't a great place to be at that time of the year. December – only a few days away – and January were the only months that Helmand saw any proper cloud or rain.

Billy was one of the last down to the flight line.

'Oh you prize arse,' Geordie greeted him.

Most of us had turned up in our camouflage smocks – which were clean, uncreased and unfaded as they were seldom used and rarely washed. But not Billy; desperate to show off his wings, he was standing there shivering in his flying suit. In case any passing head of state was in doubt, *he* was an Apache pilot.

It was 7.09am and there we all were – a sizeable chunk of the Helmand Task Force's firepower – lined up like prunes with nothing to do for the next fifty-one minutes. Only Nick and Charlotte were missing, air testing in Kandahar. It would have been valuable experience for Nick; he would probably *be* Prime Minister one day.

'Come on Ed.' Billy gave me a nudge. 'Let's check out the croissant tent.'

'The what?'

'Over there. I spotted it on my way down.'

A posh-looking marquee had been erected at one end of the

runway. Its front flaps had been pinned open to reveal an urn of piping hot water, tea bags and jugs of filter coffee on a wooden picnic table. On a second table was the biggest tray of croissants I'd ever seen: hundreds of them, with mouth-watering fillings, steaming in the early morning air.

A couple of senior officers stood in the tent's entrance, so a frontal assault was never going to work. Billy and I tried our luck round the back.

'Sorry guys,' said the master chef. 'Definitely no one allowed in here.'

'Come on mate, give us a croissant.'

'I can't. Nobody's allowed any until Tony Blair has been in there.'

'Why, is he going to eat all 300 of them?'

'Look, it wasn't my idea … Oi!'

We left him to apprehend a pair of marines trying to sneak in behind him. One was holding up the far corner of the tent while his mate tried to slide underneath it.

Back at the squadron's place in the line, Geordie and Darwin had opened a book on who could get the longest handshake with the PM. It would mean holding on for as long as you could, even if he tried to tear himself away. They were also challenging the rest of the team to see who could ask him the oddest question and still get an answer.

'Just make sure it's all respectful, please. I still want a career in the army.' The Boss hated every second of this.

'I've got a belter,' said Darwin. 'Who's got a camera?'

A few of the boys had brought one down.

'Right, here's what Geordie and I are going to do. We'll ask Mr Blair if he doesn't mind a picture. When he says, "Yeah, sure, chaps, where do you want me?" we'll say, "Just there's fine thanks, sir," and hand him the camera. I bet he'll be so embarrassed he'll take the picture anyway.'

The PM's Hercules arrived a few minutes early and he emerged from the pilot's door to be greeted by the brigadier. A forty-strong travelling circus of TV cameramen, photographers and reporters poured off the rear ramp and glanced around, looking a little confused. Our desert wilderness wasn't the Afghanistan of the Tora Bora Mountains you saw on the news.

The entourage of senior brass and clipboard-wielding sub-ordinates led him to the end of the line furthest from us. The PM insisted on stopping and chatting to every group while the TV cameras did their stuff. Finally, he reached the marine mortar team alongside us. A balding bloke in a suit with an A4 pad strolled on ahead.

'Gentlemen, before the Prime Minister gets to you, I could do with a few details. What do you all do?'

The Boss turned to him. 'Who are you?'

'Oh, I'm Bob …'

'Bob who?'

'Bob Roberts. From the *Daily Mirror*.'

The revelation provoked all-round merriment; we'd thought the guy was some kind of Downing Street flunky.

'Fuck off, baldy,' and 'Get out the way, will you?' the Groundies chorused from behind us.

The poor bloke scampered off in the other direction, looking quite hurt.

'Hi guys.'

And there was Tony Blair, standing right in front of us. We'd been so busy hurling abuse at the man from the *Mirror* that most of us hadn't seen him approach.

'Gather round the Prime Minister please,' the RSM instructed.

Tony Blair was in official Prime Ministerial war zone kit: blue slacks, a navy blazer and a dark blue shirt, open at the neck. He looked tired and old. The famous blue eyes still twinkled, but huge crow's feet spread from each corner of them and his hair was more salt than pepper. He was a different man to the one I remembered walking into Downing Street nine years before.

The squadron wags had gone quiet now; everyone was a little bit star-struck. Trigger must have breathed a sigh of relief; it was immediately obvious that all the big talk wasn't going to come to anything.

Blair thrust his hand forward to each of us. There was no chance of holding onto it, even if someone did have the balls. We were given a quick, forceful shake, up and down, a momentary fix of the eyeballs and then it was onto the next bloke. Two seconds each, max. He moved incredibly quickly, clearly well drilled in how to avoid the 'I'm going to hold onto his hand the longest' game. No surprises there; he'd been shaking squaddies by the hand for years.

'Prime Minister, this is 656 Squadron, Army Air Corps. They operate the Apache AH Mk1.'

'Ah yes.' The trademark grin stretched from ear to ear. 'So you must work with the locals.'

None of us knew how to answer that, so none of us did. That kind of killed the conversation.

Someone did ask for a photograph, but instead of pulling Darwin's cheeky prank we all gathered sheepishly round Blair instead – Darwin included. The most rebellious we got was slipping the odd thumbs-up to the camera behind Blair's back as we posed up for the group snaps.

Then, just as quickly as he'd arrived, he was ushered away to the medics, the next group in line.

Billy couldn't conceal his disappointment. 'I thought he might ask us *one* question about the aircraft. He did buy the bloody thing, after all.'

Geordie was still as confused as the rest of us.

'Hang on, did you hear what he said to us, like? "So you must work with the locals." What the *fuck* does that mean?'

It was obvious Blair had no real idea of who we were or what we did. Sadly, scaring the locals half to death was about the closest we ever got to working with them. Since we spent most of our lives 3,000 feet up, he couldn't have been further from the mark. Maybe he'd offered everyone down the line the same catch-all remark. I suppose it saved having to think of twenty different ones.

The procession finished and, 200-odd hands shaken, Blair was whisked across to the croissant tent. A dais had been erected at the opposite end of it, with a loud speaker on either side. After Blair had downed his coffee, we were ordered to gather round for his speech.

A bank of raised platforms had been thrown up for the travelling media. They offered the best view, so Billy and I jumped up on one of them. It earned us an evil look from its occupier, a man with thick black glasses later identified to me as the BBC's Political Editor Nick Robinson. He didn't seem totally thrilled about sharing his platform with us. Billy and I gave him a grin.

'Here, in this extraordinary piece of desert, is where the future of the world's security is going to be played out … The only way we can ensure security is being prepared to fight for it … We will beat the Taliban by having the determination and courage to stand up to them … You defeat them not just on behalf of the people here in

Afghanistan but in Britain, and the wider world ... People back home are very proud of the work you do, whatever they think of the politicians who sent you ...'

He went on for about fifteen minutes, and finished with 'a huge debt of thanks from a humbled nation'. For that, he got a spontaneous cheer and a generous round of applause as he was swiftly channelled back to the waiting Hercules. It was an upbeat, crowd-pleasing performance and went down very well with the younger soldiers. Pride, support, courage; he knew all the buzz words twenty-year-old squaddies wanted to hear.

As far as I was concerned, the Blair magic began to fade as the Prime Minister and his flying circus trundled down the runway. Despite his well-crafted phrases and emotional expressions, he hadn't actually told us anything we didn't already know. There was no big announcement, no addition to the defence budget, no deadline for the end of the conflict, no council tax rebate for our families at home. He'd had nothing new to say. I wondered why he'd bothered to come all that way. Still, the bacon croissant had been nice.

As November became December, Alice's first situation brief proved increasingly accurate. Not only were the Taliban getting better, they were coming after us.

Close air support had changed the outcome of a lot of battles in our ground troops' favour, so the Taliban hated all Coalition offensive aircraft – but they still hated Apaches the most.

If you wanted to go after aircraft and had none of your own, you needed surface-to-air missiles. SAMs had been the preserve of the world's superpowers, but by the 1980s they had become a global phenomenon.

The missiles employed one of three different systems to track and hit moving targets: radar-tracking, heat-seeking, or laser-guided. They varied in quality, but most could detect any aircraft flying in the SAM belt – between 1,000 and 20,000 feet – from about six miles, and engage it from four.

All three types of SAMs were believed to be kicking around Afghanistan. The principal threat came from Man Portable Air Defence Systems – SAMs fired from shoulder launchers that a couple of blokes could carry around on foot. There was no shortage of them. At Dishforth, we had been briefed to expect Russian SA7s and SA14s, Chinese HN15s – and the US Stingers and British Blowpipes that the CIA and MI6 had flooded into the country during the Soviet occupation.

The good news was that although we knew the Taliban had ManPADs, we didn't believe they had many of them left that actually worked. Their biggest problem – our greatest advantage – was that their battery system decayed. This was especially the case with Stingers, and the Taliban had no means of replacing them. Even the world's most unscrupulous arms dealers thought twice about dealing with Islamic extremists because of the heat it brought down on them.

'Working SAMs are a highly prized commodity to the Taliban,' an Int Corps briefer told us. 'We reckon that the few they retain will be used only as a last ditch defence for very senior people; they'll only be fired if a Taliban or al Qaeda leader's life is under imminent threat.'

No SAMs had been fired at Coalition aircraft in Afghanistan for quite a while, so while we remained cautious, we hadn't been taking the SAM threat too seriously. Then, four weeks into the tour, they did fire a SAM at us – in Helmand, at a Dutch F16 jet bomber, callsign Ramit.

I was in the JHF at the time, watching some gun tapes on the computer. The news came through on the MIRC. There was a Military Internet Relay Chat in every HQ across the four southern provinces – a giant TV screen / video printer pumping out one line sitreps as they came in about operations ongoing over Regional Command South; a running ticker tape on the whole war.

'Jesus, have you seen this?'

All eight of us in the tent crowded around the MIRC.

'KABUL: RAMIT ENGAGED BY SAM. SOUTH SANGIN. SAM DEFEATED …'

'Bloody hell. What's going on at Sangin? Are Special Forces lifting some big player we don't know about?'

They weren't. A quick call to brigade confirmed there were no arrest operations going down in the Sangin area. In fact, troops weren't even out on the ground.

The next day, the full report came through. Lookouts in Forward Operating Base Robinson, a support base seven klicks south of the Sangin DC for the marines in the Green Zone, had heard some sporadic shooting from the west. They'd put in a call to the brigade air cell to ask if any passing aircraft might be able to take a quick peek.

The cloud base was fairly low that day. To see through it, the F16 had to drop down below it, to 3,000 feet. The shooting had stopped, so the jet tootled around for a minute or two as a show of force. A corkscrew trail of grey smoke rose from the Green Zone as the missile arced towards the F16. It passed just behind the jet, diverted by a flare, and disappeared into the clouds.

Arcing meant it was guided – a SAM. Corkscrew and grey smoke meant SA7b – a tail chaser that locked onto engine heat. It wasn't just a pot shot. It took a fair few minutes to set up an SA7. It bore all the hallmarks of a deliberate trap. Ramit had been lucky.

The incident shook the air community. It told us two things. One, the Taliban had SAMs that worked; and two, they were now very happy to attack opportunity targets. We didn't enjoy hearing either. It was a major break from their previous operating pattern.

Ramit's SAM escape threw a different perspective on an intelligence hit we'd picked up recently. Some days before the launch, a radio intercept heard a Taliban commander saying, 'Fetch the rakes and spades to hit the helicopters.' Initially, the Int cell had assessed rakes and spades meant Chinese rockets and a launcher. Now, we had to assume they meant SAMs.

Alice then delivered a series of different snippets of bad news about SAMs over the next week's morning and evening briefs.

'We believe they're planning to move a Stinger to Sangin or Kajaki.'

'What do you mean,' the Boss asked. 'Where did this information come from?'

'I can't tell you sir, sorry.'

That normally meant HumInt; human intelligence – aka: a spy. I and every other pilot in the room mentally crossed our fingers not to get the next IRT call-out to Sangin or Kajaki.

We were told that a specific Taliban commander in the north of the province, had boasted that he could listen in on all our movements. 'I have a British radio frequency and I know everywhere they go.'

It was certainly possible. Perhaps he'd taken it from the dead SBS pair in June. He couldn't hear Apaches on it as our radios were secure and codes regularly changed. But the ones in the Chinooks weren't.

Alice also told us that some bright desk officer had discovered that there were no less than five Stingers in the valley between Sangin and Kajaki.

But a second Taliban radio intercept in Now Zad a couple of days afterwards picked up the most worrying SAM intelligence of all. A commander was overheard saying, 'When the helicopters arrive, if the professional man brings his thing, fire from a distance.'

A 'professional man' and a 'thing' weren't SAM-specific, but 'fire from a distance' certainly was. It was good advice, too. It identified the 'thing' as a heat-seeking SAM. The longer the missile had in the air, the better its chance of homing in on the aircraft's engines: as the gap closed, the heat source became clearer to the missile's seeker. Translation: they were anticipating the arrival of some bloke who knew what he was doing, and then they were going to fire another heat-seeking SAM specifically at one of us.

A huge amount of SAM activity and intelligence had come in over a short period. How much of it was true and how much bluff we had no idea. That was always the problem with the intelligence game; it was a world of smoke and mirrors. All we knew was that the bastards were up to something. The ante had been upped, big time.

The feeling of foreboding with which I'd started the tour had lessened after a few successful enemy contacts. Now it was right back again. I was in no hurry to become the first British Apache pilot to get shot down by a SAM.

I decided to have a quiet chat with Carl the next time I got the chance. He wasn't just our Electronic Warfare Officer – he was one of the most clued up guys in the Army Air Corps. Only a few people in Britain would have known more about Electronic Warfare with regard to the Apache's Helicopter Integrated Defensive

Aid System than Carl. The EW manual was his Book at Bedtime, for Christ's sake. I thought I could do with a few of his reassuring stats.

'Sure Ed, where do you want to start? HIDAS is a beautiful thing ...'

'Just keep it simple and pretty, please buddy.'

Most of it I already knew, but it was good to hear it again. There was no escape from a SAM in Afghanistan. You couldn't go and hide behind a tree or a rock, and if you climbed it was worse. Instead, HIDAS took the SAM on. The Apache's Helicopter Integrated Defensive Aid System had been painstakingly constructed to defeat all known SAMs. What's more, it did it automatically.

HIDAS detected every missile threat – any laser beam that tried to track the aircraft, any radar attempting a lock onto it, and any missile that was fired at us – from a huge distance, with a web of sensors that picked up a specific UV plume generated by the missile's propulsion. Then Bitching Betty, the Apache's female cockpit warning system, passed on the message. The moment the aircraft came under threat – from air or ground – she gave us the good news, telling us what it was and where it was coming from.

When a missile was fired against you, HIDAS would automatically launch the necessary countermeasure. For a radar-tracking SAM, the Apache threw out clouds of chaff that appeared as large-sized aircraft to confuse the radar. If it was a heat-seeker, it would spray out a shower of flares – hotter than our engines – to divert it. If the missile was being manually laser-guided, Betty would issue a series of rapid (and highly classified) instructions for violent manoeuvre: 'Break right', 'Break left', 'Climb' and 'Descend'. When we were out of danger, she would say, 'Lock broken.' It was the closest she got to a compliment. What a woman.

HIDAS had never really been tested on operations. The boffins had done everything they could in the labs and on the ranges. But until you sent up a couple of guys and fired a ManPAD at them, you wouldn't know for sure how well it could cope.

'So what do we do in the meantime?' I asked.

'Just trust in the aircraft.'

Just when I'd started to feel a little better …

SAMs weren't the only threats we faced. HIDAS could do nothing to defeat conventional 'line of sight' weapons. We were just as vulnerable to old-fashioned bullets as anyone else. Rifle and RPG fire wasn't necessarily a big concern for us. An AK47 had an effective range of 800 metres. RPGs were timed to explode at 900 metres or on impact, though they could be doctored to achieve twice the distance. We generally stood 2,000 metres off enemy targets because the power of our weapons and sensors allowed us to.

Higher calibre anti-aircraft guns were a different matter. The Taliban had a lot of them, mostly ex-Soviet stuff. Anti-aircraft guns were single-, double- or quadruple-barrelled and put down a phenomenal rate of fire. Afghans used them as ground weapons, firing them horizontally at each other.

We liked the 14.5-mm Soviet ZPU the least. Each barrel could crack out 600 rounds of ammunition per minute, lethal up to 5,000 feet in the air. Luckily they were prized pieces of equipment, and not in limitless supply.

DShK's, or Dushkas as they were nicknamed, were more common than ZPU's. Firing a slightly smaller round, a 12.7-mm, they had a range of 4,000 feet. Every tribal chief normally had access to a Dushka for his tribe's protection – they were that common. And they caused us a lot of grief. Only good flying – and a sizeable helping of luck – had stopped a British helicopter from being shot out of the Helmand skies thus far.

It was rare for a full day to go by without at least one helicopter getting some incoming. It had been like that ever since we'd arrived in Helmand; the statistics defied belief.

By the time of their departure in September, the Joint Helicopter Force had counted more than fifty close calls from enemy ground fire on Apaches, Chinooks and Lynxes. 16 Air Assault Brigade saw a lot more than we did: rounds had passed through or bounced off all three machines. A Dushka bullet went straight through the tail boom of Darwin's Apache on his very first combat engagement in May – he hadn't known until he landed. Another large calibre round had hit a second Apache's rotor head, bouncing straight off it. If the rotor head had broken, the aircraft would have fallen out of the sky.

During the first month of fighting in June, a Chinook's fuselage had been riddled with bullets while coming into land to insert Paras north of Sangin, and one of its passengers seriously wounded. And a young female Chinook pilot – on her very first combat sortie – had a bullet enter through her side door and pass through her seat, inches behind her chest.

Nobody had yet been killed by ground fire. That had amazed us on our return. And as the year drew to a close, it was a living miracle that it was still the case.

From the generals in Whitehall who read the damage reports all the way down to the young pilots who just got on with their daily flights, everyone was in full agreement: it was no longer a case of *if* a helicopter got shot down in Helmand, but *when*. And now that the Taliban seemed to have got their hands on a shed-load of working SAMs that moment seemed an awful lot closer.

But something was being done to address the Taliban's ever more proficient supply of men and arms. The brigade had a plan. And it was one hell of a good one.

OP GLACIER BEGINS

Smashing the Taliban's supply chain to smithereens was 3 Commando Brigade's first objective with Operation Glacier. Five days into December, we had a ringside seat at the second.

Things in Garmsir had gone from bad to worse. The Taliban still believed they could dislodge the Brits, as they had done before. And they were giving it their all. The fighting had deteriorated at times to hand to hand combat; it was like something out of the Zulu War.

The marines' every movement in or out of the DC compound drew withering sniper fire. The Taliban also launched daily attacks on the commandos' lookout post on a neighbouring hill to the south.

The compound was at the edge of the town. Its western flank was protected by the north–south running Helmand River and the Green Zone narrowed to a funnel point to the north, so the Taliban hit it from the east – from the cover of Garmsir's five- or six-street grid – and, even more vigorously, from the farmland to the south. The fields and orchards offered the enemy excellent natural cover. With its regular treelines and deep irrigation ditches, they could move with impunity to within 100 metres of the British compound, then open up with AK47s and RPGs, supported by WOMBATs and mortars.

Barricaded inside the DC and on the top of JTAC Hill (as they'd christened it), the marines replied with air strikes, heavy machine guns and 105-mm artillery called in from a gun line set up for them in the desert. Every enemy shooting position in the few square kilometres around them had been pummelled five times over.

Garmsir used to boast a busy high street and bustling bazaar, but all the locals had moved out to escape the Taliban regime. After the schools were closed and rebellious farmers beheaded, its shabby streets were deserted. Skeletal buildings lay derelict amongst the debris. Whenever the shooting lapsed, an eerie silence fell. 'Even the birds have left,' its defenders said.

Every so often, when Colonel Magowan's southern battlegroup could cobble together the resources, the marines would push the Taliban back from their ramparts. And that's where we came in. HQ Flight was rostered on Deliberate Taskings, so the job of giving close air support to one such counter-attack fell to us. It was the best kind of mission; going in dirty, shoulder to shoulder with the troops, was what made flying an Apache such a joy.

The objective of the attack was to clear a square kilometre of farmland to the DC's immediate south, up to a long east–west treeline. The marines couldn't hold the ground; they didn't have the spare men. But in the process they'd learn about the enemy's routes of approach, kill those who were well entrenched, destroy their fortified positions, and perhaps buy the garrison a few days' breathing space.

Two Royal Marine companies were moved in covertly overnight, and the objective area was heavily bombed and shelled. At 10am, the two companies stretched along the main road and advanced slowly south. An RAF Harrier was on station to give them initial air cover. We were tasked to arrive forty-five minutes later.

Trigger hogged the front seat of our Apache again. I didn't put up a fuss. He was enjoying himself so much I didn't want to take the smile off his face. We checked in with their JTAC, Widow Eight Three, and he told us it was going well. The enemy were not standing and fighting. Caught out by the size of the marine contingent and with no time to reinforce, they were falling back, offering only sporadic 'shoot and scoot' fire as they did so. The JTAC gave us the positions of all the friendly forces.

'Ugly callsigns, we believe Taliban might be infiltrating a large compound 300 metres to the south of our limit of exploitation. I would like you to fix them there and destroy them.'

I took us three klicks straight south on the western side of the river, and banked hard left to hook us in behind the target.

'Okay, I've got five Taliban entering the compound now.'

The Boss started to get excited again. 'Looks like they're trying to get into cover before the marines reach the treeline and catch them in the open.'

'Weapons?'

The Boss zoomed in his TADS.

'Yes. The last bloke's got an RPG. And they're running.'

I looked down at the MPD by my right knee. All five were now running diagonally through an orchard within the compound's outer wall. They must have heard our rotor blades; we were only 1,500 metres off. Sunlight glinted off the working parts of their AK47s.

'Affirm boss. They're enemy all right. Get 'em.'

'Five One, firing with thirty Mike Mike.'

Trigger put three bursts of twenty rounds into the group. The RPG man and the guy in front of him were torn apart by the shrapnel, but the three leaders made it into a reinforced adobe hut in the south-east corner. The Boss put another two bursts onto the front wall, gouging great chunks off it, but these things were built to last and we weren't sure how much was getting through.

Billy had come round from the north. 'Five Zero, I saw men running in the direction of that hut before you engaged the orchard. I reckon there could be quite a few of them in there.'

'Copied, thanks. Let's get a bomb on it.'

Topman, the Harrier pilot, said it would be a few minutes before he could set up a run, so the Boss delivered a Hellfire through its letterbox whilst Billy pinned the Taliban inside it with harassing cannon fire. The missile collapsed half the roof, and we got the Harrier to stick a 500-lb GBU in there for good measure. By the time we'd finished, there wasn't anything left of it.

The marines had reached the treeline, clearing all enemy from the target area. Widow Eight Three told us to look into a few more isolated compounds south of them for any enemy movement. There was none. True to form, the Taliban had gone to ground in a plethora of well-prepared hiding places.

'Ugly callsigns, come north-east of the treeline and hold there. We're going to drop all the compounds with 105-mm.'

Salvo after salvo of artillery rounds would dislodge the Taliban from their hideouts. They'd break for better cover and the fast air and Apaches could bomb the merry hell out of them; good old-fashioned scorched earth tactics – as effective for the marines today as they were for the Carthaginians 2,200 years earlier.

There wasn't a civilian within ten miles of the place; we could see that ourselves from the unkempt state of the fields – so the marines were keen to make the most of the firepower they had that day, and give the Taliban a licking they wouldn't forget. I checked our fuel level. Ten minutes left on station.

'Boss, we're not that far off chicken. Might be a good time to RTB for a suck of gas, and to bomb up the aircraft again ...' Going chicken meant you only had enough fuel to get back to base within the legal limit. The marines were under good cover in the irrigation ditches, and it would take an hour or two to bring in all the artillery fire missions they wanted. The Harrier was pulling off, to be replaced by a US F18 Hornet, and an A10 had just come on station too. It was a perfect time for us to break off.

Widow Eight Three agreed. 'The commander wants all ground callsigns to go firm for a few hours while we fix as many enemy as we can. Can you come back down to cover their withdrawal?'

We agreed with the JTAC that we'd stay on thirty minutes' notice for his call to return. We'd go back to Camp Bastion, refuel and rearm, and wait in the JHF for his shout.

The boys in Garmsir deserved to get the chance to give the Taliban what for. Until today they'd been in a living hell, just like the Paras had in Sangin during the summer. Siege warfare: their sole aim was survivability; pounded, probed, shot and wounded day in, day out, night in and night out. I smiled as I looked out of the window and saw them in the long treeline whacking the Taliban. It was a pleasure to help.

We were sitting in the loading bays midway through the 30-mm upload when an urgent voice came online from the Ops Room.

'Ugly Five One Flight, Zero. Rearm as quickly as possible. Do not close down. You are going back down to Garmsir immediately.'

We didn't want to clutter up the Apache net by asking why.

We'd find out when we needed to. A more detailed order followed as we taxied onto the runway.

'Ugly Five Zero, Ugly Five One; you are to escort a CH47, callsign Doorman Two Six, on a Casevac to collect a T1 and a T3. Then remain in support of Widow Eight Three, who is receiving very effective enemy fire.'

A T1, a T3 *and* they were still getting nasty incoming? Jesus. Carl didn't want to speculate over the radio so he sent a text.

WHAT WENT WRONG ... ALL CALM WHEN WE LEFT ...

A casualty was given one of four initial gradings by the medics on the ground. It allowed the recovery chain to know how best to prioritise their resources in response. T1 meant the casualty's life was in grave danger; he had to be recovered by air immediately. Get him to the operating theatre at Camp Bastion's field hospital within an hour and his chances of survival were significantly increased. It was what we called the golden hour. T2 meant the casualty could be stabilised but was in a serious condition and needed to get to hospital before he ran the risk of becoming T1. T3 was commonly referred to as the walking wounded – every other conceivable injury that was not life-threatening within twenty-four hours and required extraction. T4 was the least time-pressing, because T4 meant he was dead. It was hard-nosed military risk management – designed to send a clear signal about whether the recovery chopper should risk jeopardising its crew, surgeons and medics to pick up our injured.

The mighty Chinook's blades began to turn.

We still couldn't make sense of it. When we'd left, the Taliban were in disarray and it was a turkey shoot for the marines. How could the tables have turned so quickly?

MUST HAVE BEEN A LUCKY MORTAR BOMB ... BOSS

OR VERY UNLUCKY ... BILLY

There was no other way the Taliban could have got through the marines' arcs of fire.

We escorted Doorman down. The Chinook tanked it, low level at top speed, the quickest line from A to B. It landed in the cover of a berm north-west of the Garmsir bridge as we scoured the approaches. The two casualties were loaded on board and Doorman lifted again less than thirty seconds later. We checked in with Widow Eight Three.

'Ugly, Widow, we are being engaged heavily from the east–west treeline, the original limit of our exploitation.' The treeline? Wasn't that where the marines were?

'Copied. Send friendly forces' positions.'

'Friendly forces are falling back from the treeline towards the main road now.' He gave us their grids.

'Also, confirm you can see an oval-shaped series of compounds on the western side of the farmland, halfway between the treeline and the main road.'

'Affirm, I see friendlies.'

'That is the location of the tactical headquarters. That's where we were hit and took the casualties.'

The casualties in the tactical HQ seemed to have brought a swift end to the scorched earth artillery plan. If the marines now thought the Taliban had accurate grids to mortar them, they needed to move out of there fast. As they exfiltrated, the initiative inevitably swung back to the enemy.

The Boss and Billy swept the treeline with their TADSs, pouring long bursts of cannon at any glimpse of Taliban. They could see very little; these people were good. They used the trees and bushes over the irrigation ditches to follow-up unseen. The marines

149

reported one new firing position after another as they withdrew; the Taliban had infiltrated the whole of the kilometre-long treeline and were harassing them all the way back to the main road.

It called for some scorched earth tactics of our own. As soon as we were satisfied all the marines had pulled back far enough, we put pair after pair of Flechette rockets into the trees. The two Apaches took it in turns to run in, again and again, following up each time with cannon. We saw the Flechette darts strip through the higher branches, but the undergrowth was so thick we couldn't see where they landed. It was impossible to confirm any kills.

After half an hour of our bombardment, Widow Eight Three reported the two companies of marines had reached the relative safety of the main road without any further casualties. Our suppression seemed to have worked, and we were released to return to base.

They would like to have stayed out for longer, but the marines had achieved all they could in the circumstances. The attack hadn't been a failure by its own standards – despite the complete lack of territorial gain. It had been bitter and bloody stuff, with every metre of ground passionately contested then handed right back to the enemy. But this was business as usual in the hell that was Garmsir.

It is extremely hard to measure success when we take casualties. Their aim was to clear the ground to the treeline and flatten the firing points that the Taliban used beyond it. This was achieved but at a high cost. This was technological warfare on a par with World War One: Tommy over the top after the guns and Tommy falling back to his original trench. It did allow Magowan to test the resolve of the Taliban and they were most certainly up for the fight. They were strong, well armed, well trained and ferocious. It was a costly but vital mission to know where the Taliban routes were, and where their firing points in the treeline were. It would now give the marines some breathing space in the DC whilst Magowan concentrated on the big plan.

Six hours after we climbed into our cockpits, the four of us made our weary way into the JHF for the usual debrief. Alice's expression told us an already bad day was about to get a whole lot worse.

'Just so you know, it looks as though we've got a blue-on-blue situation down in Garmsir. Nothing to do with anything you put down; it was when you were on your way back to refuel. We think the F18 strafed the marines' command post, and that's what gave us the T1 and T3.'

My heart sank. A blue-on-blue. *Fuck.* Suddenly it all made sense. The Taliban hadn't managed to strike back at the marines after all. Our own aircraft had done that for them. Just when the guys were really nailing the bastards who were making their lives a misery, they got a smack from one of their own.

'The Special Investigations Branch guys have already been in,' Alice said. 'They asked if you could hang around the JOC for them.'

Every friendly fire was acutely investigated. Statements had to be taken from everyone who had been operating in the area. The SIB examined the circumstances in case of negligence then the Board of Inquiry tried to learn lessons for the future. The process often took years.

We knew then that only two things could have caused it. The F18 would have been tasked onto its targets by Widow Eight Three or another JTAC, just as we had been onto ours. Either the US pilot had been given the wrong grid or he had mistaken the marines' compound for the Taliban's.

Blue-on-blues from the air were nothing new. For every offensive aircrew, intiating fire on friendly troops was the worst nightmare of all. That day in Garmsir, the American pilot had been trying to save Coalition lives. But close air support was a dangerous and complex business, supplied in circumstances of great pressure for both ground troops and pilots. It was often very fucking close. The tiniest mistake – a number on a grid reference, the briefest lapse in concentration pulling the trigger, or the slightest movement of the TADS – meant the difference between hitting your enemy and your friend.

By nightfall that day, the Union Flag over the JOC had been lowered to half mast. The T1 had become a T4. Marine Jonathan Wigley was pronounced dead in Camp Bastion's field hospital; a mem-ber of Zulu Company, 45 Commando, he was twenty-one years old.

The Apache force was brought in on Operation Glacier two days later. We hadn't heard about it before, because we hadn't needed to. Like all covert operations, it was kept very hush hush. The brigade were only bringing us into the loop now because they needed our help.

Colonel Magowan's southern battlegroup had been doing a lot more than just holding Garmsir. And they'd be doing it for a month already.

'They've got a few jobs for us.' Our Ops Officer briefed out the basics of the plan. 'And they will take priority over all other Deliberate Taskings.'

Everything was being thrown at Operation Glacier, because it was the most ambitious plan the Helmand Task Force had drawn up since our arrival. As far back as early November, it had been decided that Garmsir could not be held successfully by British grit alone –

however steely it was proving. The periodic counter-attacks were only cutting off a few Taliban snakeheads, and they soon grew back.

We needed to put a 7.62-mm high-velocity bullet straight through Medusa's temple. That meant hitting the Taliban where it really hurt: smashing the long underbelly of their southern supply chain. They came to have a crack at us from Kandahar in the east, and the mountains of Uruzgan in the north. But the Taliban's main supply route into Helmand was from the Pakistani border in the south.

Not only would severing it reduce the pressure on Garmsir, it would also reduce the flow of men and arms to the other four contested locations, impairing the Taliban's operations across the province: up to five birds killed – or at least badly winged – with one big stone. Of course, the Taliban would eventually recover and establish a new MSR, but that would take them time – and time is what the Task Force was most keen to buy. The harder the enemy MSR was hit, the longer it would take to rebuild.

Operation Glacier had two stages: quiet and then noisy. The first was a thorough and painstaking reconnaissance of the roads they used, the places they stopped to rest, their supply dumps and command centres. Their entire southern logistical structure had to be analysed piece by piece. Concentrations of enemy fighters were the most prized targets. Only once the main concentration points had been acquired would Brigadier Jerry Thomas give the order for them to be destroyed; methodically, one after the other, and with a massive display of force. The quiet reconnaissance stage was expected to take around two months. Nothing was likely to go noisy until January. Or so we were told.

It had been no coincidence that Magowan's Information Exploitation Battlegroup had been given Helmand's southern stretch as their area of operations. The brigadier had obviously had a pretty good idea of what he wanted to achieve down there from the moment he arrived. The battlegroup was structured as a highly advanced recce unit, pulling together under Colonel Magowan's command all the intelligence gathering formations the brigade had: 45 Commando's lightly armed and highly mobile Recce Troop, C Squadron of the Light Dragoons in their armoured Scimitars, the Brigade Reconnaissance Force – the marines in-house Special Forces – and Y Troop, the expert signallers who eavesdropped on the enemy's communications. As his muscle when he needed it, he also had two regular Royal Marine rifle companies: 42 Commando's India Company and 45 Commando's Zulu Company.

The units had been discreetly sent out to track even further south of Garmsir. They would come off the desert into the Green Zone's fringes, and probe for any reaction. Some areas were quiet, others a hive of Taliban activity. They would never stay in one place long enough to give the enemy the impression they had any special interest in it. Instead, everything they witnessed was logged. If the Taliban had engaged them or they had spotted sentries, it was pinged as a hot spot and an eavesdropping station was set up to intercept all radio transmissions and phone calls.

Magowan didn't just have the use of his own troops. Every asset in the UK inventory had been laid at his battlegroup's disposal, from SBS teams specialising in close-target reconnaissance to aerial drones and a Nimrod MR2 spy plane. Fitted with a high-tech sur-veillance suite, the ageing jet followed vehicle and troop movements from 25,000 feet, for many hours and over hundreds of miles, totally unseen. Even the national intelligence agencies, MI6 and GCHQ, were tapped up for any SigInt or HumInt which might be of use.

'The operation has made some good progress so far,' the Ops Officer told us. 'They've picked up a lot more than they expected to by this stage. They've got some valuable int hits on how the Tier Two fighters come in; to be frank – it's because there are so bloody many of them.'

Huge numbers were coming through from Pakistan. They passed over the border at Baram Chah, a lawless opium trading town that straddled both countries. From there, they would be split into groups of three or four to avoid detection, put into single Toyota 4x4s, and driven at speed across the desert until they hit the Green Zone. The Helmand River ran from north to south until it bent west sixty klicks south of Garmsir into what we called 'the fish hook', and swept on into Nimruz. It was somewhere north of the fish hook that the Toyotas deposited the new combatants and the Green Zone MSR began. The exact location had yet to be pin-pointed because the recce units hadn't got down that far – but the battlegroup was confident it was only a question of time. We were impressed. It was a hell of an operation.

'So where do we come in?' Billy said. 'Skip to the chase, sir – the suspense is killing me.'

'Because we're a bit too noisy to do masses of stand-off recce and we've got enough on our plates already, our bit kicks in with Stage Two. It looks like we're getting written in big time for the kinetic assaults.'

There were grunts of approval from every attack pilot in the room.

'But there are one or two little tasks they've asked for us to help with during Stage One as well …'

HQ Flight was given an Op Glacier job on our next Deliberate Tasking shift. The Brigade Reconnaissance Force had asked for

Apache close air support for a tricky little spot fifteen kilometres south of Garmsir on the eastern edge of the Green Zone. They had some good intelligence that the place was a major Taliban hot spot. But the vegetation was particularly thick there, so they had to go in close to verify and pin down the enemy's exact location. If it went badly for them and they got smacked, they wanted us to steam in and sort it out.

We were asked to go down late morning and stand off five klicks into the Red Desert so as not to give the game away. If the Taliban heard us clattering over them, they'd immediately go to ground.

I'd finally managed to wrestle the front seat back from Trigger, so I was mission commander for the sortie. It was a forty-five minute trip from Bastion, giving us about an hour on station.

We arrived at our desert spot and I checked in with their JTAC, Knight Rider Five Five. The Brigade Recce Force (BRF) had chosen their own callsign as well: they were clearly Hoff fans. They gave us their grid, and we pinged them 700 metres from the Green Zone, in a convoy of six WMIK Land Rovers and Pinzgauer trucks – a light, manoeuvrable and well-armed force, but without any protection when the rounds started coming in.

'Ugly Five One, Knight Rider Five Five. Here's the plan. We don't want to go into the Green Zone because we think we'll get cut up. We're going to try and entice the Taliban to take a shot at us by going up on a ridgeline just before the Zone starts.'

'Nightrider Five Five, Ugly. Confirm, you actually want the Taliban to shoot at you?'

'Affirm. It's the best way to assess their location and strength. That's when we might need your help. Confirm you can see the ridgeline?'

'Affirm. We have you visual on our optics. We're due east; can you hear our rotors?'

'Negative Ugly. We can see a couple of black dots through binos, but that's about it.'

'Good. We're in dead ground to the Green Zone but we'll have some fire down for you within thirty seconds of your call. Keep us updated on what you see and pass suspect grids regularly; it will cut down on our response time.'

'Knight Rider Five Five, that's a copy; stand by for some playtime.'

We orbited in oval-shaped 'race tracks' at seventy knots, keeping 100 feet off the desert floor to stay out of view. Either my TADS camera or Billy's was on the marines at all times. Our downdraughts made wonderful patterns in the thick red sand beneath us.

'Knight Rider, Ugly. We're moving up onto the ridgeline now. Get ready.'

We saw their vehicles cautiously ascend the 500 metre slope. I actioned the cannon.

'Knight Rider, Ugly. We're now presenting the vehicles to the Green Zone. Stand by for contact.'

The second the guys started taking rounds, the Boss would power up hard and make a beeline for them. I kept my finger over my trigger, and the Boss tensed up on the cyclic. Both Apaches were now pointing towards the BRF, but nothing happened. Ten minutes and as many circuits later – still nothing.

'Knight Rider, Ugly. We're getting no response. The feeling is the Taliban might think we're looking a bit too handy in the vehicles with our weapons pointing down on 'em and that's what's stopping 'em from engaging. We're going to debus. Standby for contact. Again.'

The marines slipped down into firing positions around their vehicles, lying on their belt buckles. Another ten minutes passed. Still no reaction. Billy and Carl had started doing flying exercises, landing in the desert and taking off again.

'Knight Rider, Ugly. Okay, we're going to stand up and have a bit of a mill around the ridge. Hopefully that'll do it. Stand by.'

The figures on the ridge strolled about for five more uncomfortable minutes, cradling their rifles. It looked utterly incongruous. When that didn't work, they gathered into a group for a pow-wow by the middle Land Rover. The Boss wanted to know what Billy and Carl were up to.

'You never know when you might need to do a dust-out landing. Just keeping our skills up.'

The BRF strode purposefully back to their vehicles.

'Knight Rider, Ugly. We don't fucking understand this. Normally when we come down this far, we get shot at. Today they're not doing a bloody thing. We've decided we're going to get a brew on.'

'Confirm; you're going to do it up there?'

'Affirmative. The enemy will think we've decided they're definitely not around and, fingers crossed, they'll open up.'

The Green Zone was less than 100 metres away. They were either very brave, or clinically insane. Or even more bored than Billy and Carl. The marines separated into small groups, lit their hexamine stoves and brought out their mugs. Then the Mad Hatter's tea party began.

'This is priceless,' I said. 'HM Government is paying 20k an hour for us to watch a load of mad bootnecks have a cuppa in the enemy's back garden.'

'I hope they're enjoying themselves. It's making me thirsty. But we've only got about ten minutes of combat gas left before we go chicken. You might want to tell them to get a scoot on.'

All still quiet on the ridge. I gave Knight Rider our ten-minute warning.

'Knight Rider, Ugly. Copied. Bear with us. We've got one final trick up our sleeves.'

Twenty commandos stripped off their body armour and helmets and stood in line, weapons down and hands on their hips, facing the Green Zone. They might as well have tattooed 'Shoot Me Quick' on their foreheads. For all the reaction the marines got, they might as well have been on the Hog's Back. It was time to draw the charade to a close.

'Knight Rider Five Five, Ugly Five One. We're bang out of gas. We're going to have to disappear. The Taliban just aren't here, mate.'

'Copied. Well, we tried our best. They obviously don't want to play today. Thanks for coming down.'

We overflew the suspect patch of Green Zone on our way out, but could see nothing either. Back in the JHF Ops Room an hour and a half later, we updated Alice during the quickest sortie debrief ever. She shook her head and smiled.

'Did none of you stop to think what day it is today?'

We looked blank.

'Friday. On Friday at noon, all good Muslims go to *Jumu'ah.*'

'*Jumu'ah?*'

'Friday Prayers. I could have told you that this morning. Next time you lot get a bright idea, do feel free to ask.'

We weren't having a great run. It took 42 Commando's Intelligence Officer to steer us out of our next reconnaissance cul-de-sac a few nights later. That sortie also served to remind us that the Apache's high-tech gadgetry could only ever be as smart as the human being in charge of it.

We had moved onto the IRT / HRF shift, and got a late night call out from the Kajaki DC. Once we'd got there, the shooting had stopped and we couldn't see a trace of the enemy. To make the trip worthwhile, we decided to take a covert look from a distance at a compound that 42 Commando, the local battlegroup, had asked us to keep an eye on. They suspected the Taliban might be using it as a training camp.

We stayed three kilometres back, at about 4,000 feet and down-wind, so its inhabitants wouldn't hear us. As we began to circle, five men walked out of one of the buildings. The locals never moved around Helmand at night, so this could only mean one thing. I hit record on the TADS.

They headed in staggered file down a track, a few metres apart, turned slightly outwards with the rear marker checking back, like a well-trained military patrol. The Apache's thirty-six-times-magnification FLIR thermal imaging camera was so powerful we could pick up a heat source in an open field miles away. Just a short distance closer we could identify a human shape, so we had a grand-stand view of whatever they were about to do. It was like watching a black and white TV show. About fifty metres up the track, the men peeled off right, one by one, into the field alongside it. They moved a safe distance and crouched down, now about ten metres apart.

'Fuck me,' Billy said. 'They're in extended line; infantry tactics. They're practising battle drills.'

We couldn't engage them because they weren't armed, but 42 Commando's Int Cell needed to take a look at this.

After a few minutes, the first man got up and walked back to the path. The rest followed at roughly thirty second intervals, and once the whole group was back on the path, they patrolled back to the compound. We'd found the notorious Taliban training ground 42 Commando were after.

We projected our footage onto the big screen in the JHF. Our Ops Officer was intrigued, and popped next door to fetch his opposite number from 42 Commando. He in turn fetched his Intelligence Officer, and then the 2i/c and CO. We played the tape a third time, beaming with pride.

'What do you think of that then? Quite a find, eh? But what does it mean?'

The 42 Commando Int Officer was a wise old bird.

'Right, take it back. Here they go; they walk down the road then break into an extended line. Now, watch carefully. Zoom in on this man … here …'

He surveyed our blank faces.

'Look, he is crouching, and then he moves away. Do you see his weapon? Look carefully … there …' He pointed to the patch of ground the man had just left.

'See? He's left a heat source. Look at the size of his foot and look at the size of the heat source. Same length. Now if you zoom in on the other men, a fiver says you'll find they've all left similar length heat sources.'

We began to feel more than a little stupid.

'Gentlemen, you have captured top secret footage of an Afghan communal shit. It's a tradition; they do it for mutual protection at night. Now I'm going for one too. But don't worry, you can stay here.'

THE BOBS AND STEVE-O

The Taliban were watching us too.

A company of infantry soldiers was responsible for Camp Bastion's security, manning the sangers on its perimeter fences, and fanning out to protect the C130 runway when a Hercules came in. The soldiers' most time-consuming job by far was manning the camp's most vulnerable point, its front gate.

An almost permanent line of local trucks and lorries queued outside it, delivering a never-ending mountain of supplies to feed and equip the garrison. Most of the vehicles came from Kandahar air base, where the bulk of our supplies arrived in long-range heavy-transport planes like the RAF's C17s or chartered Russian made Antonovs. The local vehicles were held back 200 metres behind a chicane of Hesco Bastion bollards, the guards' protection against suicide bombers. They were called forward cautiously, one by one, and searched from tip to toe before being allowed in.

One night, a sharp-eyed sentry spotted a driver climb onto his cab and get on his mobile phone as soon as a pair of Apaches clattered overhead. A covert watch was set up on all the waiting lorries.

We discovered that it wasn't just one driver. Almost all of them were climbing onto their roofs to get a better mobile phone signal whenever we took off. In Northern Ireland, we used to call it 'dicking'. At some stage of their journey from Kandahar, the Taliban had got to the drivers and employed – or forced – them to report on our movements.

We'd had a nagging feeling in the weeks prior to the discovery that the enemy seemed to know we were coming. Now we knew why. Once they'd been given the nod from Bastion, they'd set a stopwatch for our reaction times to specific locations, and packed up attacking the marine patrols minutes before we arrived.

Dicking was a threat to both our safety and that of the troops on the ground. Trigger and Billy drew up new drills to try to counter it. From then onwards, Apaches never flew over the main gate, we kept all the lights off at night, and we always set off in a different direction to the one we were really headed. That was a pain too, because flying a few klicks out of our way just to fox the dickers added a minute or two to the time it took us to reach the guys. But it was crucial to try to keep ahead of the Taliban's learning curve.

They learned, we learned; then we had to learn again. It was known as the caterpillar – one end moved first, the rest caught up. And the Afghan caterpillar never stopped moving. The longer the Helmand campaign went on, the more complex the battlespace became.

While the diligent reconnaissance for Operation Glacier continued, the huge demand for Apache support elsewhere kept us frantically busy. It came from all over the province. So much so, at least one of the squadron's flights was now firing in anger in some arena every single day. We were putting stuff down at a phenomenal rate – far more than we'd ever done before. Whether it was the change in the Rules of Engagement, the increased flying hours, or the enemy's ever more dogged persistence – or a combination of the three – it was hard to tell. Sometimes, we used our weapons systems as they were originally designed to be used. Others, we just had to improvise – like the day Soggy Arm Field got its name.

We were on a deliberate operation with the marines up in Kajaki one afternoon, covering them as they fought a clearance patrol onto the Shrine and then through the Taliban-held village to its west. The enemy were putting up strong resistance, gritty compound-to-compound stuff.

We trapped six of them out in the open on our arrival and nailed them with cannon. But two of their more dogged companions, firing from the far end of the village, had pinned down a section of marines. A Joint Terminal Attack Controller climbed to the top of Falcon to direct our fire. The JTAC talked us onto the pair's grid.

We found them by stealth, heading for home and doubling back, coming out of the clouds four kilometres behind them. They were in full white dishdashes, crouched a metre apart at the edge of a track behind someone's freshly painted white house.

'That's them,' confirmed the JTAC. 'I've had eyes on them since their last engagement. Remove them as soon as possible, by any means.'

They were a challenging target. The village was inhabited; it was crawling with mopeds and animals and we had no idea who was in the house behind them. Rockets and cannon would have peppered its wall and roof, and probably gone straight through them. Due to the Rules of Engagement there was only one option.

'It's got to be a Hellfire,' Trigger said. 'ROE is simple – but the proportionality bothers me. You're my weapons guru; can we really chuck a missile into a civilian village?'

'Positive ID, ROE and clearance to engage doesn't give us a choice, Boss, but collateral damage and the family in that lovely house does. We wait till we're closer and use the gun, or kick off to the right and hit them with the Hellfire so the blast disperses into that field. If we get closer they'll bolt for the house and the family will have Terry Taliban as lodgers ...'

A .5-inch calibre sniper rifle would have been ideal for the job. But Hellfire was the only point weapon system we had. It was proportionate in this instance.

'Okay, Mr Macy. Set me up.'

'I'll set you up all right. Set you up to make Apache history.'

The Boss glanced at me in his mirror, lined the crosshairs up perfectly on the ground between the two fighters, and let rip from six kilometres. The Hellfire had not been used on personnel before. We watched the missile rise, fall to its usual angle and impact right on target. When the smoke cleared, all that was left was a two-metre-wide hole in the ground.

'Delta Hotel,' the JTAC reported.

The freshly painted wall got one final coat – toffee brown – but on the flip side, the washing was still clean and the house itself completely untouched. It took an age to figure out the battle damage but the JTAC summed up the situation perfectly. 'I think your targets may have vaporised.'

That night, after the battle, the marines on Falcon watched as the locals came out to collect their dead. The next time we went up to Kajaki, the JTAC relayed their story.

'The Taliban had a really good look around the crater area for your two guys, but they couldn't find a thing. Then one of them went about thirty metres into the next field and came back holding a soggy arm. That's why it's now called "Soggy Arm Field".

The Special Boat Service had done a fair bit of work all over southern Afghanistan with the US Apaches co-located with them in Kandahar. But every now and then they came to us. Our first request from the Special Forces Group arrived six weeks into the tour.

The JHF was just told that it was an op in the notorious Panjwayi Valley – a Taliban hotbed west of Kandahar city. We would be briefed on everything else by the SBS themselves in Kandahar on the night. They'd asked for permanent cover as they expected it to go on a bit. So two flights went over that morning: 3 Flight's Nick, Charlotte, Darwin and FOG, and the four of us.

I'd worked with Special Forces before, so the mythical aura that surrounds them no longer had quite the same effect on me. They're just normal blokes like you and me, who prefer to stick to the shadows and happen to be particularly bloody good at what they do. It was Nick's first SF operation, so he had a grin on him like a Cheshire cat from the moment he got up. Bonnie was straining at the leash.

'It's exciting isn't it, Mr M? It really is.'

'Yes, sir.' Bless him.

The other thing I knew about Special Forces was that an awful lot of their missions never went down – but I didn't want to piss on Nick's bonfire. He wouldn't have wanted to believe me anyway.

It was a fifty-minute flight to Kandahar. Around the halfway mark we passed ten klicks to the south of a remote little town called Maiwand. The Boss pointed it out. 'We studied it at Sandhurst.' It was the site of the British Army's second great Afghan disaster: 969 officers and men were massacred there during the Second Afghan

War in 1880. A massively superior 25,000-strong native force wiped out the 1st Grenadiers and 66th Regiment of Foot, throwing the nation into shock and precipitating a campaign of bloody revenge. 'A grim lesson,' Trigger said. 'They were betrayed by their local allies.'

It was always odd coming back to Kandahar after a week or so at Camp Bastion. Its giant runway and line of helicopters stretched almost as far as the eye could see, dwarfing our tiny sideshow 100 miles away. Dozens of Blackhawks, Chinooks and Apache AH64As jostled for space. Beside the military colossus of the United States, we were a bunch of pygmies. The Special Forces compound was set discreetly to one side of the sprawling base's main thoroughfare. Its Hesco Bastion walls were ringed with razor wire.

Bob, the SBS officer running the operation that night, waited for us at the front gate with a couple of colleagues. They both introduced themselves as Bob, too. Three Bobs. The normal SF drill. One of the other two Bobs was the operation's JTAC. We never found out what the third Bob did.

The Bobs walked us swiftly to a nearby building and down a short corridor. Framed photographs of Sergeant Paul Bartlett and Captain David Patten hung from the wall, their names typed neatly beneath their smiling faces.

'Sorry about your boys,' I said. 'We found them the following morning.'

'Thanks. It was a crying shame.'

We were led into a briefing room completely devoid of furniture and decoration, except for one table and a handful of chairs. A room for visitors like us, sanitised of all useful information. We would only ever know from the Special Forces what they needed us to know. It was how SF always worked. Officer Bob plonked a laptop and projector down on the table, connected them and began the brief.

The mission was to kill or capture a senior Taliban player called Haji Mullah Sahib. In his mid-fifties, he was the former governor of Helmand province. He was believed to be holed up in Siah Choy, an isolated area of the Panjwayi, in a major Taliban command post. Officer Bob showed us maps of the target area and aerial photographs of the compound. Other Taliban commanders were expected to be joining him that night.

The operation was going to go one of two ways. We'd know which by a certain time that night before we took off. If the right intelligence came in to establish Sahib was definitely in the compound, they would bomb it. There was no point in risking boots on the ground unnecessarily. If the intelligence didn't come in, a ground assault would be launched.

'You'll only be needed for the second option,' Officer Bob said. 'But the second option is looking likely at the moment.'

The second option would go like this. A large ground force of SBS would be dropped some distance off, move in and surround the compound, then give it a 'hard knock'. Nobody expected Sahib to come quietly, so the SBS force had prepared some backup. (JTAC Bob took over, and Officer Bob leaned back against the wall.)

A vast air stack would position itself above them, from a Nimrod MR2 at the very top to an array of fast air in the middle and then us at the bottom. Each aircraft was given its own height parameters so we would all deconflict; ours was from 3,000 feet down to the ground. The assault teams could also call in fire from 81-mm mortars and 155-mm artillery guns if they needed it. I'd never seen so much firepower concentrated on one small place in all my time in Afghanistan.

'It's immediate and intimate fire support that we're looking for from you. We'd like you to hang around to the south of the target area so you're ready to tip in whenever I call.'

He showed us on a map where he wanted us, asked if we had any questions, and then wrapped up the brief with one final to me, as the lead front-seater on the mission.

'Can you confirm which close-in fire support card you're using, mate? Mine might be out of date ...'

Billy knew he'd ask me that. It detailed the criteria he needed to give us, so we could bring weapons to bear. I flicked through my Black Brain to the close-in fire support card, and there he was ... *From Rocco, With Love. x.*

JTAC Bob saw Rocco immediately. 'What the fuck's that?'

'Er, it's Rocco. A squadron joke ... you see ...' I tried to explain Rocco.

'I don't know what he's talking about, Bob,' Charlotte said with an utterly straight face. She added haughtily: 'We've never seen that disgusting picture before in our lives.' The rest of my Apache colleagues took Charlotte's cue and all solemnly agreed. Silence from all three Bobs. Not even a flicker of a smile from any of them. But Billy grinned at me from ear to ear. He'd pulled off a corker.

We had a few hours to kill before we got our heads down in the Apache crews' temporary accommodation, so we sampled the R and R delights every mid-sized US base in the region had on offer. They were spread around the four sides of a giant wooden boardwalk square with a thirty-metre-long plastic hockey pitch at its centre.

There was a Burger King trailer; a Pizza Hut stand; a Subway restaurant; a dry cleaner; a local souvenir shop flogging scarves, jewellery and stone carvings; and a PX the size of an average

Sainsbury's. The Post Xchange flogged everything from giant feather pillows and duvets to video cameras and PlayStation consoles: everything you could possibly want to fight a war in extreme comfort. We settled for Tim Horton's; an air-conditioned coffee shop that served Charlotte's favourite, an apple juice with a giant chocolate chip cookie. The Americans were well entrenched in Kandahar.

The Boss and I moved on to the Joint Helicopter Force HQ's Ops Room. The call came in from Force 84 bang on the dot, as promised. The intelligence had been good. Sahib was in the compound. So they'd already bombed him to oblivion from 20,000 feet. The jets that had carried out the attack took off from locations in the Middle East. Nobody even had to leave the base. Nick sat in his sleeping bag looking crestfallen when we relayed the news.

'Bad luck Bonnie,' the Boss said. 'You'll have to be Andy McNab's bitch another day.'

We weren't going to be any use to the ground troops if we couldn't be sure we could stay up in the air. So from time to time we had to come up with a few jobs of our own.

By mid-December, Now Zad had hotted up. It seemed to have taken over from Kajaki as the Taliban's new focus of attention. The Now Zad DC had started to get pummelled, a twenty-three-year-old Royal Marine from 42 Commando was shot dead on a foot patrol to the north of the town. And they were going for every helicopter within reach.

During the morning and evening briefs, Alice started to feed through some alarming intercepts that had been picked up in the town. 'We are dug in and ready for the helicopters,' was one. Another revealed a detailed plan for a helicopter ambush employing small arms, RPGs and possibly even a SAM.

Then Nick and Darwin got shot up during an IRT shout 2,000 feet over the town. A 12.7-mm Dushka round passed through the airframe's forward left electronics bay, destroying avionics and a systems processor, before hitting a Kevlar plate and smashing into tiny pieces less than two feet from Nick. It set off all the cockpit alarms and Nick suggested they bug out, but Darwin – the aircraft's pilot – was cool.

'We're okay, sir. Is your TADS still working?'

'Yes.'

'Then put some fucking fire down there.'

They flew back gingerly, and landed with smoke pouring out of the side. Demonstrating their usual tenderness, the Groundies rushed out to film Nick and Darwin's approach for their personal tour videos in case they crashed.

It was the second time Darwin had been shot; he'd taken a Dushka round on the first tour, so he then became known as the Bullet Magnet. Then, two days later, a Lynx on a photo recce over Now Zad took a Dushka round too. Two aircraft getting hit in the same location in such a short space of time added up to a Dushka gunner somewhere in Now Zad who knew exactly what he was doing.

We obviously couldn't continue normal air operations while he was there. A dropped Apache would have been bad enough – but the thought of a Chinook going down with thirty marines aboard was what really gave us sleepless nights. We had to find the Now Zad Dushka gunner and remove him.

'I've got it,' the Boss said proudly, after a couple of hours of deep thought. 'We're going to launch Op Steve-O.'

The night before, the Boss had taken a break from the first

episode of *24* and watched a few minutes of *Jackass: The Movie* instead – just long enough to catch the scene where a bloke called Steve-O had a hook pushed through his cheek and was thrown off a speed boat by his mates so he could be dragged along as shark bait.

'That's what we're going to be, Mr Macy – Dushka bait. You and I will ramble around above Now Zad while 3 Flight hide off to one side. A nice, juicy Apache over his head is bound to lure our man out. Then Charlotte and Darwin will tip in and blow him away.'

'Right you are, Boss. And how are you going to explain this to my family when it all goes tits up?'

'Not a problem,' he said cheerfully. 'If we go down, I won't be the one who'll have to tell them.'

If any pilot on the squadron was going to attempt something like this, it had to be the Boss. He couldn't order anyone else into harm's way without first going there himself. And I was the poor sod who crewed with him. Darwin was coming along with Charlotte as his regular front-seater, for his insight into how the Dushka gunner worked – and hopefully a touch of revenge.

I could have refused to go – but the truth was I wanted to. It was a bold plan, and would guarantee one hell of an adrenalin rush. The Boss knew the aircraft as well as any of us, and he was confident the Apache could take it.

We decided to fly Op Steve-O at night. The Dushka's muzzle flash and tracer rounds would be seen easily with the naked eye whilst the heat of his barrel in the chill of the night would show up far better on our FLIR camera. And if we went down, we'd have Night Vision Goggles and the cover of darkness.

I would be flying this mission, and Trigger would provide the eyes. The four of us headed down to the flight line after the evening brief. Charlotte and Darwin were small but perfectly formed at the best of times. They were completely dwarfed by the Apache they were checking over. 'Hey, Umpalumpas,' I said. 'Do you want an extra cushion in that beast to help you see over the dash?'

'You better believe it, Ed.' Darwin looked up from the cannon. 'There'll be that many bells and whistles going off in your cockpit when the sniper sparks up, you'll be praying we can see enough to nail him before he finishes you off.'

Charlotte carried on polishing the seeker dome of a Hellfire. Maximum effect for minimum effort was more her style. 'Here's the deal, Mr Macy. You concentrate on *not* getting shot and leave the bad guy to me. If I get him first time, you sign off our annual weapons check.' She treated me to her most Sphinx-like smile. 'What do you say?'

Trigger chuckled. 'They'll do, eh?'

'Yes, Boss,' I said with a grin. 'They'll do just fine.'

The Apache was *built* to be shot. If it had been smothered in armour like a flying tank, it would never have got off the ground. It was designed to absorb incoming fire; it practically invited it – a challenging concept to get your head around if you were sitting in the driving seat.

The Apache could withstand a direct hit from a 23-mm high-explosive incendiary round. The airframe's entire skin, and the drive shaft that ran down its spine to the tail rotor, was constructed from thin alloy, so that a round could pass clean through the body without tearing a bloody great hole in it. Anything crucial to the aircraft's survival had a backup: it had two engines, two sets of hydraulics and electrics, four computers, two sets of flying controls – and if they broke we could still fly with fly-by-wire sensors. It even had two pilots.

The gunship only had one rotor head and one set of rotor controls, but both were built from electro-slag-remelt, strong enough to stop a round from penetrating. Multiple rounds could pass straight through a rotor blade without impairing its capacity to generate lift.

The fuel tanks were even cleverer. The Apache had three and they all worked independently. They were made from layers of impregnated nylon and uncured rubber. If a bullet punctured the tank, the uncured rubber would react with the fuel to create a fast-hardening foam which would seal any large hole. The main gearbox couldn't self-seal, but it didn't need to; it could run dry of all oil and still turn the rotors long enough to get back to Bastion.

By far the most vulnerable bits of the Apache were the two pink, fleshy things in the cockpit – so the floor, the side and front panels and the back and sides of the seats were lined with Kevlar plates. Nothing smaller than an artillery shell would penetrate them. The armour-plated front windscreens could take .50 cal shots head on, but the enemy were armed with more than that now.

Since bullets mostly came from below us, we were only at threat from high mountains or when we turned sharply during a fight. That was when we pushed our backs hard into the Kevlar shell and hoped for the best.

In case the unthinkable did happen, our cockpits were separated by a two-inch-thick glass blast fragmentation shield and had their own air-conditioning systems. If an RPG whipped into the front compartment, it could remove the gunner, all his electronics, his controls and even his seat, and the back-seater could still fly on. He wouldn't even smell the burning.

But every time we walked out to the aircraft no one needed to remind us of what we called 'the golden shot'; even the best pilots were not immune to a lucky round, or sheer bad luck. Otherwise, eight highly skilled US Apache crews would not have been shot down over Iraq.

It was a twenty-minute flight to Apocalypse Now Zad, as the marines had christened it. Now Zad was built in the shape of a triangle, with its flat-roofed, mostly single-storey, buildings hemmed in by towering rock faces on all three sides. It was an awesome sight; a geographer's paradise. The southernmost tip of the Hindu Kush sprang up along its western edge. Its eastern boundary consisted of a series of interwoven ridgelines that ran south to north. And the base of the triangle, to the south, was a stand-alone range, five kilometres long and 400 metres tall at its peak.

We knew the Dushka gunner was in the south-east of the town, so we planned to split up as we approached the southern ridgeline. Charlotte and Darwin would wait on the desert side, nose forward, high enough to get a visual on the town. Trigger and I would bear right through a 300-metre-wide crevasse, bringing us immediately over the gunner's territory. The Boss would target spot for the Dushka gunner, moving between his monocle and his Night Vision Goggles – and leave the flying to me.

I thought through how I was going to do it on the flight up. It would take the Dushka gunner's rounds four seconds to reach us, up at 4,000 feet, so he needed to predict where we'd be four seconds after he pulled the trigger. I had a reaction time of perhaps half a second from the moment I saw tracer, or heard the Boss's or the wingman's shout. Ugly Five One was a weighty beast and it would take a second to overcome its inertia and change direction. So that gave me two and a half seconds, maximum, to take evasive action. This was going to be a penalty shoot-out, Apache-style – except that I wanted to stay as far as possible from the ball. Two and a half seconds didn't feel like very long. And all those clever statistics suddenly didn't add up to a hill of beans. I felt like I was flying an eggshell.

I tried to think through what I'd do if we were hit. We'd lose some systems for sure. I hoped it wouldn't sever a hydraulic line. Hydraulic fluid was the most flammable thing on the aircraft, and so highly pressurised it would go off like a volcano. The next round would ignite it and we'd turn into one big fireball. Even the heat from the engines could set it off. Jesus, what then?

I realised I was fingering the fire extinguisher buttons top left of the dash. *Stop it* … I'd disappear up my own arse if I carried on like this. I wrenched myself away from the endless succession of what ifs … Charlotte and Darwin had the lead.

'Five Three, five klicks from the crevasse now,' Darwin said. 'We'll start to break off left and cover you through the gap. Good luck guys.'

They banked, and the crevasse opened up in front of us. Ninety seconds and we'd be through it. Gripping the cyclic and collective, my hands were so clammy I could feel them sticking to the insides of my gloves. I actioned the gun, moving my head side to side to check it was still slaved to my eye. It was. I flipped the trigger guard and rested my finger on the red button. A breath away from firing.

'Thirty seconds, Boss.'

I thrust my spine as hard as I could into the Kevlar seat, and buried my arse as deep into the foam pad as it would go. I took a deep breath.

'Copied. Just keep her belly flat as a pancake …'

It was the fourth time Trigger had said it since we'd launched, but the closer we came to the enemy the more vulnerable we felt. I knew that, and the Boss knew I knew. His palms must have started to sweat as well.

The Taliban mounted a permanent lookout on the crevasse. I hoped he hadn't nodded off; this time we actually wanted to get dicked. The jagged edges of the rock face reached out at us from the shadows, and it's fair to say I was shitting Tiffany cufflinks. *Jesus. Here we go.*

'Five One, over the target in … five …'

I clicked off the radio. Four was always missed from the countdown. It allowed someone at the other end of the net to jump in at the last second to call everything off.

'Three …'

Click.

'Two …'

Click.

'One …'

Click.

'Now.'

'Visual. We're looking.' Charlotte did her best to sound reassuring.

I put the Apache into the gentlest anticlockwise sweep I possibly could, banking a fraction to keep us turning. As the aircraft tilted to the left, I leaned my head to the right but peeked over the Kevlar side panel, determined to catch the first tracer round as it began to burn.

In daylight a sniper set the range on his sights, taking gravitational forces into account, and he was guaranteed a hit as long as the wind didn't blow the round off target. His sights weren't calibrated to fire nearly ninety degrees upwards, and he'd almost certainly miss with the first round or burst of automatic fire. If he was firing single shot, the tracer would enable him to re-aim for a second- or third-round hit once he'd seen where the first round went; if automatic, he'd keep the trigger pulled and guide the jet of tracer onto the target like a big red laser gun.

'And that,' I told Trigger, 'should buy me a second or two to save your sorry arse, sir.'

We completed one full orbit. It took two minutes, and felt like a lifetime.

'Keep the turn tighter, Mr M, or we'll be too far away from him.'

It was all very well for Trigger. The Kevlar came up to his chest, while the back-seater was exposed from the waist upwards unless we were dead level. Why couldn't I be a short arse like Darwin?

Six feet in front of me, Trigger was also frantically quartering the ground. The two sets of crosshairs in my monocle whipped backwards and forwards across the same piece of ground, colliding repeatedly and passing through each other as we searched the ghostly green compounds, hedgerows and trees for the glow of a man.

We wouldn't see the AA gunner on anything other than FLIR, but it picked up heat, not light. We would only spot his rounds with the naked eye. Killing him wasn't our job, but seeing him so he didn't kill us was. We completed a second orbit, and then a third. *Why isn't this fucker firing?* Any more of this and my heart was going to hammer its way out of my survival jacket.

'Do you think he can hear us?'

'Hell, yeah. We're right over his head.'

Charlotte came on. 'Five Three, can't see any movement down there at all.'

'Neither can we.'

After what must have been at least our tenth orbit, the Boss came up with another brilliant way of getting us shot.

'Okay, Elton – now's your chance. Roll the aircraft and slap the blades about a bit.'

'What do you mean, "slap the blades about a bit"? You've got Kevlar up to your tits!'

'Come on, you pussy. Just give the blades a bit of a slap so he definitely knows we're here.'

'Don't worry, he fucking knows.'

I threw the aircraft ninety degrees onto its right side for a second or two, righted it again, and then chucked it left. Each time the blades clattered away, slapping hard on the air.

'Now the whole of Now Zad knows.'

We still saw nothing on the ground.

'Do it again.'

'At this rate everyone down there is going to try and hose us down for keeping them awake.'

I rolled right and left twice more. Still nothing. Round and round we kept on going; we must have done two dozen circuits.

After thirty minutes over the target area, I started to relax. If the sniper was going to have a go, he would have done so by now. He'd had more than enough time to set up and open fire. Last time around, he'd hit Darwin within ten minutes of his arrival.

'Do you want me to put the lights on, Boss?'

'Erm … no, I don't think we should do that …' Trigger replied in all seriousness. Jesus … He'd actually considered it …

'Five Three this is Five One; he's not down there.'

We were just wasting time and fuel.

'Five Three, I agree,' chipped in Darwin. 'This geezer doesn't piss about. He's gone.'

'All right, we'd better knock it on the head.' The Boss didn't bother to hide his disappointment. 'Let's RTB.'

I pointed the nose south and pulled power. It still came as an immense relief to pass over Now Zad's southern ridgeline and into the safety of the desert.

There wasn't much chat on the way back and no game of Apache Triv either. The Dushka gunner was still out there. We all knew we'd have to keep coming back until we killed him.

The aircraft were tied up for the next two nights on other deliberate taskings so the next Op Steve-O was pencilled in for seventy-two hours later.

Then a Harrier filed a sitrep about a munition drop in south-east Now Zad. He'd been circling high above the town, working to the DC's JTAC, and had spotted a group of men setting up an anti-aircraft gun in the back garden of a compound. He must have been too high for them to have any idea he was there. The JTAC gave the Harrier permission to engage, and he dropped a 500-lb bomb on them. Topman got the Taliban and the AA gun in one go; they got a new swimming pool. And helicopters stopped taking Dushka rounds over Now Zad.

Charlotte and Darwin were even more delighted than we were. Next time, it had been their turn to provide the bait.

HAPPY CHRISTMAS

The weather turned in mid-December when the Helmand winter kicked in. The rains arrived and the temperature started to plummet at night; before long it fell below freezing.

The Taliban in the Green Zone were largely on foot, so they hated fighting in bad weather. A diehard few continued to put up a token resistance, but when it got cold most of them retreated to their northern mountain refuges.

We welcomed the brief change in tempo. It allowed us to think about Christmas. Wherever I had been deployed, it was always a big deal, a special occasion that helped lighten the monotony of operational life – even if you did have to work all the way through it. It was also the time we particularly missed our families, so we all did our best to make it a really special occasion.

The Groundies got into the festive mood early. A few of them decided to introduce a bit of extra cheer by writing a letter to the GMTV presenter and *Daily Mirror* columnist Fiona Phillips, signed with a nom de plume. The letter was forgotten about almost as soon as it was posted. Nobody expected to see it published – but it was, immediately. Fiona even penned her own reply.

I AM writing on behalf of a group of pilots and ground crew serving in Helmand, Afghanistan, who provide 24-hour helicopter support for troops on the ground. To help the nights pass quickly, we are looking for pen-pals.

Al Pache, Joint Helicopter Forces (Afghanistan)

Forward Operation Herrick, BFPO 792

FP: *No sooner said than done, Al. Anything for our boys!*

A week or so later, the first bag of mail arrived. The next day there were two bags. And two more the day after. Soon, hundreds and hundreds of letters were pouring into the JHF; so many that nobody knew what to do with them all.

People from all walks of life had replied, from Royal British Legion members and nice old ladies to mums and dads with serving sons and daughters. Most of them just wanted to wish us a Happy Christmas; some fancied a flirt, and one or two took the trouble to explain precisely what they'd like to do to a nice man in a uniform while their husbands were out at work.

One young refueller peeled open a crimson envelope containing a photograph of a gorgeous brunette posing in nothing more than a bra, knickers and suspender belt, attached to a handwritten note: *Al – if you want to see more, write more ...*

The boy couldn't believe his eyes. 'Whoa! Look at this, lads!' He sprinted down to the flight line, photo in hand.

That was it. The dam broke. The Groundies invaded the JHF en masse. They even brought up the missile truck, determined to pinch as many of the mailbags as they could get their hands on. Billy and I watched them cluster around the bird table like sniffer dogs, in search of the most promising offer.

It didn't take them long to discover that the kind of invitations they were looking for were in pretty short supply – but they were swiftly consoled by the extraordinary number of thoroughly decent people who cared enough about the sacrifices they were making to have taken the trouble to wish them a Happy Christmas. And before long, with a little encouragement from the vets, a stream of thank you letters was making its way back home.

For some of the youngsters of the squadron, it was their first Christmas away from home; a daunting experience for anyone. Charlotte had told us it was the only part of the deployment she was dreading – but her friends and family back home were clearly doing their best to cheer her up. I popped into 3 Flight's tent to see if anyone fancied a brew and was confronted by the biggest pile of presents I'd ever seen, beautifully wrapped and carefully piled on a spare camp cot: six feet long, three feet wide and four feet high.

There were a few for Nick, one or two for FOG, none for Darwin; at least 80 per cent of them belonged to Charlotte.

'Hang on lads,' one of the guys said. 'I've got a great idea …'

Charlotte burst into the JHF a few hours later, her face white with shock. 'I can't believe it! Somebody's stolen our presents.'

'*What?*' We did our best to sound suitably horrified.

'They were all laid out on a bed, ready for Christmas, and someone has stolen them. I can't believe it. Who would be so mean?'

Always the perfect gentleman, Nick sprang to her support. 'I can't believe someone would actually *steal* Christmas presents. What a low down, rotten thing to do.'

FOG was more philosophical. 'No guys, we should have known better.'

'Quick,' I suggested helpfully. 'Go and report it to the police. They'll seal the main gate and then search the camp –' Charlotte charged across to the RMP office before I'd even finished speaking.

The coppers didn't let us down. The two SIB sergeants escorted her straight back to her tent, but as she was about to lead them in, one of them blocked her path.

'Sorry ma'am, you can't go in there,' he said gravely. 'It's a crime scene.' And his partner slapped two strips of blue and white police tape across the entrance.

'But all my stuff is in there! When can I go back in?'

'Well, we'll need to dust the place down for prints. That'll mean getting someone down from Kabul, which will take a few days, I'm afraid. And at this time of year … ooh, you're looking at after Christmas now. Sorry.'

Not only had 3 Flight lost their presents, they'd also lost their tent. All they had to live with was a wash bag and the few meagre possessions they'd taken down to the IRT tent. We were finding it increasingly difficult to wipe the smiles off our faces.

We'd found three Father Christmas hats and beards and filmed ourselves tiptoeing to the cot, looking furtively left and right, stuffing all the presents into big black bin bags and giving a 'Ho ho ho' to the camcorder as we made off with them. We'd locked the presents in a couple of big green weapons cases in our tents at first, then had the bright idea of driving them down to the RMP office and roping them into the plot.

We planned to show our film to Charlotte and the others before triumphantly reuniting them with their gifts on Christmas Day. We were quite proud of it; we even managed to secure a cameo appearance by the celebrity chef Gordon Ramsay, who'd flown out for a few days to cook Christmas lunch for the troops. We approached him in the hangar during a tour of the flight line. He was well up for it.

Looking as mean as he could, he rasped: 'Hello 3 Flight, and

Happy Christmas. Do you know where your fucking presents are yet?'

I also asked him rather sheepishly to sign a recipe for Emily's mother's Clootie dumplings, a heavy Scottish cake she made by the truck load.

'I can tell she's a Jock,' he said, handing it back to me. 'She's making it with fucking margarine!'

Charlotte grew progressively quieter as Christmas Eve approached. Homelessness, presentlessness and family separation were getting to her. We began to feel guilty enough to bring Darwin in on the plot. He'd told his family not send out any presents; he wanted to celebrate with them on his return – so he had no axe to grind. He'd know whether we should call it off.

'Don't worry about Charlotte,' he assured us. 'She's pretty tough; she'll be good with it.'

So we kept on going – never dreaming that, after a few hours, Darwin would buckle under the pressure of living with our secret. By that night, the weasel blabbed to Charlotte, Nick and FOG. We discovered his treachery after she let it slip to the Boss, and someone overheard.

The drama of the missing presents now gripped the squadron. Trigger finally stepped in on Christmas Eve. He told 3 Flight their presents were safe and sound with the RMPs. 3 Flight tried to pretend they'd never cared about them in the first place. Honours were just about even – though we still had a score to settle with Darwin-the-Rat.

HQ Flight were up early on Christmas Day for a deliberate tasking. We had to escort a Chinook on a series of resupplies to the three most northern district centres. It was tedious stuff and went on for hours. We were in the cockpit – air or ground – for most of the day. It was bitterly cold and the weather was dire: low cloud and drizzling rain. Camp Bastion turned into a quagmire, and we squelched all the way to the flight line.

'Like Christmas in the World War One trenches,' Carl moaned. 'But without the footie.'

Kajaki was furthest away, so it was our first destination. We went the long way round – low through the eastern mountains at 1,000 feet – to avoid SAM traps. We hadn't seen the mountains in the rain before, and it was an eerie experience. Great slabs of glistening silver-grey rock towered either side of us, punctuated by puffs of marshmallow cloud. It felt like we were on our way to Middle Earth. Everything was deathly quiet; we were on silent drills because of the Chinook's insecure radios.

Carl could see well enough to fly, but there was no harm in having a backup in shit like this. So for the only time on the tour I flicked to the radar page on my left-hand MPD and switched on the Longbow's Terrain Profile Mode.

The US Apaches flew without their Longbow Radars in Afghanistan and Iraq. Initially designed to help destroy armoured columns, the Americans said they were no use for counter-insurgency. They swapped them for more weapons weight. Our Rolls Royce engines were strong enough to carry the Longbow and all the weapons we'd need.

The Longbow's Ground Target Mode was extremely handy for spotting vehicles at a distance, or well out of the TADS line of sight. It pinged anything moving or static up to eight kilometres away, in any direction. But Terrain Profile Mode was even more useful on a sortie like this. The Longbow mapped out the lie of the land up to two and a half kilometres in front of us. On the MPD, it showed terrain below us as black, terrain within 100 feet of us as grey and terrain above us – terrain that we'd hit – as white. It projected an electronic zigzag graph across our monocle so we could identify the hills and valleys ahead of us. TPM meant we could fly in all weather, day and night, at ultra-low level, at great speed and totally blind. Carl got us through the spooky mountains off his own bat, but it was always nice to know TPM was there if we needed it.

After Kajaki, we hit Now Zad, then back to Camp Bastion, south down to Lashkar Gah where the Chinook had passengers to pick up, Bastion again, and finally back up to Forward Operating Base Robinson near Sangin.

The clouds finally began to clear on our last leg over the desert, treating us to a perfect blood orange sunset.

'I can see clearly now the rain has gone ...' I started to sing.

There was never going to be a better moment.

'Five Zero, Five One; there's something rattling by my door. Check the nearside of my aircraft with your TADS, will you?'

Billy pulled level with us and Trigger swung his Day TV camera onto our cockpit.

'Ho, ho, ho!'

I'd taken off my helmet for a few seconds and pulled on a red and white Father Christmas hat to give them a wave. For the first time since we'd got up it began to feel like Christmas Day.

We were back too late for turkey and stuffing in the cookhouse, so we scrubbed up and joined the squadron party. It was being held in our newly acquired recreation tent. A stage and makeshift bar were set up, the place was rigged out with tinsel and a sparkly silver tree, and we all piled in to enjoy a rare drink.

Alcohol was banned for all British troops across Helmand. On Christmas night a special exception was made and everyone was allowed two cans of beer. Only the four IRT / HRF pilots had to stay dry. They went to the party in full flying rig ready for the call-out if it came. Luckily, it didn't.

Every section performed a sketch, taking the mickey out of all the squadron characters. These could go on for hours, but the good ones were comic genius. Instead of a sketch, 2 Flight played us a film they'd spent countless hours crafting, a pastiche of *Top Gun* with footage from the movie edited in.

The highlight of the evening was Darwin's Kangaroo Court; all the better because he had no idea it was coming. As soon as the entertainment finished, he was held firmly by both arms and tried then and there. The charge: 'Wilful betrayal of the Warrant Officers and Sergeants' Mess by forming a secret alliance with the officers – namely, by telling them who had their Christmas presents.' The jury agreed it was a most heinous offence. There was a prosecution, a defence and the Boss was the judge.

'Right, bring in the guilty bastard.' Trigger opened the proceedings. The evidence was presented with all the venom of a Stalin show trial. Darwin was left with little choice but to plead guilty.

'Guilty is the correct plea,' Trigger decreed. 'You have been convicted and I hereby sentence you to wearing your flying suit and helmet throughout the whole of your next evening meal in the cookhouse.'

We sat on our cots at the end of the evening and opened our presents. The Boss joined us, and set up his camcorder so he could send the video home to his kids. We took it in turns. I opened my kids' presents first and then Emily's. She'd written *Open Last* on one; by the time I got round to it, everyone else had finished.

'Right, Mr Macy, only one left.' Trigger grabbed his camera. 'I'm going to film you opening it.'

I undid the bow and unwrapped a beautiful little red box. I

thought it would contain cufflinks or something, but there was a tiny Christmas stocking inside it. In the stocking was a tiny card. I couldn't speak.

'Come on Mr Macy, what is it? Hey guys look, is that a tear on Macy's face? Macy's crying!'

I rediscovered my voice. 'I'm not crying; my eyes are sweating. And take that camera out my face.'

'So what's she written then?'

She'd written four words. *Congratulations. We are pregnant.*

I raced to the telephones. Emily was four months gone. Going back to Afghanistan wasn't planned, and we never dreamed we'd be this lucky. She kept the whole thing a secret for as long as she could so as not to worry me.

'Don't worry about me, I'm just relieved I can tell my family now. Don't do *anything* stupid; I don't want to be forced to name him *Ed Macy*. Especially if he turns out to be a girl.'

'*Ed Macy*?'

'Yes, that's what he'll be called if you do something stupid. Are you carrying the angel?'

When I got back to the tent, all the others had gone to sleep. I poured myself a whisky from the emergency-only bottle I kept hidden in the bottom of my bag. I was going to be a father for the third time and I was the happiest man in Camp Bastion. That was worth a dram in the dark.

The only downside about Christmas on operations was that it finished. Afterwards, the squadron hit the usual post-big occasion blues. We were halfway through the tour, with another two months to go and no more cans of Christmas beer to look forward to. And fatigue was setting in.

The longer we were out here, the more knackered people looked. Since everything we did was devoted to saving life or taking it, the mental pressure was intense – and not only in the air. One sloppy drill by a young refueller or one of the boys loading weapons on the flight line could be catastrophic. Keeping 100 per cent focused for 100 days without a break was tough, especially if you were eighteen years old.

Everyone's workload was horrendous because we were still brand new – we were developing and learning lessons on the Apache and changing procedures every single day. Everything had to be evaluated and reported, be it weapons functions for me, aircraft threats for Carl or the flight envelope for Billy.

Afghanistan took its toll physically too. The climate – wind, sand, heat and cold – was relentless. Young guys came back looking like men. Undisturbed sleep, as our Crew Rest Period rules required, was the last thing we got in a sleeping bag on a camp cot with perpetual aircraft noise and people coming and going all night.

Cumulative fatigue was the official name for it – burnout for short. It was hard to spot because we were all weathering at the same rate. As the tour went on, the Boss made a point of policing Crew Rest Period ever more religiously. He had to give direct orders.

'Geordie, bed, *now!*'

It would be left to his 2i/c to police the Boss, who was the most reluctant of all to leave the JHF. One or two started to get a little fractious, but most were too professional for that. People became quieter, preserving their energy for the job. The senior guys had to make a real effort to keep up the banter and morale.

Little accidents could happen easily. For pilots that might mean overtorquing an engine; for Groundies, putting rockets in the wrong tubes. Billy dragged all the pilots in for a brief the day after Boxing Day, and warned them to be careful about getting bitten by the aircraft.

'My advice is, take a little bit longer doing everything you do. You may all think you're absolutely okay. I promise you, you're not.'

The constant stream of VIP visits was yet another addition to our workload. It wasn't just the political party leaders – a constant stream of defence ministers, foreign ministers, shadow defence ministers, shadow foreign ministers, military chiefs and foreign military chiefs passed through Bastion. They thought they were doing us a favour, showing their solidarity with the chaps. We could never tell them they were a pain in the arse. VIPs tied up valuable airtime and resources; they all needed to be choppered about, and of course they all wanted to crawl all over the Apaches. Even Billy started to get bored with his bigwigs speech.

The one VIP we always had time for though was General Sir Richard Dannatt, the Chief of the General Staff. After years of faceless chiefs burying their heads in the sand and toeing the government's line, General Dannatt infuriated the Prime Minister by speaking out – questioning policy in Iraq and calling for better soldiers' pay and housing. A true soldiers' friend, his honesty made him the most popular chief we'd had in a generation, and perhaps since Monty. He was also Colonel Commandant of the Army Air Corps, so we liked him even more.

General Dannatt's latest visit coincided with this period. Trigger showed him around the flight line, Billy did his spiel in the aircraft and I went last with a weapons brief.

'Right sir, this is our Ops Room and this is Mr Macy,' Trigger said. 'He's going to show you some gun footage.'

'Terrific, I'm looking forward to this. Where do you want me?'

I escorted him to a chair. I'd prepared shots of a missile attack, a rocket attack and a gun attack from a big contact south of Now Zad a few nights previously. Before I ran the tape, I gave him a quick description of the contact's location with the help of a large-scale map of Helmand province stuck to the white partition wall upon which we projected the gun tapes.

Everyone takes down posters differently. I always remove the bottom blobs of Blu-tack first. And I thanked God that I did that morning.

As my hands moved to peel off the top blobs, my right palm brushed over a laminated surface. Something had been stuck on the partition wall behind the map.

I froze.

'Something wrong, Mr Macy?'

I flashed Trigger a look, and knew he'd guessed what – or more precisely, *who* – was lurking behind the map.

'No sir. Blu-tack's a bit stiff, that's all. One second.'

In one fluid movement, I managed to slide my right hand underneath the map and Rocco, unpeeled them both and dumped them under a table.

There was a muffled groan from the JHF's back room.

'Well done, Mr Macy,' Trigger said with enormous relief.

General Dannatt looked puzzled. With Rocco subdued I played the tape and the general left looking very pleased with our shooting.

As usual, the culprit never came clean. He denied everything, but I blamed Geordie. Only he would have had the balls, panache and sheer stupidity to have attempted a 24-carat Rocco blinder.

The Boss took longer to get over it.

And from that moment onwards, Rocco mysteriously disappeared.

Just before New Year, we had another bitter reminder of the dangers lurking in the south of the province. A lance bombardier from 29 Commando Regiment, Royal Artillery, was killed when his vehicle drove over a landmine in the Garmsir area. A young lad with him lost his right leg.

Billy stuck a Hellfire and a shed load of 30-mm into it to stop the Taliban getting their hands on it. They later named a forward operating base in the desert after the killed soldier; FOB Dwyer became the permanent 105-mm gun emplacement to support the Garmsir DC.

There were strong suspicions the landmine had been planted by the Taliban – another tactic we were seeing more often. The Mujahideen wrought havoc for the Soviet Army by burying anti-tank mines in their path.

The New Year did give us something to look forward too, though. By the beginning of January Operation Glacier was ready to go.

READY TO GO NOISY

Nine weeks of tough and dangerous work had gone into it. There had been a few false starts and a fair number of close shaves, but the southern Information Exploitation Battlegroup had stuck it out. By 1 January, Colonel Magowan's men declared they were ready for Operation Glacier to go noisy.

The Taliban main supply route from Pakistan had been mapped. Not only did the battlegroup know their enemy's main base locations, but they'd also pinpointed tunnel systems and ammo dumps. They'd discovered that they moved covertly between them disguised as local farmers. Now they were ready to destroy the lot. The marines' .5-inch calibre Barratt sniper rifle was pointing right at the heart of the Taliban octopus, and they were about to pull the trigger.

They had located five enemy concentration points, each performing a different function in the Taliban's sophisticated logistics chain: pampering, preparing for and then pushing their warriors into battle. These had been designated as Operation Glacier's primary targets.

The plan was to prosecute one target at a time, moving steadily northwards. The furthest, more than twenty kilometres south of Garmsir, would be hit first (Operation Glacier 1), and the closest – two kilometres south-east of the Garmsir DC – would go last (Operation Glacier 5).

As each attack proceeded, survivors and forward groups would be funnelled north, and with their command chain broken, the old men in Quetta would have nowhere to send reinforcements. The retreating Taliban would finally be trapped in one killing zone at Garmsir.

They were going to follow the example of the old bull at the top of the hill, one of the marine officers explained. 'The bull's young son says to him, "Dad, let's run down and jump on one of those cows in that field." "No son," the old bull replies. "Let's walk down, and jump on them all."'

Brigade believed that the destruction of the Taliban's southern MSR would leave their operations in turmoil across half the province, and that they'd be unable to mobilise enough manpower for anything more than the odd pot shot on the Garmsir DC. Once they were on their knees, the southern battlegroup would make sure they kept them there.

The offensive stage of Operation Glacier would begin on 11 January, and the brigadier wanted all the strikes completed in a month. Our Apaches would be needed on every one of the Glacier attacks. Our combat punch was to be utilised on Operation Glacier 1 as it never had been before. And it coincided with HQ Flight's turn on the rota for a deliberate tasking.

Alice gathered us for a general intelligence brief nine days before. 'You're going,' she told us. 'So you'd better know all about it.' The target was a command post used as a reception area for all new recruits from Pakistan. This was where the Toyota 4x4s hit the

Green Zone after their long slog across the desert. On arrival, they were fed, rested, briefed and organised before being sent forward to the next link in the chain. It was the Taliban's equivalent of Kandahar air base.

The post sat on the east bank of a north–south running canal near the village of Koshtay, twenty kilometres or so south of Garmsir. It consisted of three large rectangular buildings – the living quarters – surrounded by a cluster of huts, a mosque, two courtyards, gardens and an orchard. An imposing place by Helmand's standards, it used to be the old district governor's house – but it wasn't thought to house more than fifty enemy fighters at any one time.

'The only thing we're not being told is who initially pinged the place,' Alice said intriguingly. 'The battlegroup's Int Officer says it wasn't them. Apparently it was "intelligence sources".'

Alice didn't need to spell it out. We all knew what that meant. Spooks. What colour, shape or nationality was anyone's guess. MI6 and GCHQ ran their own operations throughout Afghanistan, as did the CIA and the NSA, France's DGSE, Pakistan's ISI and God only knew how many other 'friendly' foreign intelligence services. The place was crawling with them; always has been. One thing was for sure – we'd never find out.

Glacier's first target was the most important strategically – the Taliban's linchpin between Pakistan and Helmand. If the link was well and truly broken, it would take them a lot of time and effort to reconnect. Attacking the site would do the Taliban serious psychological damage too. Foot soldiers and senior leadership alike would know that we knew exactly where they were and what they were up to. Some of their senior commanders were also believed to work out of Koshtay, marshalling their ranks from the rear. Taking them out would be an additional bonus.

The full set of orders for the operation arrived from the battle-group seven days later, with the classification 'Secret'. Trigger picked it up from the JOC's Communications Cell after lunch on Tuesday, 9 January. He gave it a quick flick and came to find us.

'Guys, I think the four of us had better go into the Tactical Planning Facility right now. Cancel whatever you've got on for the rest of the afternoon.'

We sat down and read through it together. The orders were highly detailed and the timings incredibly precise. They gave us maps, sketches and aerial reconnaissance photographs of the site. It was an extraordinary piece of work. And it told us we were making Army Air Corps history.

'Fuck me sideways,' Billy breathed. 'We're really going sausage side this time, aren't we?'

There would be no ground assault. Instead, a B1B Lancer strategic bomber was going to open the show with the mother of all hard knocks. It would drop ten different bombs on the Koshtay site at once – four 2,000-pounders and six 500 pounders. Then it was our turn, to mop up any survivors.

As the bombs were falling, we would begin our run-in on the target from the desert, so when the dust cleared we'd be ready to start shooting. It was made clear to us that no buildings were to be left standing, and no people left alive. With five tonnes of explosives down their necks, all within an area of 150 square metres, we weren't expecting a huge number.

Koshtay was under the highly covert surveillance of our old friends, the Brigade Reconnaissance Force. It's what the BRF did best, and many of them went on from it to join the SBS and SAS. Creeping up on the site through bushes, undergrowth and waterways, they had observed a disciplined sentry system. Two guards patrolled the road that ran in front of it, perpendicular to the canal, while at least two more manned the lookout posts. The sentries changed over every thirty minutes.

The BRF's JTAC – Knight Rider Five Six – would control the air attack from a vantage point on the ground as close to the target as he could get, 500 metres north-west of the site. We needed eyes on the target at all times during the attack, in case a busload of nuns and schoolchildren were out on a stargazing field trip.

The JTAC and his twenty-four-strong protection team – including two snipers – planned to bag up all their kit and swim the Helmand River two kilometres to the west of the site and then yomp to the vantage point. They would be laid up there from 0300 hours.

A Nimrod MR2 was tasked for the operation, flying at 27,500 feet and feeding a live video link to Colonel Magowan and the Brigade HQ in Lashkar Gah. There was acute interest in Glacier 1; nobody wanted to miss a second of it. Then callsign Bone One One – the B1 from Diego Garcia atoll in the Indian Ocean – would drop his bombs from 25,000 feet, impacting precisely thirty minutes later, giving us an H hour of 0330 hours.

For the Apaches, it was a phenomenal task. We would be carrying out the first deep raid the Corps had ever flown. For the first time on a live operation, we'd be on our own over enemy-held territory. So far we'd fought hand in hand with the guys below us. If we went down this time, there would be no ground troops nearby to come and help us out. The BRF was too small and lightly armed; it'd have a job exfiltrating safely itself. A rescue bid would only be launched once brigade was sure we'd evaded capture; until then, we'd just have to fend for ourselves.

It was a whole new ball game. But the extra risk didn't temper our excitement – it added to it. We were chomping at the bit.

'I've got butterflies,' Carl said. 'Bring it on.'

We finished reading the orders at 4pm. The attack was set for the early hours of 11 January. We had an awful lot to prepare in less than thirty-six hours.

It was down to us to seamlessly dovetail our Apaches into the plan. Split second timing was essential. We worked out exactly where we needed to be and when, and went through every eventuality.

Koshtay was 100 kilometres from Camp Bastion as the crow flies, the furthest we'd had to fight so far. Long distance wasn't a problem though; we could hit a target 250 klicks away on our normal set-up and still have enough fuel to return to base. Slap on the five additional fuel tanks we could carry – in part of the gun magazine and off the four weapons pylons – and we had a strike range of almost 2,000 kilometres without having to touch down; London to Marrakesh, Malta or St Petersburg.

Where we were going, we wanted to take some proper weaponry. So we calculated a fuel / weapons split that gave us ninety minutes over the target, just in case we'd need them. We went for a Load Charlie again, but Hellfire-heavy – giving each aircraft six missiles.

Koshtay was a job for the two most experienced front-seat gunners. Billy took the back seat to fly the Boss, as Ugly Five Zero. Carl would fly for me, Ugly Five One. The Boss was mission commander.

Word that we were doing a deep raid spread around the squadron like wildfire. Everybody's blood was up, including the Groundies' and the Ops Room's, as every sortie was a massive team effort. We would be making Corps history. The twelve other pilots who weren't flying it were green with envy. Conspiracy theories were rife.

'Saving the best ones for yourself, eh Boss?' Nick said. 'What a coincidence it just happened to be HQ Flight's turn for a deliberate task.'

Trigger just smiled knowingly. But Nick's turn would come.

At lunchtime on the 10th, the ministerial permission we needed for Op Glacier 1 finally came through. We were hitting the place cold and firing the first shots, which we very seldom did. With all the paperwork in place, the brigade confirmed it as a go.

The four of us had a kip after lunch, since we weren't going to get much sleep later. At sunset we went down to the flight line for a final walk around the Apaches and loaded our kit.

'Just double check your LSJs, chaps,' Trigger said.

It was a good point. Our survival jackets were vital if we got shot down; they contained everything we might need to keep us alive on the ground apart from our personal weapons. I went through every last pouch.

To squeeze so much into one man's waistcoat was a masterpiece of design, and the reason they were so bloody heavy. The deep left front pocket was easiest to grab for a right-handed pilot like me. That's why it contained the most important piece of kit – a very powerful multi-frequency ground-to-air radio with which we could talk securely to anyone above us or at a distance, through burst transmissions. It was also fitted with a GPS system and a homing beacon that could be picked up by satellite.

Three pockets were sewn into the front right-hand side of the jacket. The top one contained a signalling pack – an infrared or white light strobe and a signalling mirror. The middle held a survival pack: a matchless fire set – cotton wool and magnesium metal with a saw blade to ignite it (matches ran out and could get wet) – fuel blocks, a nylon fishing line, hooks and flies, a foil blanket, high energy sweets, tablets to purify dirty water, a polythene bag, tampons to soak up water, two Rocco-sized condoms that could each carry a gallon of water, a compass, a candle, parachute cord to rig up shelters, three snares, a wire saw, a needle and thread, camouflage cream and a medium-sized Swiss Army knife. The lowest pocket was packed with the things you hoped you'd never need: antibiotics, morphine-based painkillers, three elastic dressings and adhesives, two standard dressings, a safety pin, Imodium tablets to stop the shits, a razor blade, dextrose high energy tablets, sun block, insect repellent and a pair of forceps.

We kept a six-inch-long Maglite torch and an emergency extraction strap with a black karabiner in another small pocket, just next to the zip. A large pouch sewn into the back of the jacket contained a metre-square waterproof, tear-resistant nylon escape map that you could also use to shelter from the sun or rain. Alongside it we kept two litre-sized foil sachets of clean water.

Back up at the JHF we formulated an escape plan for the mission. We had one for every location we went to, and for every pre-planned sortie we flew. If we did go down over Koshtay, we'd all know exactly what to do.

Apache pilots underwent the most intensive escape and evasion training of anyone in the UK military, alongside Harrier pilots and Special Forces personnel. All three worked behind or over enemy lines, so faced the greatest risk. It was a gruelling sixteen-week course, and as the squadron's Survive, Evade, Resist and Extract Officer, Geordie gave us regular refreshers

The first emergency drill was always the same – talk to your wingman and tell him where you are. He'd know you'd gone down, and would be doing his damnedest to keep you alive. If the threat on the ground allowed it, he'd swoop down, land next to your aircraft and you'd have about three seconds to strap yourself onto a grab handle forward of the engine air intakes with your own strap and karabiner.

We practised the drill every now and then, but no Apache pilot in the world had ever done it on operations; it was fraught with danger for everyone concerned. Putting an aircraft on the ground in a battle made it incredibly vulnerable, which was why the MoD pencil-necks had written into the Release To Service rules that it was only to be used in dire emergencies. If they had it their way, it would have been out of the RTS altogether.

First, of course, we had to survive going down. There were no ejection seats in an Apache; it was dangerous enough standing beneath a turning rotor blade. If our aircraft went down, we went down with it. It concentrated the mind. So much so, that experienced pilots would always subconsciously scope for the safest place to crash-land.

Should the worst happen and we found ourselves on the ground, it was going to be immediately obvious if Trigger and Billy were going to be able to pick us up at Koshtay. If they couldn't – which was almost inevitable – we'd try to get as far away from the aircraft as possible. The Apache would act like a magnet for the enemy, so we wouldn't even hang around to destroy its clandestine equipment; someone else with a big bomb would take care of that.

It would be dark, which was a great advantage. Maybe only a handful of Taliban would see us go down. Five minutes later though, the word would have gone round. By daybreak, we'd be the focus of a massive and coordinated hunt.

Once clear of the aircraft, we'd head due north or south and then west as soon as we could. Our best hope of escape would be the GAFA desert, preferably by dawn. We'd either find the BRF there or get picked up. It was only four klicks away – but we'd have to cross the raging Helmand River and possibly the canal on the way.

We'd move at night and hide in daylight. We'd keep switching on the radios to speak to anyone we could see or hear above us. They'd be up there, waiting for our call. And above all, we had to stick together – two pairs of eyes and ears were always better than one, and one of us might be injured.

After the 8pm brief, we tried to get a few hours' sleep. The Boss took the cot next to mine so we wouldn't wake anyone in his tent.

'It's strange, isn't it?' he said as he climbed into his sleeping bag. 'I'm going to bed now, knowing that when I wake up, I will deliberately go out and kill people.'

The Boss grappled with this idea for a few moments as the opening credits of *24* rolled on the laptop beside him – but only for a couple of minutes. The next time I looked, he was fast asleep, his head tucked into the crook of his arm.

I couldn't sleep a wink. I just lay on my back in the darkness, going over every eventuality again and again, trying to visualise how I would deal with them. How to get out of the Green Zone if we went down was the challenge that preoccupied me most. There'd be no chance of a rescue. How fast was the current in the Helmand River? Would we reach the GAFA by dawn? If not, where would we lie up? Must remember to keep away from livestock, especially dogs; they'd give us away immediately. What if I was incapacitated and Carl was okay? Carl would have to run. I'd make him. He'd get nowhere trying to carry me. What if he was injured? I'd have a tough time lifting him and all that strawberry cheesecake. But I couldn't leave him – I'd never be able to live with myself. No; I'd stay and fight to the end – and save the last two rounds for ourselves.

It didn't matter how hard I tried, I couldn't get one picture out of my head: me standing alongside a burning aircraft with Carl unconscious at my feet and the Taliban swarming towards us … Wouldn't it just be Sod's Law if I got it tonight? Emily was four and a half months pregnant … I saw the look on my kids' faces as they were told that this time their dad wasn't coming back … And I knew for certain that this *had* to be my last tour.

But would I have ducked out of it there and then, given the choice? Not for all the tea in China.

The alarm clocks went off at 1am. We dressed in silence, pulses racing, and popped into the JHF to pick up our Black Brains and check for any changes in plan. There weren't any. We walked down to the flight line in the cold night air and fired up the aircraft at 1.55.

There were a few extra start-up procedures to run through in the cockpit before a night flight. Sound was often difficult to place, so keeping the aircraft as dark as possible gave us a much-needed edge. We knew the Taliban had NVGs – probably supplied by Iran – so we didn't want to make it any easier for them.

Bat wings were sheathed below the left and right windows of the cockpit for us to pull up and shield the glow of our MPD screens – the only light source in the cockpit.

Carl needed a few more minutes to adjust his monocle. At night, he was 100 per cent reliant on it – it was his only window on the world. Other military pilots used NVGs, which magnified ambient light sources 40,000 times. We had Pilot's Night Vision Sights instead.

The normal flight symbology was projected into the pilot's monocle, but it was underlaid with the image of the 'Pin-viss', a second infrared lens sitting above the TADS bucket.

Through the PNVS thermal picture, we could see landscape in total darkness, as well as anyone moving below us. 'If it glows, it goes,' the instructors used to say – though not in the handbook.

Like the cannon, the PNVS lens was slaved to your eye. It followed the direction of your right eye, though a fraction more slowly than the gun, so there was a momentary lapse between desire and action. It was mounted above the TADS on the aircraft's nose, so the perspective was slightly out of kilter too, as if your eyeball had been stretched twelve feet out of its socket.

Flying on PNVS low level at 140 knots was the hardest thing to master on Apache training; it was like driving down a pitch black motorway with no lights, with a hand clamped over one eye, a twelve-foot-long tube capped with a green lens strapped to the other, and the speedo needle brushing 161 mph ...

We learned how to do this by 'flying in the bag'. Our entire back-seat cockpit was blacked out with panels, while the instructor sat in the open front. It wasn't a great place for claustrophobics.

'Please God, just let me get through,' we'd pray. Fail three test sorties in the bag, and you were out. Passing gave you the world's greatest high.

Despite Carl's whingeing, I knew I was in good hands with him flying me that night. His was the best pair of night hands we had.

We were all set in good time. No need for calls; we just slipped out of the bays with two minutes to takeoff.

We lifted silently at 2.10am. Billy led us a few klicks north to dupe any Taliban dickers then backtracked south-west across the A01 Highway, and hard south once we were into the empty desert, our Hellfire-laden machines invisible against the GAFA's sky.

OP GLACIER 1: KOSHTAY

It was a thirty-five minute flight to our holding area in the desert. We'd chosen a spot fifteen kilometres due west of the Taliban base at Koshtay, giving us a run-in time onto the target of four minutes and three seconds. Nobody would hear us that far out; we'd do racetrack patterns at seventy knots and fifty feet off the ground until the time came.

Carl and Billy kept the aircraft 200 feet off the ground as we headed south. We would normally have gone lower to prevent detection, but the Dasht-e-Margo lived up to its name and was void of all habitation.

The Boss and Billy were 500 metres to the left and marginally in front of us. The TADS FLIR camera was slaved to my eye; I could see them clearly with my right eye, but in the complete absence of ambient light, my left eye might as well have had a patch over it.

It had been a while since I'd been a gunner on a night flight. I used some of the transit time to re-familiarise myself with the feel of the firing grips. The front seat had exactly the same controls as the back seat, as well as a bloody great targeting console bolted into the middle of the dash, at the centre of which was a three-inch TV screen providing an additional display for one of the cameras or sensors. I selected the Longbow FCR option. If there was anything remotely threatening in the desert, it was sure to find it and give us a heads up so we could box around it. A large metal PlayStation-like grip sat on either side, with buttons and cursors galore to control the cameras and weapons. Each grip also had a trigger: the right for the laser range finder and designator, the left to kill.

I moved my thumb and fingertips across the buttons, rockers, switches and pads, instantly recognising each different shape and function, and ran through a dozen different combinations until I was completely comfortable. It didn't take long.

The night was unusually still for January. It made me fidget even more. I needed to keep myself occupied. I tried chatting with Carl but he wanted to concentrate on his flying. I sparked up the Automatic Direction Finder (ADF), a radio navigation system we used to pick up homing beacons in bad weather, and absentmind-edly scanned the local stations. I'd already preset the channels with the strongest signals to help counter the boredom of desert flying.

Apache pilots never met any Afghans. Life in the cockpit was remote from the real life of the country; it was the one disadvantage of the job. The nearest we could get was listening to their radio. We all used to do it. Local Pashtun songs were my favourite.

A Pakistani station broadcasting at 900 kilohertz was often the clearest. I tuned into a mullah in mid rant. I had no idea what he was saying, but he sounded pretty angry about something; maybe he didn't like having to whip up the faithful at ten to three in the morning.

'Hey Carl, check out the ADF Preset 1. I think they're onto us. "Come out and kill the mosquito pilots," they're saying. "The infidels are nearly here."'

Carl remained unmoved. 'I'm not listening to it, Ed.'

'Okay buddy, suit yourself.' I turned the volume back up in my helmet.

This was getting more surreal by the minute. The infidel-hater had been replaced by the opening chords of Beethoven's *Fifth Symphony*. So there we were, armed to the teeth at the dead of night in The Land That Time Forgot on our way to give a whole load of Taliban a rude awakening, and an insomniac radio producer somewhere in Baluchistan had managed to provide us with the perfect soundtrack.

As we reached the holding area, Trigger put a call into the BRF's JTAC. I turned off Beethoven as Knight Rider Five Six whispered, slowly and softly. We knew he was in position and perilously close to the enemy before he told us.

'Ugly Five Zero, Knight Rider. I can't get hold of Bone One One. Can you try to establish comms with him? We need his time on target.'

The Boss made several calls, each of them unanswered. Sometimes prearranged fast air left their arrival right to the last minute. We'd all just have to wait.

Two fresh icons popped up on the map page on my left MPD. Our Radar Warning Receiver had just pinged two other air assets over the battlespace, tens of thousands of feet above us. Their radar codes identified them as the Nimrod MR2 and a Predator UAV. We hadn't been told about the Predator. We often weren't.

Five minutes later, at 3.20am, a southern US drawl broke the silence.

'Knight Rider Five Six, Knight Rider Five Six. This is Bone One Three. How do you read, sir?'

'Bone One Three, Knight Rider Five Six, Lima Charlie. We were expecting to hear from Bone One One.'

'Affirmative, sir. The pre-planned B1 has gone unserviceable in Diego Garcia. We are a B1 and we have been tasked to you as the airborne alert from the Afghanistan stack. How many targets do you have for us?'

The BRF JTAC whispered his reply. 'Bone, Knight Rider. I have many targets. How many grids have you been given and how many bombs can you drop in one go?'

He could drop a maximum of ten in a oner and had not been given any of the pre-planned targets. Knight Rider asked him if he could have all ten.

'That's an affirmative.'

'Okay. Stand by to copy ...'

The JTAC read over each and every fifteen-digit grid and four-figure altitude in the same strained whisper. It can't have been easy with Taliban sentries on the prowl and no wind to hide any noise.

'Target Number One.'

Pause.

'Priority target.'

Pause.

'Forty One Romeo ... Papa Quebec.'

Pause.

'One Zero One ... Three Two.'

Pause.

'Two Double Four ... Four Zero.'

Pause.

'Altitude ... Two Two Five Seven ... Feet.'

Pause.

'Target Number Two ...'

It made for painful listening, and it took for ever. I copied the ten grids down as well and cross-referenced them on the map. Each of the three accommodation blocks was getting a 2,000-pounder and the middle one was getting two; one in each half. The four highest priority buildings would be on the receiving end of enough 500-pounders to flatten the Pentagon. The B1 could carry a total of twenty-four GBUs or sixteen thermonuclear gravity bombs.

'Bone, Knight Rider. Read back.'

Bone had to repeat each and every grid and altitude correctly to ensure that he wasn't going to rain down merry hell on innocent civilians.

There was a pause as the B1's offensive systems officer tapped in the grids.

'Bone, Knight Rider. Call Time on Target.'

It was 3.29am.

'Knight Rider, Bone. TOT in four-zero minutes. I am nine-zero miles to your south.'

Bloody hell. He's still in Pakistan, about to cross the border.

'We haven't got the fuel to wait all night for these jokers,' Carl grumbled.

They'd slashed the time we'd have over the target by almost half. We'd started off with ninety minutes and now had barely fifty. And that was only if Bone dropped when he said he would. Bone's problem was that he had to programme each bomb with the coordinates of the starting and finishing points of its journey. To ensure pinpoint accuracy, he also needed to radar map the ground beneath him and then commensurate the grids.

'Let's just hope they're all still fast asleep.'

Many orbits later a third air icon flashed up on the map page, a jet heading towards us from the south. The B1 was now close by. Bone spoke again at 4.05am.

'All stations, Bone One Three. Time on target in five minutes. Bone is running in.'

It was our cue. Billy and Carl held back for another sixty seconds to ensure we didn't catch any of the blast, and pointed the aircrafts' noses hard down for Koshtay. The two Apaches were neck and neck, fifty feet from the ground and going max chat. Trigger and Billy were 500 metres to our left. We'd divided up the workload by splitting the target area in two. They'd take the northern half of the site, working north to south; we'd take the south, working south to north.

'Ugly callsigns, Knight Rider Five Six. You are cleared hot to engage any leakers on the bombs' impact.'

I shifted forward and hunched over the gunning grips. The moment that lazy Texas voice told us his bombs were in the air, Carl and Billy would climb hard to our engaging height. We should hear Bone when we had around five klicks to go. We didn't. Bone came on at the four-kilometre mark instead.

'Bone is off. No drop, repeat no drop. Resetting.'

Fucking hell.

'Steady tu –' Billy began.

'Slow turn,' Carl unintentionally interrupted.

God only knew why Bone didn't drop. It could have been for any one of a dozen reasons. It wasn't the time to ask. We needed to reset immediately. We were less than 4,000 metres from the target. Any closer and they'd hear our rotors. A gentle 180-degree turn was crucial to stop the blades chattering and why both pilots made the same call: we could blow this big style.

'Ugly, Knight Rider. I can hear you. Move back, move back.'

We cruised back towards our holding area. *Shit*. More time down the drain. It would take Bone at least five minutes to reset, and another five to run in. We were down to forty minutes of combat gas. One more delay and we'd have to go home. It was already agonising, and about to become humiliating. We'd have to tell Knight Rider that he'd have to drop with no follow-up, or delay ninety minutes so we could gas up back at Bastion.

The next time there was no mistake; Bone was early.

'Bone One Three is off hot. Twenty-six seconds to impact.'

I hit record on the left grip; I didn't want the rest of the squadron to miss this. But we were still six kilometres out. 'Climb, climb, climb!'

Keeping their speed up, both pilots heaved on their collectives to max torque and began a rapid climb. We soared up to 2,500 feet and I slaved my TADS straight onto the Taliban camp. I made out the line of seven tall, bushy trees directly in front of the complex, then the canal in front of the trees. No movement from what I could see. That was good. It was still pitch dark.

'BUSTER,' the Boss ordered. Our nose tipped forward momentarily before the big stabilator wing on the back of the Apache levelled us out again. We couldn't risk any delay between the bombs' impact and our arrival over the target.

But where were the bombs? My clock: they'd been in the air twenty seconds, but it felt like an eternity. I looked out of a side window and my left eye made out flicks of tree below. My right confirmed the desert was ending and the Green Zone about to begin. Jesus, we only had a few klicks left to run. I looked back at my MPD. A pattern of tiny pinpricks of heat fell towards the earth, angled towards the seven trees.

At 4.13 on the dot, all ten of the B1's GBUs exploded directly in front of us. A series of stroboscopic flashes melted into one blindingly bright light, followed a split second later by cylinders of angry orange flame. The biggest explosion I had ever seen played out in total silence; we still couldn't hear a thing in the cockpit. The whole complex had turned white on my FLIR.

'Did you see that?' Billy was beside himself.

'Awesome.' So was Carl.

'And then some!'

'Kick right, Carl.'

We couldn't make it out in the dark and the FLIR would see right through it, but it would be there – the fallout from the blast site: earth, brick and humanity, all vaporised.

'Ugly Five Zero is looking for the northern sentry,' Trigger said, as Billy banked their Apache away from us. Then: 'I've got him, he's still there. Engaging now.'

The sentry must have been sheltered within the mosque's safety distance. Trigger opened up with his cannon, but his quarry had slipped into the small, roofless outbuilding through a doorway on its northern side. 'He's taking cover in the sentry post ... Engaging ...'

He squeezed off two further bursts. The second threw the sentry around like a rag doll until he finally slumped motionless against a wall. The smoke and dust was starting to clear at ground level, though it still hung high above us. As we circled I scoured the complex for any sign of movement.

It was like the B1 had dropped a nuclear bomb. The trees were stripped of their branches and star-shaped scorch marks covered the earth. There wasn't a single crater. The living quarters on the southern edge of the target and the L-shaped building had totally disappeared. Not a single brick remained. The B1 Lancer had set all the fuses to super-quick. The bombs had blown apart the buildings – and everyone inside them – before they'd even landed. Not surprisingly, I couldn't see any runners, but one long single-storey affair remained standing by the edge of the canal.

'Knight Rider Five Six, Ugly Five One. I have one building still intact. It's on the southern side of the target. Confirm you want it destroyed.'

'Ugly Five One, that's an *A*-ffirmative. Engage all remaining target buildings with Hellfire. Leave nothing standing.'

Carl banked hard right, taking us back the way we had come. There was enough heat from the place to indicate it was still inhabited but too much around it to allow me to lock it up. I'd need a straight line of sight to it all the way in.

'Ugly Five One. Running in from the west with Hellfire.'

I flicked the weapons select switch with my left thumb; right for missiles. On my right MPD I lined up the crosshairs on the middle of the target's front wall. My left MPD told me that a missile on the right wing had spun up and was ready to go. The dog was well and truly ready; it just needed a glimpse of the rabbit.

'Confirm we're on the correct side, Carl.'

It was imperative that the missile didn't pass in front of the camera lens on launch as its heat haze would have destroyed my line of sight on my FLIR image. If it did, I would lose the target and have to keep searching for it whilst the Hellfire sped on, in search of my laser beam. Carl eased down his foot pedal, moving the aircraft's nose a fraction to the right. Perfect.

'I've stepped on it, Ed. Clear to engage.'

I flipped the guard and pulled the laser trigger with my right index finger whilst maintaining enough thumb pressure to keep the crosshairs on the centre of the building. My left index finger also flipped its guard.

At 2,000 metres, I pulled the weapons trigger, 'Engaging with Hellfire.'

A one second pause. No bang, judder or jolt – just a rush of jet propulsion as it slipped gracefully off the right rail.

'Missile off the rail and it's away.' Carl treated us to the usual pilot's running commentary.

MSL LAUNCH flashed up on my TV screen.

'Missile climbing, Ed.'

My entire focus shot to the thumb cursor on my right grip. The helicopter swayed slightly, but I had to keep pointing the laser beam bang in the middle of the building. For those seven seconds, it was the only thing that mattered in the whole world.

Two seconds later, *MSL LAUNCH* was replaced by the Hellfire's Time of Flight countdown in seconds:

TF 5 ...

'Missile levelling off now. Missile coming down.'

TF 4 ...

Shit. As we closed on it, I saw a cool ridge running through the middle of the target, front and top – two buildings, joined together.

TF3 ...

To do the most damage, I needed to hit each section individually.

TF2 ...

I adjusted the crosshairs to the right side of the building.

TF1 ...

As I centred them on the apex of the walls the missile struck, smack on the laser beam. A flash, followed by a billowing cloud of dust as the roof lifted. The dust cleared to reveal a huge chunk missing from two-thirds up the front of the building. The right-hand and back walls had collapsed, bringing down the roof. The left-hand side of the building still stood firm.

'Good hit, mate.'

'Take us back out for another run-in.'

'I've got the second sentry hiding behind a tree near the remains of the northern accommodation block,' the Boss reported. 'I need to get in close.'

'We're clear,' Carl called.

'Engaging with cannon.'

I swung the TADS across in time to see the earth and a low wall erupt beside the base of a bare tree fifty metres south-west of the mosque. As Carl banked us back in to the target I saw the lone heat source drop to the ground from behind the trunk. Trigger was in his element. My adrenalin was pumping like a piston engine too.

Carl pushed Billy north to give us a clear shot. I put a second Hellfire into the cooler stripe where the roof met the inter-connecting wall. Two minutes and twenty-one seconds after the first Hellfire impacted, the building was in ruins, but I caught a glimpse on the left of my screen of a small guardhouse still standing twenty metres to its north-east. We were just 1,000 metres off now; could I get it on the same run?

'Hold it steady, Carl. Going for one more.'

'No, Ed. There's not time left for –'

'Firing Hellfire!' The third missile streaked off the rail to my right, between two skeletal trees. It never had time to climb, or even to count me down; it just slammed straight into the middle of the six-foot by six-foot building, reducing it to rubble.

The Boss came on again, cool as a cucumber.

'Ugly Five Zero has got a leaker, running east. Stand by ...'

'Engaging with cannon.'

I couldn't see anyone in my half of the target area, so I swung my TADS sharp left to catch his second burst cut straight through the guy's path. He was hurled forward, a metre off the ground, then hard down on one side. The 30-mm round that hit him had failed to explode, but it hadn't done him any favours. It had powered straight through his back and out of his chest, leaving a hole the size of Trigger's clenched fist.

Only the mosque was left without a scratch. They were strictly off the target list. It was where Trigger's leaker had appeared from. And if there was one, there would be more. We needed to nail them before they reached their DShKs and Stingers, and our fuel clocks were ticking.

'Okay Carl, bring us in close. Complete sanitisation now.'

Carl threw us into an anticlockwise orbit as I scanned the southern half of the site. Nothing.

'Ugly Five Zero, Knight Rider Five Six. Intelligence from higher has identified a further enemy compound at the following grid. Ready to copy.'

Intelligence from higher?

'Ugly Five Zero has identified a building in the northern sector.' The Boss hadn't finished with his half of the target yet. 'Pass grid to Five One. Five One acknowledge.'

I was only too pleased to copy.

'Break ... Break ... Engaging with Hellfire.' The Boss was doing an increasingly bad job of disguising his excitement.

I copied down Knight Rider's grid, punched it into the keypad and slaved my TADS thermal camera to it with a push of a button. It was a small, chisel-shaped compound surrounded by fields, 200 metres directly east of the Taliban base. Whoever wanted us to have a look at it wasn't part of the stack. We'd be able to talk to the Nimrod, and the B1 had a radar. 'Higher' was either connected to the Predator feed, or had picked up a SigInt hit from the place – or both.

High and to the east, I zoomed into the chisel-shaped compound as three men ran through its main entrance and ducked into the first of the five single-storey buildings inside it.

'Runners to the north, closing in fast on the compound.' Keeping a broad sweeping arc – out of Billy's and Trigger's way – Carl had spotted two more sprinting down a path to the south. We hadn't seen them leave the complex, which made them a fresh target; I needed permission to engage.

'Knight Rider, Ugly Five One. Two men heading south towards the second compound; confirm clear to engage?'

I flicked the weapons switch forward, tracked him with the crosshairs and began lasing to update the gun's range to target.

'Knight Rider Five Six, you are clear hot –'

'Firing with thirty Mike Mike.'

I gave the path a burst as the first runner reached the nearest building, throwing up mud and dust. The second runner was still 100 metres short. He'd stopped to see his mate get through and knew he wouldn't be so lucky.

I centred on him and squeezed off a twenty-round burst. I saw the heat of the rounds arc down and knew they were going to miss him too. Bollocks. He stumbled as the ground erupted behind him then legged it into the field.

I aimed off, slightly to the left of him, as he picked up speed and angled back towards the compound. The cannon thundered beneath my feet and the heat pulses shot towards him, close enough this time to catch him with a few fragments of red hot metal. He stumbled back towards the path and rolled down the bank of a tiny irrigation ditch. It may have looked like good place to hide, but he was glowing from his exertions. I moved the crosshairs onto him, adjusted them a little further this time to compensate for the inaccuracy of the gun, and gave him another burst of twenty. His running days were over.

'Knight Rider, Ugly Five One. I have got at least four individuals complete in the buildings within the second compound.'

'Copied. You are cleared to destroy all the buildings in that compound. Intelligence from higher says they're Taliban commanders.'

'Higher' was clearly exceptionally well informed. The first three runners had turned right and the one I'd missed had gone left. That meant Taliban in at least two different buildings now.

'Carl, set us up for a missile run from the north. I'm giving them two Hellfires at once on the first run.'

It could work if I was quick. Really quick. Carl told Billy that we would hit the first three buildings and break back north-east after each engagement. Billy would run in straight after us from the west to take out the remaining two and the one attached to the compound on the southern edge, breaking south-west.

I focused the laser beam on the right-hand building and let Hellfire Number 4 go at 4,000 metres. It shot from under the left wing, climbed, levelled and dived. Still holding my laser trigger, I launched Number 5, so I had both missiles locked onto the beam. The instant I saw Number 4's white flash, I slewed my crosshairs ten metres east, onto the apex of the building immediately left of the entrance. Hellfire Number 5 screeched into it four seconds after the crosshairs had gone stationary.

We'd come so far in we were now 'Danger Close'.

'Ugly Five One resetting and ...'

Carl threw the aircraft onto its left side and powered up violently; the G sucked my arse deep into the seat.

'... clear.'

'Ugly Five Zero running in from the west with Hellfire.'

I craned my neck to keep my eyes on the compound. There were still three buildings untouched. If these guys really were senior

Taliban commanders, they'd have a SAM close by. We couldn't give the bastards a single second to pull it out.

'Carl, just get us round as quick as poss.'

'I am, I am …' The engines screamed as he ratcheted up the torque. The poor guy was doing his best.

'Engaging,' the Boss called.

A thousand metres would have to do. 'Right, bring us in now, Carl.' We needed to cover each other; we couldn't have both aircraft turn tail on the enemy.

As Trigger's Hellfire impacted on the far south-easterly building, Carl rolled us back to face the compound. I waited for Five Zero to get clear before aiming Hellfire Number 6 at the building immediately to the north of the one they had just destroyed. We were far too close to it, but had run out of choices. I squeezed the trigger 650 metres out then Carl wrenched us around in the tightest turn I had ever experienced.

As the Apache lurched upwards, I went from twelve stone to nearer thirty. My head, encased in its helmet, NVGs and monocle, immediately tried to bury itself between my shoulder muscles. I didn't have time to brace myself. I didn't even have time to reach for the steel grab handles on the roof frame. I threw my hands onto the console and held it fast.

My monocle drilled into my cheekbone as it pressed against the console's brow pad. My harness clamped down on my shoulders and the survival jacket forced the chicken plate deep into my bladder. I felt the blood rush from my head to my feet, now pinned firmly to the floor. As the foam cushion in the seat was squashed flat and my haunches dug into the Kevlar base, I heard myself give a low moan. Carl rolled us back out level, and normal transmission was resumed.

Billy and Trigger were turning inbound for their next Hellfire. We were out of missiles, but needed to provide cover for them as they ran in. We didn't get the chance.

'Ugly Five Zero, Knight Rider. Intelligence from higher; there are enemy in a compound by the canal two hundred metres north of the original target. Stand by for grid.'

'Ugly Five Zero. Running in from the west with Hellfire. Ugly Five One you take that target; I've got two buildings to finish off here.'

There was an awful lot of smoke and dust in the air so Carl swung us away from the hornets' nest and over to the west side of the canal. It kept us out of Ugly Five Zero's way and gave me a better view.

The new compound was the furthest north of a cluster of three. We held off 2,500 metres south-west of it, so as not to spook the enemy and to give Carl eyes on our wingman.

I picked up a series of white shapes on my FLIR and zoomed in: four men stood in a group against the high compound wall. One had what appeared to be an RPG alongside him. Two others had a moped in front of them. A donkey flicked its tail disconsolately in the top left-hand corner of the compound, thirty metres to their west. I needed to confirm that this was the correct target, but there wasn't a single unique identifying feature.

'Knight Rider, Ugly Five One. Can you confirm the target precisely?'

'Ugly Five One, Knight Rider. I am told there are people in the north-east corner of the compound. You are cleared hot on those people.'

Yes, but who was telling him all this? And was I definitely looking in the right compound? Knight Rider couldn't know; he didn't have eyes on. The targets were getting progressively further from the main Taliban base. I didn't want to open up on third party information without better clarification. If I was going to kill, I needed to be 100 per cent sure.

'Ugly Five One. I need something to hang my hat on. Can you give me more information on the target?'

'Ugly Five One, this is Knight Rider Five Six. Higher has cleared you hot onto that target.'

'Ugly Five One. Give me a unique feature or tell me who's buying my weapons. I must confirm that we are both looking at the same target.'

'Ugly Five One, this is Maverick Zero Bravo. How do you read?'

Maverick Zero Bravo? Who the hell was that? No callsign I'd ever come across. The voice was short and clipped, its nationality indistinguishable; I put the accent as mid-Atlantic at best. I flicked through the top pages of my Black Brain; no joy there. Maverick wasn't a callsign we'd been given for the operation. But it was impossible for him to be on the secure net if he wasn't authorised so he had to be 100 per cent bona fide.

'Maverick Zero Bravo, Ugly Five One. Lima Charlie. You, me?'

'Maverick Zero Bravo. Lima Charlie also. Stand by … Can you see the donkey in the north-west corner of that compound?'

'Ugly Five One. Affirm.' But that didn't mean a thing. Everyone had a bloody donkey!

'Maverick Zero Bravo. Another man will join the four in the compound,' the clipped voice continued. 'He will walk past the donkey.'

Sure enough, a fifth man appeared a few seconds later and walked behind the donkey to join his companions. *Bloody hell, that's clever.* It was good enough for me. Whoever and wherever he might be, Maverick Zero Bravo must have been controlling the Predator feed. *He* must have been 'Higher'.

'Ugly Five One will prosecute that target with rockets; stand by.'

'Bring her in Carl; we're going to use Flechettes.'

Carl rolled us out, pointed the nose north-east and began to line up early. I actioned the rockets. The steering cursor flashed up on my screen.

'Four rockets. Come co-op, Carl.'

I positioned the crosshairs over the group of five and began to lase.

'Match and shoot, Carl.'

'Match and shoot … Stand by.'

'Ugly Five One. Engaging with rockets.'

Carl steadied the rocket steering cursor on the crosshairs as the fifth man approached the moped.

'Firing … Good set.'

Four bright orange flashes and four rockets whipped towards the centre of the crosshairs on the MPD. They looked good. Less than a thousand metres out, the white-hot cradles that had held the Flechette darts inside the rocket broke away, twisting and jinking through the air as the darts themselves flew at near hypersonic speed towards the target. Two seconds later 320 searing pinpricks blossomed across the north-eastern corner of the compound and its far wall. The five men hit the deck; we needed to nail them big time before they got busy with the RPG.

'Smack on, Carl. Don't break, we're going for another four. Match and shoot.'

The rules stated that after one volley of rockets we must change heading to avoid colliding with the Flechette cradles. I was utterly mission focused; they were no longer a factor. I'd seen them drop off the screen.

Carl let rip again from 1,500 metres. The second concentration was even tighter – a ten-metre circle, max.

'Good work, buddy. And another four.'

Carl pulled the final trigger at 1,100 metres.

The second the rockets streaked past our windows I flicked up for gun. Three final bursts from the cannon – slightly offset – would finish the job.

We had flown through the wake of twelve rockets and the environmental control system couldn't handle the pollutant saturation. The acrid stink of rocket propellant seeped into the cockpit and burned into my nasal membrane. A few seconds later, we were almost over the compound. I zoomed in the FLIR for a thorough battle damage assessment (BDA).

The moped was in pieces, and the RPG launcher broken in two, with its warhead still in place. Where the five men had been, there were heat sources galore across the ground and wall, but none in any recognisable human shape. I found another heat source scanning left, but still standing on four legs and looking okay. The donkey had escaped unscathed, but the five men had been shredded.

'Good arrows, good arrows,' Maverick Zero Bravo purred.

'Ugly Five One, target destroyed.'

'Ugly Five Zero, target destroyed also.'

Knight Rider had been waiting in line. The Nimrod had pinged enemy movement in two long sheds east of the canal, 500 metres north of our original target. It was a perfect job for Bone, but Bone had a more pressing engagement with an airborne fuel tanker.

I picked up the frustration in the BRF JTAC's voice. He couldn't see any of these new targets. He had become a relay station for the eyes of others. At least he no longer had to whisper.

It was our third new target. There were clearly even more Taliban down at Koshtay than the recce had established. They hadn't just confined themselves to the central complex; they'd spread their tentacles into the adjoining compounds too. The whole kilometre-square neighbourhood was a seething mass of Taliban.

'Five One is out of Hellfires.'

'Five Zero. Copied. You check out the original target for movement and I'll take on this target. All buildings in the chisel have gone. No leakers.'

The Boss and Billy stuck their final two Hellfires into the sheds whilst we surveyed the area of the battle. There were no leakers; the place was finally silent.

I checked the clock: 4.54am. I brought up my Hellfire *Shot at* page on the MPD. Hellfire 01 struck the target at 23:52:02 Zulu – 4.22am. We'd been fighting solidly for thirty-two minutes. And we were almost out of combat gas.

'Knight Rider, Ugly Five Zero. Ugly callsigns have five minutes left on station. Is there anything else you want us to do?'

'Ugly callsigns, Knight Rider. Affirmative. RTB, rearm and refuel. We have more intelligence. Callsign Bone One Three is coming back on station any minute to hit more targets for Higher. We'll need you back down as soon as you can.'

We'd put down twelve Hellfires, twelve rockets and 360 cannon rounds; an Apache record for one sortie. And still they wanted more. It couldn't get any better.

A GOOD NIGHT'S WORK

We flew a fifty-four-mile straight line back to Camp Bastion, taking us right past the Garmsir District Centre and over huge stretches of the Green Zone. We radioed back a list of what we needed and Kev and his boys were waiting with it all in the arming bays.

It was like a Formula One pit stop: fuel first, then 30-mm, rockets and six Hellfires loaded simultaneously. It was all hands to the pump. At one point I spotted Kev carrying a 100-lb missile on his own; I could have sworn he was smiling. They worked their socks off and got us out of there in twenty-five minutes.

More than three hours in the cockpit normally made me feel as though I was sitting on a bag of golf balls, but tonight I seemed immune from it. Perhaps it was because I'd never sat still; it had been a roller coaster of a ride.

All four of us were on an incredible high during the transit there and back. In his usual modest fashion, Billy texted us his Distinguished Flying Cross citation for the mission – par for the course when he thought a sortie had gone even moderately well.

The secure text messaging system had only four lines of text and 176 character spaces. He used them all:

*4 GALLANTRY LEADERSHIP + AMAZIN FLYING SKILL
HEROICS ON AAC 1ST DEEP RAID 4 KEEPING BOSS
CALM WHEN HE GOT TOO EXCITED THE DFC GOES TO
WARRANT OFFICER CLASS 1 WILLIAM SPENCER AAC*

We checked in on station over Koshtay at 6.14am and it was as dark then as it had been when we left.

In the eighty minutes we'd been away the geography of the battlefield had changed yet again. Maverick had obviously wanted more work done. Judging by the size of the heat splash on the ground, it looked like the B1 had plonked a 2,000-pounder bang in the middle of it. It must have been a super-quick fuse too. All the buildings in the compound where Maverick had asked me to engage the five Taliban had disappeared. There was nothing left; no heat sources whatsoever.

'Looks like it was curtains for the donkey, buddy.'

Knight Rider Five Six and his small party from the Brigade Recce Force had withdrawn. They couldn't risk hanging around in the middle of an enemy-controlled area of the Green Zone in daylight.

Maverick Zero Bravo appeared to have knocked off for the night too, now the back of the Taliban in Koshtay had been broken. The Nimrod MR2 – callsign Wizard – was spotting for targets with his equally powerful cameras instead. It had already directed Bone One Three to drop 2,000-pounders on the Boss's sheds, but Bone had pulled off station again.

The Boss tried to speak to Wizard and couldn't get a peep out of him. We knew Lashkar Gah would have the downlink, but we were too far away to establish comms with them. We'd had a satellite phone fitted to our version of the Apache for just such an occasion. Trigger dialled up the JTAC at Brigade HQ in Lashkar Gah, Widow Seven Zero. With no conference facility, Billy relayed the call to Carl and me.

'Ugly Five One, Five Zero. The Boss has got Widow Seven Zero on the bat-phone in Lash. He has fresh targets from Wizard; stand by for talk on.'

I followed the irrigation ditch south-east from the chisel-shaped compound for 300 metres.

'Five One has a large compound on the south-west side and two smaller compounds on the north-east side of the ditch, approximately fifty metres beyond the footbridge.'

'Five Zero. Affirm. Wizard watched injured Taliban making their way across the bridge towards those compounds. You take all the buildings on the south-west of the ditch; we'll take the east.'

The sky began to lighten as Billy and Carl put us in broad orbits above the compounds. As Carl and I came round, I saw two smart-looking 4x4s parked a few hundred metres down a dirt track which ran alongside the ditch. That was a Taliban indicator if ever there was one; a local could never have afforded one. Either reinforcements were arriving or, more likely, they'd come to collect their wounded.

'Stand by, Carl. I think we might have a shoot on here.' I had the gun and the crosshairs ready. I saw a flicker of movement on the canal side of the compound. 'East a bit more, buddy.'

As we cleared the eastern wall, two men were trying to get inside the place. They had left what looked like a locked gate near the canal and staggered along the wall, looking for an opening. One was holding up the other, and they scrabbled about, increasingly desperate to find another entrance. Neither seemed to have weapons on them. I hit zoom as they drew level with the building on the inside of the compound.

The one being carried had clearly been in the battle earlier; the heat stains on his head and tattered clothing must have been blood.

He appeared only to have one arm and his left foot was missing. Squirming like trapped rats, they were a truly pathetic sight.

Then I spotted an RPG launcher and an AK47 fifteen metres behind them, on the ground, just short of the ditch. They must have dropped them when they heard our rotor blades. So they knew the drill.

'Ugly Five Zero, Ugly Five One. I have eyes on two Taliban trying to get into the first compound on the west side of the ditch. Confirm clear to engage.'

'Ugly Five Zero. Affirm. Widow has cleared us to engage any targets and all buildings with Taliban sheltering in them.'

The duo was bang in the centre of my crosshairs, but I hesitated. My cannon rounds would chew up the house on the other side of the wall for sure, along with whoever was inside it. I had clear orders, but I couldn't bring myself to pull the trigger. I kept thinking: what if it was *my* kids in there?

All I needed was for them to give me a few more feet ... They finally found the gate and scuttled inside. They stayed as close to the wall and then the house as they could, desperate for somewhere to hide.

It was a typical Afghan compound, forty metres long and twenty-five wide, with a floor of hard-packed dirt, divided in two by the house where it extended from the eastern wall. Behind it was a solid stone oven and a chicken coop, a big stack of firewood, cooking pans, matting, a goat and a toilet. The other half was empty.

The uninjured fighter pushed against the first of the house's three doors, but it didn't move an inch. Struggling to keep his companion upright, he eventually managed to bounce him along the wall to the next one. It too was locked.

I would finish them as they rounded the corner if the last door was also impassable; Carl put me in position to do so with minimum collateral damage. As they hobbled towards it, the injured man collapsed; he'd probably passed out. Could I fire? Shit, no, not quite – they were within a metre of the house and it was guaranteed to get some of my splash. This fucker knew what he was doing. I stuck my crosshairs on him like glue. He banged hard on the third door.

I could now make out the building with my naked eye. Dawn hadn't quite broken and there was no colour in my vision, but I could see the two fugitives increasingly clearly. The door opened and he pulled his unconscious comrade inside by the shoulders, leaving a trail of blood in their wake.

Ten seconds later, five children of varying sizes burst out of the same door and huddled together in the open courtyard. They were afraid of being outside, but clearly didn't want to go back in. They stared at the doorway and suddenly began pushing each other into line. The smallest one clung to the tallest and wouldn't let go. The others were clearly agitated. They must have been receiving orders from inside the house.

As dawn broke they looked up at us in unison and waved madly. I zoomed in tight on their faces. Their ages ranged from about two to perhaps twelve. And every single one of them was terrified.

'Look at your TADS screen, Carl.'

'I'm seeing it. Scum of the earth.'

'Carl, that scum is using innocent kids as a shield to protect his sorry arse.'

The children shuffled back to the door and stopped outside it. As we swarmed, they followed our every move. Every orbit we did saw each of them turn with us. I told the Boss what was happening.

'Ugly Five Zero. Wizard's orders are to destroy any building with Taliban occupants. But I am instructing you: *Do not engage that house.*'

I had no intention of doing so. Our ROE were simple. We'd kill any amount of Taliban, but never at the risk of even one innocent life. The Boss informed the Widow that he was not prepared to authorise the engagement of our target as he had better situational awareness than they did. Good man.

The wounded Taliban was as good as dead, if he wasn't already. His companion was too savvy to come out into the open until we were long gone. I looked forward to meeting him another day.

It was now three-quarters light. A deep red dawn filled the eastern horizon, and the sun would begin to pop up out of the Red Desert at any minute. We swarmed over the compounds up and down the irrigation ditch for a few minutes more and I poked my TADS inside it, hunting for survivors.

The more I looked, the more I realised we wouldn't be putting any more rounds down that morning. The daily routines were beginning to re-establish themselves: women carried bowls out of their houses; teenagers fed goats and started fires. The men stayed indoors while we were overhead, terrified they'd get mistaken for Taliban.

'Ugly Five One is seeing a normal pattern of life here and negative targets.'

'Five Zero. Copied; my thoughts too. I'll inform Lash that we can't engage any of these targets due to civilians. Let's sweep the initial target and conduct some Battle Damage Assessment.'

Carl swung us west, back to the main Taliban complex, to film the battle's aftermath with our TADS cameras for the battlegroup to analyse. The first rays of sunlight dusted everything below us a delicate pink, then bright, flaming orange as the sun's crest popped over the horizon. I looked out of my right-hand window as we passed over the complex. It was only then that I realised the full extent of the devastation we'd caused.

It looked like the old pictures of Hiroshima. The earth was still smouldering; the wisps of battlefield smoke hung low in the chill morning air, giving the place a strange, dreamlike quality. The trees that had survived were charred and skeletal. The huts we'd Hellfired were mounds of darkened rubble; the 2,000- and 500-pounders had reduced everything in their path to powder.

Trigger's leaker lay where he'd fallen, the huge hole in his chest now a dark ring. His first sentry was still slumped in his guardhut, but the one hiding behind the tree hadn't died immediately; he'd crawled nearly forty metres towards the mosque.

'Check out east, Ed. Here comes the burial party.'

A long line of women and a few unarmed men began to fan out from the far irrigation channel and made their way slowly towards the complex. We'd seen this before. After a battle, the Taliban forced the locals to scour the ground for their dead. One or two members of the burial party were probably Taliban directing the operation; they knew they were safe as houses.

Behind them two local women emerged from a domed wicker hut, halfway up the path where I'd gunned down the runner. A jumble of legs and feet stuck out of its arched entrance. They must have been piling up the corpses inside. A man in a black dishdash ducked down and crawled into the hut. When he backed out he wiped his hands on the ground before he stood up.

Fifteen minutes later, the Boss told Lashkar Gah we had everything.

*　　*　　*

Unsurprisingly, after Billy had awarded Trigger his DFC (Distinguished Flying Cross) via text, the graveyard humour ran riot on the flight back.

As we passed Garmsir, the Boss said he'd check in with the incumbent JTAC to check all was still quiet with them. It was the opportunity I'd been waiting for all night. I jumped in before he could make the call.

'Ugly Five Zero, Five One. I had a message passed into the cockpit during the upload. The JTAC in Garmsir has switched to the alternate frequency due to atmospheric interference on primary.'

'Copied. What's the frequency?'

'Don't know. I can't find my comms card. Sorry.'

Cue the Boss flicking through his Black Brain to the frequencies page. And there it was. *Do you suffer from erectile dysfunction? Put the pleasure back in your life with a little blue pill …* Below the headline there was a photo of a good-looking middle-aged man staring disconsolately into his Y-fronts. Geordie had torn the Viagra advert out of a magazine.

'Very funny, Elton.'

I couldn't believe it had taken the whole night for Trigger to look up a radio frequency.

Rocco hadn't been seen for three weeks and we were worried that he'd been taken prisoner. The conspiracy theory had it that the Boss had hidden him because he was so alarmed by the stunt during General Dannatt's visit, but nobody could prove it. Two days before Glacier 1 was launched, Geordie and Darwin came up with a plan to smoke Rocco out. We'd Rocco Trigger relentlessly by other means until he had the Italian Stallion released.

We had a strong cup of coffee back at the JHF, courtesy of Billy, who'd lost Apache Triv on an excellent HIDAS question from Carl. Then it was into the debrief. The Ops Officer had crunched a few stats during our second sortie.

'Well, Mr Macy, aren't we Flash Harry this morning. Not only was that the fastest pair of Hellfires ever fired by the British Army, it's also the first time we've had two in the air from one Apache at the same time in combat.'

I was so consumed by the mission, I'd had no idea.

'As for you, Boss, Kev Blundell tells me you've passed your £1 million of Hellfire marker. And for all of you: that's the most Hellfires ever fired in one mission. But I imagine you don't need me to tell you that.'

We debated the one aspect of the mission that had puzzled us all – the identity of 'Higher'. Maverick Zero Bravo was a new callsign on all the pilots, as well as everyone in the JHF.

'I tried to look it up,' the Ops Officer said. 'It's not in any of the battlegroup's orders and it's not on the Air Plan. It's not Colonel Magowan; you spoke to his JTAC. And it wasn't Brigade either; they were Widow Seven Zero. I can't find any reference to Maverick Zero Bravo anywhere.'

We asked discreetly around over the next few days. Nobody in Camp Bastion had heard of the callsign either. We even checked the list of all registered callsigns in theatre and couldn't find it there either. Maverick Zero Bravo didn't seem to exist. And yet from somewhere outside Afghanistan, he had access to excellent live optics and intelligence as well as our highly secure net. And he'd been given the authority – presumably by the brigadier – to order instant strikes. That sort of power wasn't handed over lightly.

There was only one explanation. Whether Maverick was in

Vauxhall Cross or Langley, Virginia, there was no real clue. 'Good arrows' was an American military phrase, but our JTACs controlled US pilots and picked up their lingo too.

We had already been led to believe that the Koshtay complex's initial discovery had been made by the spooks. We couldn't hold it against them if they wanted a ringside seat at its destruction.

The full Battle Damage Assessment for Operation Glacier 1 arrived from Lashkar Gah forty-eight hours later. We knew it had been a good night, but it was even better than anyone could have hoped.

The strike was estimated to have killed between eighty and 130, double the initial projection. The figure was not more precise because nobody knew how many Taliban were asleep inside the barracks when they got frazzled. Three of their senior commanders were among the dead, including a big fish by the name of Mullah Fahir Mohammed. Intercepts from across the Pakistan border in Quetta revealed urgent discussions had begun about the need to restructure their southern command. They were shitting themselves, and they didn't know where or how hard we'd hit them next. Which was exactly what we wanted.

The BDA also revealed that the complex had housed a jail. Thirteen Afghan prisoners may have died inside it. It was rumoured that the jail had been known about all along and that was the reason it required a Whitehall signature. Sometimes that's the way it goes with strategic targeting. I'm glad I didn't know that before-hand.

A brief press release went out to the British media celebrating our brave troops' 'capture' of 'a Taliban regional headquarters'. It sounded better than saying we had stonked 100 new recruits into blazing oblivion along with their commanders without putting so much as one marine's boot into the place.

I was pleased to have played my part in stopping the influx of new fighters with the Corps' first Deep Raid, but the fate of the thirteen prisoners left me empty, and I wasn't in the mood to celebrate much after that.

Meanwhile, the harsh realities of life on the ground in Helmand continued.

Two days after the Koshtay raid, another twenty-one-year-old marine from 42 Commando was killed during close-quarter fighting in an enemy compound near the Kajaki Dam. Darwin and Charlotte had been out supporting the clearance patrol. I was in the JHF when they came back, waiting to scrutinise their gun tape. They looked pretty shaken up.

'Everything okay, Tony?'

'Not really mate. A guy got shot at point blank range right in front of us.' He'd run round a corner as a Taliban fighter stepped out of a doorway.

That was one of the disadvantages of our powerful surveillance system. Sometimes we saw things in graphic detail that we didn't want to remember. There was nothing Darwin and Charlotte could have done for the boy. But that didn't mean his death wasn't going to haunt them. Unlike gun tapes, memories couldn't be locked away in a safe.

There were two new arrivals from Dishforth that week. The first was an instruction yet again upping the amount of hours we were allowed to fly the aircraft. We were now up to 415 per month, or fourteen hours a day. The Chinook and Lynx hours had gone up too, but not as steeply as the Apache's. Needs must; and it was all the Joint Helicopter Command could do to respond to brigade's ever greater demands on their woefully limited Afghan resources. We knew there was still no new money for the extra spares; as always, someone somewhere would be robbing Peter to pay Paul. Soon, Peter would have to declare bankruptcy.

The second arrival was our new Commanding Officer. Lieutenant Colonel Neil Sexton had taken over the reins of 9 Regiment at the back end of the year. Now he was coming out to command the Joint Helicopter Force in Kandahar. That made him Trigger's immediate superior in the operational chain of command.

As the new CO, Colonel Sexton was an unknown quantity to most of us. We hadn't had time to connect with him in the few weeks before we deployed. We knew he was unashamedly ambitious – but that was no bad thing. He wasn't Apache trained as the previous CO had been. On the other hand, he'd done a lot of time in the simulator so he understood the machine and the demands on its aviators.

I had liked our outgoing CO. He was hugely popular and a great extrovert. I wondered how I'd get on with the new one. It wasn't long before I found out.

OP GLACIER 2: THE JUGROOM FORT

All the bigwigs were delighted with the attack on Koshtay, from the generals at PJHQ in Northwood to the brigadier in Lashkar Gah.

Happiest of all though were the hundreds of young marines of 3 Commando Brigade out on the ground. Word about the raid had spread fast up and down the platoon houses and district centres of Helmand province. The guys had taken a pasting from the Taliban in the three months since they'd arrived. Now we'd given a bit of that pasting back. Not just in self-defence for once, but a really good, hard offensive kick where it hurt – right in the Taliban's bollocks.

The brigade were now keen to capitalise on the enemy's disarray. For the first time – possibly in the whole Helmand campaign – the Taliban were on the defensive. The brigadier wanted to keep it that way. The order came down to launch Operation Glacier 2 as soon as possible. So the next carefully targeted attack was set for the early hours of Monday, 15 January, just four days after the Koshtay raid. Again, Attack Helicopters were heavily written into the plan.

This time it was 3 Flight's turn on the Deliberate Ops roster. Nick and Charlotte would fly in the gunners' front seats with FOG and

Darwin behind them; callsigns Ugly Five Two and Ugly Five Three respectively. Nick, the senior of the two front-seaters, was mission commander. A chorus of surly grunts of approval from pilots echoed around the evening brief when the Boss announced it.

'Yeah, about time someone else apart from HQ Flight got a peachy job,' was the refrain. Envy was still rife over Koshtay.

We didn't mind. We'd had more than our fair share of excitement down there to last us the rest of the tour. Instead, our flight were on the IRT / HRF shift – the quick reaction force to scramble for any emergency in the province. But judging by the amount of stuff they were going to be chucking at Op Glacier 2's target before the assault, we reckoned that there was only a slimmer than slim chance that the four of us would have anything to do with it. Yes, it was going to be another whopper all right. If we'd got the cherry, 3 Flight were getting the icing.

The second target on Op Glacier's list of five was the second furthest away from Garmsir, nine kilometres south-west of the town, continuing the plan to funnel enemy fighters north and ever closer to our killing zone while depriving them of anywhere to retreat. It was also the largest of all five.

Glacier 2's mission was to destroy the Taliban's main forward operating base in southern Helmand – their Camp Bastion. It was a giant, high-walled rectangular compound, 200 metres long by 100 wide, on the banks of the Helmand River where the Green Zone borders the GAFA desert in the west. It certainly looked the part of a sinister enemy hang-out. It was extremely well fortified, with stone and adobe walls ten feet high and three feet thick, and guard towers at each of its four corners. It was known locally as the Jugroom Fort.

Jugroom was originally constructed centuries ago to defend the area from a river-borne invasion. Nobody knew exactly when or by whom. Alexander the Great might have had a hand in it, for all the locals could remember.

With the river to its south and a canal running close by its western wall, the fort had lush poppy fields to its north. A deserted village stood along its eastern flank; the locals had moved out long ago, and only returned during the hours of daylight to tend the fields.

It had been pinged as a target early on during the recce; every time ground troops passed anywhere near it they received a ferocious volley of fire. From the air, the Nimrod MR2 footage revealed that the guard towers had been recently reinforced, and were permanently well manned. It also confirmed that the place was of huge tactical importance to the Taliban. Just as we were airlifted into Camp Bastion from Kandahar air base – our initial arrival point in the country – so their fighters were moved up from Koshtay to Jugroom on the next stage of their journey to the front line. There they would be rested, fed, equipped and briefed, then pushed forward to individual battlegrounds: Garmsir, Sangin, Musa Qa'leh, Now Zad and Kajaki – wherever they were needed. Our knowledge of the base's layout was patchier. Inside was believed to be a command centre building, several barracks blocks and a large underground weapons cache.

Force 84 was initially offered the job of taking it out. But the SBS said it was too big for them. You didn't hear a full squadron of Special Forces guys saying that too often. It wasn't their type of target and they didn't have the firepower if it turned into a big scrap. The planners were undeterred. The intelligence suggested there were no more than twenty to thirty enemy fighters inside the fort at that time. It was midwinter, so the number of new arrivals would naturally be down.

Colonel Magowan planned the operation from deep within the Desert of Death. The plan was an excellent one. He didn't just want the fort – he wanted to dispatch as many Taliban as possible along with it. Magowan's Fragos – Fragmented Orders: the fragments of the operation that the pilots needed – were read eagerly by Nick, FOG, Charlotte and Tony.

The scheme of manoeuvre was simple: first, the place would be pummelled relentlessly with a massive bombardment from fast air and artillery. It would begin at midnight and last for four hours. An incredible total of 100,000 lb of bombs dropped by B1s would test the Taliban's resolve. If they still wanted to stay around and defend it after that, the fort would be every bit as significant as the colonel thought.

Then, at 4am, he would launch a ground assault, move into the fort, and effectively plant an ISAF flag on its ramparts – a red flag to the Taliban's raging bull. They would counter-attack with all available manpower – probably with their trademark encirclement manoeuvre. Zulu Company would then withdraw swiftly just before dawn – leaving the Taliban fully exposed. Magowan's *pièce de résistance* would be to send in the Apaches to pick them off and identify any hidden bunkers they attempted to escape into, so fast air could close them down – for ever.

Instead of the SBS, the assault would be done by the 120 Royal Marines of Zulu Company, 45 Commando, with supporting fire from 105-mm light-guns and the Scimitar armoured vehicles of C Squadron, the Light Dragoons.

3 Flight got the specifics for their part in the mission from the Detailed Tasks and Timings section of the Fragos. They were to be on station at 0330 hours local. The bombardment would cease and they would be cleared into the target. Their initial mission was to

destroy any Taliban seen on or attempting to escape the fort complex. Their 'Be Prepared To' task: to provide close-in fire support for Zulu Company as they moved into the fort. 3 Flight's final mission: to destroy any remaining Taliban when Zulu Company withdrew back across the river. They were then to return to Bastion, rearm, refuel and be prepared to redeploy to the fort to cover the troops as they pulled back into the desert. The Annexes to the Fragos contained the usual aerial photographs and sketches of the fort, along with a list of enemy vehicles known to operate from it.

'It looks like someone's done their homework for this one,' Nick said approvingly.

There were no call-outs for the IRT / HRF on Sunday, the day before Glacier 2 was launched. It gave me a chance to catch up on a mountain of paperwork – as mind-numbingly boring as I always found it. Time not fighting was time wasted in my book. But the Boss had encouraged me to write a paper for a new type of thermobaric Hellfire that I was after, and I'd finally made a start on it. If Monday was quiet, too, I just might be able to finish the bloody thing.

On Sunday night, the Boss had gone over to Kandahar for a meeting with the regiment's new Commanding Officer. Geordie backfilled his place on HQ Flight, as he often did. The four of us woke up as usual at 6.45am on a chilly but crystal clear Monday morning. We were in the special IRT / HRF tent, fifty metres from the Ops tent. I'd had my shower and shave, and was sitting on my cot bed doing up my boot laces and ribbing Geordie about missing his hairdresser's car when the insecure Motorola radio crackled into action. It was 7.05am.

'Superman – Batcave – Roadrunner.'

It was Comic Heroes theme week for the radio codenames.

Superman was code for the IRT, Batcave meant the Joint Helicopter Force Ops Room, and Roadrunner meant as fast as your legs can carry you. Carl and I were the IRT that day. I grabbed at the radio.

'Superman to the Batcave: Roadrunner.'

In twenty seconds, we were up and over the Hesco Bastion wall on our homemade ladder and into the Ops Room. The watchkeeper was waiting for us.

'It's a Casevac, guys. A single Apache to protect a CH47 down to Garmsir.'

The drill was well practised by now. Without another word, Carl ran straight out and jumped into the Land Rover. His job as the pilot was to get down to the flight line and flash up the aircraft immediately. I snatched my Black Brain from the secure locker, and with Billy now at my side, I ran onto the Joint Operations Cell tent next door to get a better idea of what was going on.

'It's a busy morning.' The 42 Commando 2i/c looked stressed. 'The yanks have had a serious RTA in Nimruz province. They rolled a vehicle and have got two T1s and two T2s. It's a benign area so we're sending two Chinooks out to them; there's only one left here now. It's the stand-in Casevac and it's going to Jugroom Fort; that's the one you're responsible for.'

He gave me a grid for the Chinook's landing site.

'How many casualties?'

'Five.'

That wasn't good. They shouldn't be taking casualties more than three hours after the ground assault was supposed to have gone in.

'All gunshot wounds,' he added. 'Don't know what state they're in yet.'

'Why aren't the two Apaches down there going to protect the CH47?'

'They're busy fighting.'

Billy and I gave each other a knowing glance – here we go again. The Taliban weren't giving up Jugroom Fort without a proper ding dong. Things were obviously not looking too good, but whatever the problem was, I didn't need to know about it. We just needed to get that Chinook down there sharpish.

I ran the final 500 metres to the flight line. The air chilled my lungs as I mounted the berms and ran up out of the ditches. Carl had already got the Auxiliary Power Unit running but the Chinook 100 metres to our left was empty. The RAF guys only need five minutes to flash up a Chinook. As soon as I slammed my cockpit door shut, Carl threw forward the engine power levers and our rotors began to turn. A minute later, he radioed into the Ops Room.

'Ugly Five One, ready.'

We waited for the Chinook – then it dawned on us: the IRT / HRF pair had just left. This one was not due out for two hours, so the crews would have been sleeping during the shout. Another busy day for the RAF. Just as the Chinook started to turn and burn, the second surprise of the day arrived. 'Ugly Five One, this is Ops, hold. The CH47 will go down alone. Wait out for more information.'

Now what was this about?

'Look who's coming,' Carl said. Billy and Geordie ran across the flight line towards the Apache alongside us as the Chinook lifted and thundered over their heads.

'Ugly Five One, this is Ops. You will be joined by Ugly Five Zero. You are now going to RIP with Five Two and Five Three down in Garmsir. RIP time is 0820 hours.'

'Ugly Five One copied.'

'Ugly Five Two will brief you en route. Out.' We'd be lucky if we could make that.

So we're going to do a Relief in Place with 3 Flight. We rarely did unplanned RIPs on deliberate attacks. There just weren't the spare aircraft or crews. It meant only one thing – life was under immediate threat down there, and would continue to be for the foreseeable. Things had obviously gone badly wrong.

Billy and Geordie flashed up in record quick time, 'Ugly Five Zero Flight Airborne at 08:01 hours.'

'Ops, good luck.'

A minute into the flight, Billy came through on the Apache FM radio net. 'Ed, I've got a problem mate. Both our VU radios are tits. Crypto has dropped out; we have no secure voice.'

'Bloody typical,' Carl said.

'Copied Billy. What do you want to do?'

Carl was right. This was a certifiable pain in the arse. Billy was down as mission commander for the day, as he'd planned to requalify Geordie on his flying skills if we were called out. Losing his VU radios meant he was off both the mission net for the operation and the Helmand-wide air net. The only people he could speak to securely over his two remaining FM radios now were the other Apache crews and our Ops Room – that meant nobody on the ground down at Jugroom, and not even the JTAC, so he'd have no way of following the battle. Normally we'd have gone back and Billy and Geordie would have jumped in the spare. There was only one answer when the clock was ticking for an urgent RIP like this, and we all knew it.

'Screw it, let's press on. Nick is already well short of gas.'

The mission commander was now flying deaf.

'You better take tactical lead, Ed.'

'Okay. My lead. Carl will relay.'

'Copied. Thanks.'

I was now the point man with the outside world, while Carl listened in on the mission net and repeated everything to Billy and Geordie on the FM channel. Billy had to maintain command of the mission though, as he'd had a more comprehensive briefing on the battle. In our Apache I had mission lead but Carl was still the aircraft captain; we hadn't had time to change our paperwork earlier that morning.

Billy sent an encrypted burst transmission. 'Check data, Ed.'

With the push of a button Jugroom's coordinates joined the tactical situational display on my MPD's black map – the fort's four corners were outlined alongside the firebase overlooking it on the western side of the river, six klicks east of our artillery's gun line in the desert.

'Good Data.'

The TADS was cool now so I readied it for the mission. The focus had jammed close up on me, making it utterly useless. The FLIR was shagged but at least the day TV camera was working. It was like opening a bag of tools to find you had a pair of pliers but no adjustable spanner. I could still do my job but it was going to be that much harder.

I broke the news to the rest of the flight, which was greeted by more groans from Carl. Billy would have to sort out all the thermal imagery we needed. This was getting complicated, even for seasoned multi-taskers.

We were cruising at 138 mph at an altitude of 5,000 feet, heading on the most direct line south over the GAFA, with Billy and Geordie about half a mile back to our left. It was a sixty-two-mile flight directly into the low and blinding winter sun. Even my visor couldn't save me from having to squint.

Fifteen minutes into the flight, the casevac Chinook shot right

LEFT: Ammo Sgt Kev Blundell paying his respects on Christmas Day.

BELOW: A DShK hit on Darwin's Apache.

ABOVE: A message for the Taliban at Koshtay from arming point 2.

RIGHT: Ed and Carl's Hellfire page with Billy and Trigger in the background flying home after the Koshtay deep raid.

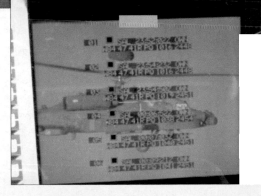

MAIN PICTURE: An Afghan National Policeman overlooking the Lashkar Gah Green Zone.

ABOVE: Rockets fired in quads.

Hellfire fired by Ugly Five One and guided by Ugly Five Zero at Jugroom Fort. CLOCKWISE FROM RIGHT: Missile 4m away, the missile impacting, the energy explodes at 5 million PSI, blowing the roof off, blowing the back wall off, clearing out all the Taliban and totally engulfing the entire building.

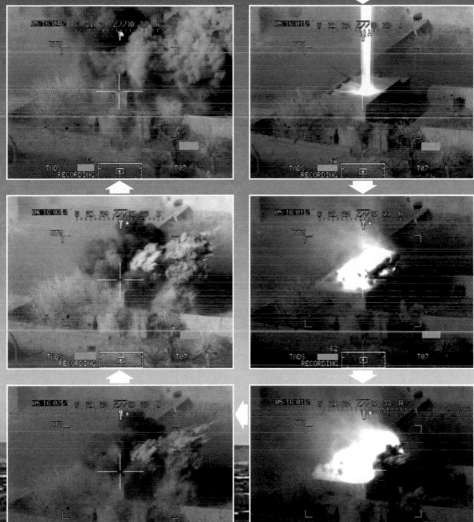

ABOVE LEFT: The rescue team for Jugroom Fort.

LEFT: The rescue briefing in the desert.

BELOW LEFT: Lt Col Rob Magowan MBE RM – the loneliness of command.

MAIN PICTURE: Mountains that surround Now Zad and the Green Zone, providing cover for the DShK gunner to shoot the helicopters.

TOP: On the wings of the Apache ready to go.

ABOVE: Ugly Five One with Capt Dave Rigg (left) and Mne Chris Fraser-Perry riding to the Fort.

RIGHT: Ugly Five Zero with RSM Hearn, filmed by Ugly Five One.

TOP LEFT: A true account of the rescue by the military artist David Rowlands. Ed Macy (with pistol) in front of Mathew Ford.

ABOVE LEFT AND LEFT: The Jugroom Fort before and after January 15th.

LEFT: 3 Flight (left to right) – Charlotte, Darwin and Nick where the marines strapped onto the Apache during the Jugroom Fort rescue, and FOG.

BELOW: Investiture ceremony at Buckingham Palace (left to right) – Nick (DFC), Geordie (MC), Dave Rigg (MC), Ed (MC) and Billy (DFC).

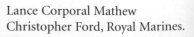

Lance Corporal Mathew Christopher Ford, Royal Marines.

under us on the way back to Bastion. It was a mighty quick turn around and they were bombing it, flying low and straight – route one. It meant the casualties were in a bad way. We'd heard over the net that they'd then be loaded up to the gunnels with ammunition for the 105-mm guns which needed an emergency replen.

At fifteen miles to go, I checked in with the JTAC. 'Widow Seven One, this is Ugly Five One, how do you read?'

'Widow Seven One, Lima Charlie.'

'Ugly Five One are two Apaches, Ugly Five One and Ugly Five Zero. We have 600 rounds of thirty Mike Mike, forty-eight rockets and eight Hellfire missiles. We have the usual amount of playtime.'

'Widow Seven One copies your last. You'll need to route west around the gun line as they're firing onto the target.'

'Is there any way we stop the guns and route direct?' A big loop into the desert to go behind the guns would lose us a few minutes and we'd miss the RIP time.

The reply was firm and impatient. 'NEGATIVE. We have a situation here. Wait out.'

The JTAC was obviously having a bad day; we didn't want to compound it. We didn't subscribe to the 'large sky, small round theory' and didn't fancy testing our armour plating with a 105-calibre shell. We would comply. Then everything changed.

'Ugly Five One, this is Widow Seven One. No longer five casualties. Now four casualties and one MIA.'

I felt the rush of adrenalin and the all too familiar taste of metal flooded into my mouth. It was preparing me for fear.

'All other troops have withdrawn, but the MIA is still on the objective. Repeat, the MIA is STILL on the objective.'

My mind flashed back to Sangin in June – our search across the fields for the two SBS lads. Looking down onto the desert floor I pictured what I had seen that day and remembered what the Taliban had done to them. Acid leaked into the hollow space in my lower abdomen. I could have put it down to missing breakfast, but I knew myself too well. Christ, not again.

Carl was on the ball immediately. He relayed the news to Billy and Geordie and shoved his cyclic forward. The aircraft's nose dipped and the rotors growled as we accelerated to full speed.

'Fucking hell,' Billy said. 'What the hell is going on down there?'

I tried to think it through. How the hell had they lost someone at the fort, and then all withdrawn without him? The Taliban were clearly still holding the place. Now they might have one of our guys, too.

There was a silence as the four of us shared the same thought. The memory of Sangin wasn't the only thing disturbing me. There was also the fresh intelligence about the bastards' plan for a TV skinning.

Geordie broke it. 'Check Data.'

A text from Billy was waiting for us. It read *MIA ... NOT ON OUR WATCH*.

I radioed in our reply. 'Good Data. Affirm.'

Widow Seven One checked back in. 'Ugly Five One, be aware Ugly Five Two Flight are chicken. They've only got enough fuel left for a direct flight back to base. They're going off station now. We need you on station immediately to help locate the MIA. Send ETA.'

The bright green number in my monocle dropped from 11 to 10.

'Ugly will be with you in ten minutes.'

'We had to bug out without being able to look for him ...' Nick's voice sounded tired and despondent. 'We're both completely out of gas and low on ammo too. We've been fighting solidly for an hour and a half. Stand by ...'

Nick checked out with the JTAC before continuing.

'We were held over the desert to the south-west for the initial bombardment then cleared in to look for leakers as Zulu Company prepared to cross the river. We saw a few Taliban, dispatched them with cannon. The place was devastated, apart from the north-east watchtower and main building. Five Three took out the watchtower and we both destroyed the building, all with Hellfire. We continued to observe but nothing moved. The place looked like Monte Casino.

'It all started to go wrong just before H-hour. Zulu Company weren't ready to move. The ground assault was put back so we went back to rearm and refuel. When we returned they still weren't ready. They didn't end up going in until just before 0700. The lost time must have given the Taliban a chance to reinfiltrate. We don't know how they got back in.'

The marines' twelve-strong column of Viking tracked armoured vehicles had crossed the river at an especially shallow point but dawn was already breaking. Their vehicles stopped in a line adjacent to the point one of the 2,000-lb bombs had blown a gaping hole in the fort's southern outer wall.

The marines had debussed into the poppy field and pepper potted forward towards the wall. As soon as they got there, five of them were hit by a volley of machine-gun fire. A hail of small arms and RPG fire cascaded down the canal and from the village to the west. It was mayhem.

'We covered them as much as we could with Hellfire and cannon, but it wasn't enough. With five serious casualties they were in a whole world of pain, and had no chance of continuing the attack. It was now light and the Taliban had already begun to encircle them. The order was given to withdraw. We put down everything we could to protect them on the way out. I used all my cannon rounds …

'The first we knew of the MIA was a few minutes ago, after we pulled off target. He was one of the casualties. We've no idea where he is or how it happened.'

'That's all copied. Thanks, Nick.'

'Ford – that's the MIA's name. Lance Corporal Mathew Ford. Good luck guys. I'm sorry.'

He had nothing to apologise for. Getting the marines out of that hornets' nest without any more casualties was a miracle in itself. Tony and FOG would have been flying harder than ever to keep up with the thrust of Nick and Charlotte's offensive.

Colonel Magowan now faced every commander's worst nightmare. There was no point in the marines going back in without knowing where Lance Corporal Ford was. With the weight of fire from the fort and the surrounding villages, it would have been suicide. The marines were still firing from the ridge in a desperate attempt to suppress the enemy. It was all they could do for Ford until they knew where he was.

FINDING MATHEW FORD

We rounded the gun line as all three 105s sparked up together. A series of concentric pressure rings surged out of each barrel across the desert floor, then disappeared in a cloud of grey smoke. Inside our air-conditioned chariot, I didn't hear a whisper.

Carl threw the aircraft into a hard left turn, and then righted her again a second later. The Power Meter Indicator flashed up in my monocle as we pulled G. The torque was up so high we were within 10 per cent of blowing up the engines. Carl kept milking them for everything he could get. We were going balls out now. If the Taliban hadn't got Ford, every second counted. At times like this, Carl was the man to fly with.

'Eight klicks to run. On target in two and a half minutes.'

'Thanks Carl. Keep south and east of the fort. The guns are firing onto the village west of it.'

Plumes of dark smoke were now clearly visible on the horizon directly in front of us. It was time to go to work. I pressed TADS on the 'Sight Select' switch on my right ORT handgrip, and the camera inside the nose turret jumped into life. I hit the 'Slave' button; the Apache knew where Jugroom was. As quick as a flash, a black and white image filled the MPD: smoke spewing from the fort. The river ran north–south in the distance. A hodgepodge of bushes, trees, walls and buildings was shrouded in a billowing cloud of dust. Every few seconds, a shell or heavy-calibre tracer round exploded with a tiny flash of light and a fresh puff of smoke.

The Taliban would try to get Ford into a building and obscure him from our optics as soon as they could. But searching for something outside, in a Green Zone battle, was already a nightmare from this distance.

'Ugly Five One is ready for a talk on. Where exactly was the MIA last seen?'

The JTAC was quick. 'There is a major bend in the river, with a tributary to the east and a canal running north off it …'

I zoomed in closer.

'Copied. Confirm it's the one running into the smoke?'

'Affirm. There's a track on the eastern side of the canal running north. It is then bordered by a canal on the west and a wall on the east. That wall is the beginning of the fort. Copied?'

'Copied. Visual with the wall.' The adobe and stone battlement glowed in the low sun.

'The furthest our friendly callsigns got was about a hundred metres along that track. Stand by for a grid.'

Grid 41 R PQ 1142 3752 Altitude 2257 feet. I punched the info into the system as he gave it to me then slaved the TV camera to it. The screen showed the fort's south-west corner, next to the towpath.

I looked for a unique feature to confirm I had the correct starting point for the search; I still needed to be 100 per cent sure. 'Ugly Five One is visual with a wall at the grid. About fifty metres east, away from the canal, is a bomb crater where it has been demolished.

252

Confirm I am looking at the correct wall?'

'Affirm. That was their limit of exploitation. We believe they were in the vicinity of that crater when they got contacted.'

'Copied. We're searching now.'

Carl relayed to Geordie. We were closing fast now, so I zoomed out as wide as I could on the TADS to get a better overall picture. We were almost at the edge of the desert. The marines' firebase sat on top of a berm, beyond which the ground plummeted to the river. Dozens of commandos were in position, in WMIKs, Vikings or on their belt buckles, all of them desperate to do their bit to get their mate back. Light Dragoons' Scimitars were lined up alongside them.

As we passed over their heads, Carl pulled back hard on the cyclic, virtually standing the aircraft on its tail and catapulting me hard into my straps. He needed to go from 161 mph to nothing on a sixpence; if he didn't we'd overshoot the fort by a mile in a matter of seconds. He banked gently to the left as Billy and Geordie banked right and we began a lazy three-quarter wheel circuit. A white object flew a few hundred feet over the fort and across my TADS screen. We weren't the only people watching.

'Keep our height up Carl; there's a UAV flying around low-level, buddy.'

'I see it. Don't worry; you won't get me low-level over that place.'

Billy and I broke up the ground we needed to search.

'Let's start at the last known sighting. Mate, can you take everywhere north of the wall? Carl and I will take the southern side in case he's crawled down to the river.'

'Affirm,' Billy said. 'We're on it.'

The radios were going ape-shit now. Even though it had only just been announced, Ford had been officially MIA for thirty minutes and word had spread. Every man and his dog were asking what was going on. Widow Eight Three, a second JTAC working with the gunners, was asking for sitreps to better his targeting. Then there was Nick's voice calling urgently for more fuel and ammunition on the FM.

I could make out at least three different levels of command on the mission net, including Zulu Company's OC, Colonel Magowan, and the brigade HQ in Lashkar Gah. It was a given that the CO of 45 Commando would be listening in, and Trigger, who should now be back at Bastion.

A Predator UAV and a Nimrod MR2 circled somewhere way above us. Their downlinks were being pumped into every HQ, fuelling the frenzy. Every rubberneck within reach would be crowded around the feed screens. With an MIA, everyone wants in. Over a hundred minutes had passed since the initial contact; they'd be hanging on every word.

Yup, the mission now bore all the hallmarks of a classic cluster-fuck. The cascade of voices in my ears made it almost impossible to concentrate. They all had a job to do, but I wished they'd all shut up.

I focused the TADS on the corner wall. The image gleamed in the bright sunshine. I moved the camera slowly down the towpath south; in the direction which Mathew Ford would have aimed to withdraw. Carl saw where my TADS was headed in his monocle and tracked east towards the crater.

Twenty seconds later: 'Ed, I've got an unusual shape. It's about forty metres along the wall, on the southern side.'

'Okay, stand by.'

I shifted the TADS onto Carl's line of sight. A large, S-shaped blob lay sprawled on a raised bank about ten metres shy of the crater, two feet away from the wall – exactly where the JTAC said the marines had been contacted.

It looked like a body, lying on its side. I felt a surge of excitement – then got a grip on myself. This wasn't the time or the place for an outburst of wishful thinking.

Carl continued the wheel turn, bringing us perpendicular to the blob. I swept the surrounding area. There were no more bodies; this one was on its own.

I flicked the TADS's Field of View button on the left ORT grip with my thumb and magnified the picture nearly five times. It filled a third of the screen. It was definitely a human body. But was it one of theirs, or one of ours? Let it be him. *Please let it be him …*

'Good spot, Carl. We have a body. Drop us down to 2,000 feet, mate.'

'That puts us in RPG range of the fort, Ed …'

'We can take it. Just twenty seconds at 2,000; that's all I need.'

'You'll have to make it fifteen. Then I'm going to have break right because of the artillery.'

We dropped and I studied the body throughout Carl's 180-degree turn to the north-west. It was lying on its left side, thighs up at ninety degrees to the torso, feet slightly apart, arms outstretched. It was a natural position to lie in, not contorted, and that was a good sign. The chest looked bulky, another good sign … Osprey body armour and an SA80 rifle? Looked like it. I waited for a better view as we turned. *Shit* – the camera couldn't pick it up in the shadow. It was only 8.44am and the sun was still low.

'Five seconds left, Ed.'

Now square-on to the body, I flicked the TADS into the largest zoom. Final confirmation: trousers and jacket were a similar shade to the ground, and patterned exactly like mine – British DPM.

'Breaking off, Ed. Sorry. We've got to turn out of the guns.'

'No problem, Carl. It's him. We've got the MIA.'

We'd found our man. But was he still alive? The moment I announced we'd found him the whole world would want to know.

We came round again, higher. I couldn't detect any dark patches on his clothing; so, no heavy blood loss – as far as we could see. His helmet was on, fastened tight and without deformation. His face was intact, eyes closed and mouth just slightly open. I felt a rush of relief. He looked peaceful; as if he was sleeping. No obvious signs of wounding. Had he collapsed through exhaustion? The marines carried an awesome amount of kit into battle these days.

'Let Billy and Geordie know, buddy. Ask Billy to use his FLIR for a heat source.'

That would give us a good indication of whether our guy was still alive. It was just five degrees celsius outside, cold enough to chill a dead body in half an hour.

'Will do.'

At least the Taliban hadn't got him. Establishing that was our number one priority. The entire brigade's actions for the next week depended on it. If he was alive, he was unconscious. But why? If he'd been bounced off the wall he could be concussed for ages. I didn't want him to be unconscious. I wanted him to give us a little wave to tell us that he was pretending to be dead so the Taliban didn't come for him.

A giant fountain of soil and dirt erupted on the other side of the canal, 100 metres away from the man we now knew to be Mathew Ford. He was Danger Close to the gunners' nearest shells …

Being on the raised bank wasn't so good. It put him in clear line of sight of the enemy in the western village. It was surely only a matter of time before they saw him, artillery barrage or not.

He couldn't be bluffing the Taliban, could he? Surely he would have done that from the relative safety of the ditch. He must have been concussed …

'As soon as you can, Carl, I need both of our eyes back on Mathew, in case any of those scumbags make a run for him. I'll tell the chain of command.'

Carl threw the Apache over his right shoulder and rolled her out 180 degrees, giving us both eyes on again. I gave Widow Seven One the news, and heard it echo repeatedly down all the commands. They were desperate to plan their next move.

'Ugly Five One this is Widow Seven One. Is he alive?'

I'd already told him we didn't know, and repeated it.

'Ugly Five One, please confirm if he's dead or alive.'

Billy had looked through his FLIR. 'He's got a heat source mate. A strong one. His extremities are still hot too. His hands are almost the same temperature as the rest of his body.'

It was the strongest sign of life we could get without actually seeing him move.

'Ugly Five One can confirm he is warm but has not moved. There are no obvious signs of death; assumption is, he's alive.'

An immediate response from a new callsign: 'Ugly Five One, this is Wizard.'

Wizard? It was the Nimrod MR2, 20,000 feet above us. They only ever relayed messages from way up the food chain. That morning, it was the brigadier.

'Ugly Five One, Sunray says do not let anyone get anywhere near the MIA. Ground troops will re-cross the river and recover Lance Corporal Ford ASAP.'

The brigadier had given the order. The rescue was on.

The big question now was would the marines get to him before the Taliban?

I kept my eyes glued to Mathew whilst Carl described the ground to me. Somehow the western village was still filling up with enemy. It was still almost entirely intact; the night's bombardment hadn't touched it. Though the artillery shells had left scorch marks on the walls, they hadn't brought the buildings down. We'd spotted tracer and muzzle flashes from most of the huts, as the Taliban engaged the marines' firebase on the berm. Whenever we got too close, they gave us a burst too – and a couple of RPGs for good measure.

The river still only had one crossing point. There was only one way the marines would get to Mathew, and that was right past the village. There was no two ways about it – they'd get another horrible smacking, if they got through at all.

Billy was the first to frame the thought. 'Ed, we've got to take on that village. The marines are screwed unless someone flattens it before they get there.'

'Not to mention what the wankers in there could do to Ford,' Geordie chimed in.

I told the JTAC and asked for permission to engage.

He didn't fuck about. 'Ugly Five One this is Widow Seven One. You're cleared hot onto the village. Destroy the position in preparation for the rescue.'

'Copied. The buildings have multiple rooms and look pretty strong. Hellfire may not be best suited. Request fast air to assist ASAP.'

'I have called for close air support. Do what you can in the meantime. But do not, I repeat, do NOT let anyone get near the MIA.'

We divided up the workload between the two Apaches. We needed to keep one aircraft pointing at the fort at all times so the

Taliban knew we'd shoot them if they went for Ford. Carl and I watched Mathew from a half-moon-shaped orbit in the east while Billy let rip on the village. Then we swapped roles. As I slaved my crosshairs up and down the fort wall, Geordie and Billy began their first run from the south-east at 9.03am.

'Engaging with thirty Mike Mike.'

I glanced up from my TADS to see his cannon rounds tearing into the first of the fifteen huts and buildings, spitting great lumps of earth and rock out of the walls and igniting the straw roof. Billy got off four good twenty-round bursts before Geordie had to break off. Every ten seconds, another three 105-mm shells pounded down on the village too. Two long, barn-like buildings had good arcs of fire up the towpath and onto Mathew. On his second and third attack runs, he planted Hellfires and raked them with 30-mm, collapsing their stone roofs on the fighters inside.

We swapped over. I could still see a series of holes dug into the eastern wall of one of the barns at ground level – little holes a few inches wide, enough to poke a muzzle through. My bet was that the Taliban snipers had covered themselves with mattresses, to protect themselves from our frag. I smacked a Hellfire into the wall and took it down. My adrenalin was up. With my second, I dropped the roof of a smaller building with three sniping ports, ten metres further north. The mattresses wouldn't get in the way of those puppies, that was for sure. Widow Seven One piped up as we swapped roles again.

'Ugly, we are taking heavy incoming fire across here at the firebase. Every time you turn away from the village it's RPG Central out of there.'

We must have killed a fair few by now, but our pummelling hadn't distracted the bastards at all. There had to be dozens of them down there, but we'd seen no movement between buildings since we'd begun our onslaught. How the hell were they all getting in? Billy broke in as Carl began our third run.

'Stand by, stand by; he has moved.'

'Say again Billy?'

'Mathew Ford has moved. I say again, he HAS moved.'

'Stand by. Break off, Carl.' I shuffled my backside in the seat to get more comfortable. My pulse started to race. Carl turned sharply right back into the fort and I slewed my TADS back onto Mathew. His feet and hands were still in the same position. He looked no different to me.

'Are you sure, Billy?'

'One hundred per cent. He has moved. He's alive.'

If Billy was sure he'd seen him move, that was good enough for me. I told the JTAC. This was big news, and it upped the ante considerably. Another tidal wave of chatter burst over the net. Now the marines knew they had a life to save.

But Billy had been thinking.

'Ed, I've got an idea. Ford needs to be moved *now*. He's alive, but clearly badly injured. He could be dying right now.'

'Affirm.'

'Well, we could pick him up ...'

'Say again?'

'We could rescue him. You stay up, we'll go down. One of us gets out and straps him to the side of the aircraft. You know, like our downed aircraft emergency drill.'

'Stand by.'

If he'd moved he was probably badly hurt, because he wasn't moving a muscle now. Or he was unconscious. Either way, he needed help fast. I thought it through. It was ludicrous; we had no

FLIR and they had no access to the mission net. More importantly still, I'd picked up unconscious bodies before. There was no way one person could shift Mathew to the Apache and strap him on alone. I consulted Carl and he agreed.

'I know what you're saying Billy. But we've got a U / S FLIR and you wouldn't be able to lift him on your own.'

Billy paused. 'Okay, I'll speak to the Boss.'

He called Trigger on the secure FM net. He'd made a beeline for Camp Bastion's Joint Operations Cell on his return from Kandahar, to follow the battle and sort out a contingency plan.

'Negative,' was Trigger's response.

'But he's still hot and we think he's just unconscious. We can get him back.'

'NEGATIVE,' Trigger said, more firmly still.

Billy wasn't giving up that easily. There had been no word on exactly when the marines we're going to cross. He was convinced it was Mathew Ford's best chance. Thirty seconds later, he came back on to me.

'Let's do it together, Ed.'

'What?'

'Let's both go down there; then two of us can get out and carry him.'

It was still totally impractical. We'd get cut to pieces if we both went. Every time we turned tail they'd volley-fired RPGs at us.

'Look Billy, Zulu Company are going to recover him. We have no top cover and the whole place is filling up with Taliban. Sure we'd get in, but we couldn't get out of there without a massively well-coordinated fire plan and shit-loads of top cover.'

Billy fell silent.

'Okay, I've got a better plan. Let's go and collect two marines each and fly them into the fort to collect the casualty. It'll be much quicker. You coord the fire plan and 3 Flight can give us top cover.'

'Stand by.'

I looked at Mathew Ford's body. Strapping someone to the side of the aircraft was an emergency drill only ever to be used to rescue downed Apache aircrew. We'd rehearsed it as part of our escape and evasion training, but only on the ground and never with engines on or the rotors actually turning. That contravened MoD health and safety guidelines. In sixteen years of Apache operations, the Americans had never lifted any ground troops on the wings.

However, it was theoretically possible. We were all carrying our emergency straps as routine equipment, and the grab bars were right there behind the canopy. The only other aircraft we had available were the Chinooks, and they'd just set off back to Bastion, low on fuel, after dropping more ammo at the gun line. Besides, a great big flying cow like that would get shot to shit down there. Unlike the Apache it wasn't designed to take rounds …

We were the only airborne option. It *was* possible. Maybe it could work …

Billy had the bit between his teeth now. I'd seen him like that before. He was like a bulldozer; nothing got in his way. But this needed serious cool. If it went wrong, we'd lose a whole load more men, and gift the Taliban eighty million quid's worth of Apaches. It would be enough to make those boys believe in Father Christmas. And it could lose us the whole bloody campaign.

I tried not to let on to Billy that I was coming round to his idea. The truth is, I was. When Billy was this confident, his track record was 100 per cent spot on.

'Listen Billy, we could only do it if Nick and Charlotte came back to give us top cover …'

That was all he needed. He was straight back onto the Boss.

'Listen, sir, the ground troops are nowhere near ready to cross. I want to get two men on each aircraft and fly them into the fort to recover the casualty. Ed thinks we can do it too …'

Bollocks.

'Can you send 3 Flight down to assist?'

'Billy, listen to me,' Trigger said. 'We've been on the phone to Lashkar Gah and they have said it will be a ground rescue.'

'Okay, sir. If I land, just confirm I will be disobeying a direct order.'

'Affirmative. You will be. You can't land both aircraft, you have no top cover.'

There was an uneasy five-second silence.

Then the Boss came back on. 'I am launching 3 Flight to come and assist you.'

He paused, to allow the message to sink in.

'Don't do anything until the other aircraft arrive. I have no situational awareness and you have the bigger picture. If you think it will work, you'll need permission from the ground commander.'

'Copied, sir. Thank you.'

Billy didn't need to prompt me. I was straight onto Widow Seven One. He was working out of Magowan's HQ, and would only have been a few feet away from him.

The JTAC's response was swift and uncompromising. 'Negative. That request is denied, Ugly Five One. Zulu Company is going to rescue him.' He added, 'We don't want cowboy missions,' in case we hadn't got the message.

Carl began to relay it to Billy and Geordie but I stopped him halfway through.

'Don't tell Billy the "cowboy missions" bit. He'll flip.'

Carl wasn't going to. Billy was angry enough anyway.

'Right, well, if the marines are going to do it, they'd better fucking well get on with it. They're running out of time. This place is filling up like Wembley on Cup Final day. I hope they realise that.'

We were all pissed off. With Nick and Charlotte dealing death and destruction from above us, coupled with a good arse-kicking fire plan, we'd convinced ourselves we could do it. Neither of us had taken our sights off Mathew, but we'd left the village alone for five minutes while the debate had raged. Billy and Geordie began another run in to attack with a Hellfire while Carl and I stayed where we were.

I looked briefly out of the canopy window to see it explode with pinpoint precision. Something caught my attention by the river bank directly south of the fort. Movement? It couldn't be; the Taliban would have had to cross the canal to get there from the village. Nobody had come out of the fort; we were sure of that. Ditto the trees to the east.

'Did you see something by the river, Carl?'

'No.'

Maybe I'd imagined it. Better just double-check. Nothing.

'Do us a favour, buddy, break off from Mathew for a sec and pull over to the east. But keep your eye on him.'

'Will do. I have Mathew.'

'Set a course so it looks as if we can't see the fort.'

I slewed my TADS down to the river as we banked right and rolled away. Anyone watching would think both Apaches were heading out. I picked up five black rings on the embankment, evenly spaced, ten metres apart, where I thought I'd seen the movement. I'd wondered what they were when we first arrived. I kept scanning the area. Nothing happened. Carl held the Apache so that the TADS was looking backwards.

'Just keep it on that line a few more seconds, Carl. Let's try and sucker them out.'

And bang, out popped a black-turbaned head from the second ring to the right, followed by a puff of smoke from behind him then a cloud of dust as he loosed off an RPG at the firebase. Quick as a flash, he disappeared again.

Tunnels. The black circles were part of a fucking tunnel system. Where did they lead to? Had the black turban been in there all along? We'd had no idea about them – nobody had. Maybe he'd shot the five marines from there …

My stomach turned to liquid. Zulu Company had been surrounded the second they drove in there. Black Turban would only have been fifty yards away from them when they got to the wall. And now he was only fifty yards away from Mathew.

GIVE ME FOUR VOLUNTEERS

'Billy, Taliban in the tunnels thirty-five metres south of Mathew. Engaging. Watch my strikes.'

As soon as Carl managed to flip us around enough, twenty of my cannon rounds went straight down Black Turban's hidey-hole. No wonder it was RPG Central at the firebase.

I put another burst of twenty down Black Turban's hole for good measure, and then another twenty to collapse each of the four other tunnel entrances. There was no way of knowing if any of the 120 rounds had hit anyone, but if we hammered them hard and fast enough, perhaps we could scare them away. At least they'd know we were onto them.

Billy continued to hammer the village with 30-mm HEDP rounds. Maybe there were tunnels under some of its buildings too. It would explain how they were infiltrating so fast.

Billy had used up more than half his Hellfires, so he switched to rockets and planted eight HEISAPs over a fifty-metre radius into the main cluster of buildings. Their charges were powerful enough to penetrate the walls, pelting the occupants with stone and debris, followed by a killer pressure wave. We switched over guard and attack roles.

'My gun. Firing.' Slaving the cannon to his right eye, Carl looked straight down at the back end of one of the buildings hit by Billy. 'I've got movement in the village.'

He was right; as his first rounds flashed and exploded on the stone, eight Taliban sprinted from the other end of the building. He gave them three more bursts of twenty before they reached cover.

'Good shooting, bonny lad,' was Geordie's verdict.

We were back on strike now, so I sent a Hellfire straight into the building that the lone escapee had just reached. They didn't like our rockets, so I slammed eight Flechettes – containing 656 five-inch-long Tungsten darts – into the village centre. The darts could penetrate armour, so they'd get through those walls. Flashes of bright orange light erupted on each side of the aircraft as we came in again.

'Long-range missile launch,' Bitching Betty announced. 'Six o'clock.' The flares continued to pour off. My neck cracked as I threw my head rapidly back and to the right. I could see Carl follow suit.

'Ugly Five One, missile launch six o'clock.' Carl's voice sounded laboured. He pulled as hard as he could on the cyclic to throw the Apache onto its back. 'Billy and Geordie are chucking flares too.'

We'd been locked on at exactly the same time, but no missiles had passed our windows. The two pilots compared notes.

'Geordie, we've just had a long-range missile launch from the south-east. Confirm the direction on you.'

'South east. Long range too.'

'Where the bloody hell is it then?'

All four of us craned our heads round. There were no telltale smoke trails to give away the firing point.

'Maybe it was the sun. Our systems could be playing up.'

'On both aircraft? You're the Ewok, Carl.'

'Yeah, I know. That's bollocks. I don't like it.'

Did the Taliban have a SAM down there now? They'd certainly had enough time to ship one in. Apaches had been scrapping over the fort for six hours now. If it was a SAM, it must have misfired. There was definitely something down there, but God knew what. Widow Seven One had more bad news.

'Be advised Ugly Five One, Zulu Company will be a further thirty minutes. Keep suppressing for their assault.'

Billy was livid when Carl relayed. '*What?* For fuck's sake … How much time do they think they've got?'

It was now 9.48am, and we'd been on station for an hour and eleven minutes. We'd prepped the area for a rescue *now*, not in half-an-hour's time.

'We're not going to be able to do this for much longer you know, Ed. I'm down to one Hellfire, sixteen Flechettes and 120 thirty Mike Mike.'

'Copied. We're stuck between a rock and a hard place. If we slow down on ammo, we lose Mathew. If we continue at this rate and they're not ready, we lose Mathew when we run out of ammo. I've only one Hellfire, eight of each rocket type and 80 thirty Mike Mike,' I reported in return.

I got back onto the JTAC.

'Widow Seven One this is Ugly Five One. We're depleting our ammunition. We could really do with some fast air on the village.'

'Affirm Ugly Five One. Still no fast air on station. I've requested it three times. I'll request it again.'

We had to keep the pressure up. We swapped over again, and Billy launched his last Hellfire and eight more Flechettes into the village. Rather than swap again, Carl launched our last missile whilst I kept eyes on Mathew, and Billy gathered it with his laser and guided it down onto the roof of a building that posed a direct threat to him. We'd never done that before in combat. We'd never had to. A bolt of blindingly white light shot straight up into the air.

'An alleluia missile.' Billy sounded impressed.

Even though it now resembled an ancient ruin, battered by endless battles across the centuries, the JTAC reported outgoing fire from the village yet again. We were hammering them, but they kept on coming.

They couldn't possibly have been there all along. There wasn't a building that hadn't been dropped by five million-lb-per-square-inch of Hellfire, smashed to pieces by HEISAPs, torn apart by Flechettes or torched by the M230's High Explosive Dual Purpose cannon rounds.

The Taliban must have worked out the Mathew Ford situation by now. Why else would two Apaches be pummelling a shitty little village when there were no ground troops in sight? And why else would they have kept coming into our thunderous shower of lead, frag and fire? It was pretty obvious now: Zulu Company weren't ever going to get back in there without fatalities.

Geordie got a second missile lock. His Apache pumped off another eight flares. 'Long range, from the south-east again. No smoke trails. I'd love to know what the hell that is …'

We tried to ignore it. It was going to take more than a Taliban SAM to make us abandon Mathew. But whatever it was, flying around smack bang in the middle of the SAM belt was now getting spooky.

Carl and I ploughed sixty more cannon rounds into the one building left that could afford a firing solution onto Mathew. The main wall collapsed on the second burst and the rest followed suit. The village was burning and we still couldn't see any Taliban moving between buildings.

It wasn't just our ammunition that was running out. At 10.02am, Carl called 'Bingo'. Bingo meant we were running low on gas. It was a call for the squadron commander's ears – it was the last moment an RIP could be ordered and launched, because in thirty minutes' time we'd only have enough fuel left to get back to Bastion.

'Yeah, I'm Bingo too,' Geordie chimed in.

The Boss acknowledged.

Our own clock was ticking down too. That made Billy even more impatient. He told Geordie to loop over the firebase on their way round for an attack run on the village so he could take a peek at Zulu Company. Now Billy really did his nut.

'Ed, I can't believe it. They're still sitting on their Bergens. Their helmets are off and some of them are smoking. Nobody's even told them to mount up.'

'You're joking.'

'Nope. They look like they've been told to wait.'

'But the JTAC said they'd be assaulting in ten minutes.'

'Those lads are going nowhere.'

Billy's voice rose an octave. 'We're going to lose Ford, you know. He went down at what, 7am? That's three hours ago.'

'I know, mate.'

'He's just not going to …'

'WIDOW SEVEN ONE, THIS IS TUSK.'

Billy's voice was drowned out by a new voice on the air net. American, and professional.

'Widow Seven One, Tusk is now on station and ready for trade.'

An A10 Thunderbolt. Top news. A fast jet with serious strike power that could do the enemy some real damage. It could also protect Mathew; it packed a Gatling Gun. Carl relayed to Billy and Geordie. Then more good news, this time from the Boss.

'Ugly Five Zero and Ugly Five One, 3 Flight en route. They'll be with you in figures Two Zero minutes.'

Billy heard that one himself. That was it. Billy's waters broke.

'Right Ed, that's it. We've got our air cover coming, and Tusk can watch Mathew while we're gone. I want to rescue him with Royals on the wings, and I want to do it now. We *need* to do it now. Get on the net and make it happen.'

'Okay, stand by.'

I knew he was right. We had an A10 here, and Nick and FOG, with Charlotte and Tony, on their way. We had about twenty-five minutes of combat gas left, and the Taliban were getting stronger by the minute. The stars would never be better aligned for an Apache rescue attempt. We had one shot at this, and that shot was now. My blood was up too. Mathew was now kipping in the Last Chance Saloon.

'Take us over the firebase will you buddy?'

It was still a huge call, and I wanted to see Zulu Company with my own eyes.

'Will do,' said Carl, and began to bank. Billy was spot on. They were still sitting on their Bergens waiting for the order.

I only had one question left. 'Carl, can we really do this *and* get the aircraft back to Bastion?'

Carl made a swift calculation. 'Yes. Just.'

Right.

'Billy, affirm. I'll push the ground commander until he gives us a go. Stand by.'

I could see Billy and Geordie running in, rockets exploding just shy of a thousand metres from their aircraft and showering the area with darts.

I got back onto Widow Seven One and explained exactly what we wanted to do and why. 'Zulu Company are not ready. We are,' I finished. 'All we need you to do is sort out the fire plan from the artillery and fast air.'

'Stand by.'

There was a thirty-second pause.

'Ugly Five One, negative. Zulu Company are going to do the rescue.'

Wrong answer from the JTAC. Time to up the ante.

'Put Charlie Oscar on.'

'The CO?'

'Affirm. The CO.'

It was time to talk to the organ grinder, Colonel Magowan.

'Stand by.'

Another twenty-second pause.

'Charlie Oscar speaking.'

'Charlie Oscar, Ugly Five One. What is your immediate plan?'

'Zulu Company will cross the river to recover Lance Corporal Ford.'

'How long is it going to take them to get ready?'

He sighed loudly enough for me to hear. 'They say they'll be ready in ninety minutes.'

What? I must have misheard.

'Confirm, NINE ZERO minutes?'

'Yes, H-hour is at 1130 hours.'

There was obviously some sort of problem with Zulu Company. We didn't have time to go into it.

'Sir, we can be across and back in five minutes maximum, but need to move now.'

'How?'

He bloody knows how. This is wasting time.

'Give me four volunteers and we'll be in and out with Ford in two minutes.'

'But I don't have any pilots.'

Pilots? What was he on?

'No sir, *we* are the pilots. I just need four marine volunteers. They will be strapped onto the wings of the Apaches.'

'We don't have any straps.'

'*We* have the straps; we will strap them on ...'

It dawned on me that this was the first time Magowan had heard any of our plan. None of the messages had got back to him. I explained the whole thing as succinctly as I could.

'Give me two minutes to think.'

'Tell him we don't have two minutes, Ed,' Carl said quietly over our internal intercom. He was watching the fuel level and the delay was getting on his tits.

'We don't have two minutes, sir.'

'Give me twenty seconds then.'

Utter silence. For the first time all day, the mission radio net went quiet. Half of Helmand province was listening in now, and everybody was waiting for Magowan's answer. You could have heard a mouse fart. He only took ten.

'Ugly Five One, this is Charlie Oscar. Your plan is approved.'

'Roger. We will be with you in four minutes.'

Now we're really going to have to do this ...

'Billy and Geordie, it's a go.'

'Copied. You sort the fire plan with the JTAC and we'll lead you into the desert. You spoke to the CO so he'll be expecting you to brief the volunteers.'

'Okay, Billy. Just give me twenty more seconds on station.'

Widow Seven One was already briefing up the A10 on how to

protect Mathew. I stepped on their conversation because we didn't have a second to lose. I had some terminal controlling of my own I wanted to complete. If we were pulling off, I wanted Black Turban's warren nailed first.

'Break, break. This is Ugly Five One. Tusk, I've got a tunnel system I would like you to destroy.'

'Copy that. Go ahead Ugly Five One, I'm ready.'

'Tusk, from the fort's southern wall go south thirty-five metres to where the canal and the river join. Can you see five black circles?'

'Visual, sir.'

'That's the tunnel system I want destroying. Now, confirm that you can identify the MIA on the southern side of the wall, thirty-five metres away.'

'I have a good visual on the prone friendly just west of the crater, sir.'

'He is well within Danger Close but there is no ricochet risk, and the ground is soft. Are you sure you can make the shot without hitting the MIA?'

'I'm sure. I'll get it right on the nose sir, don't worry.'

'Copied. You're cleared hot on the tunnels.'

The A10 climbed up to 15,000 feet to set up his run, then dived. At 5,000 feet he opened up with a giant, six-second burst from his GAU-8 Gatling gun. The GAU-8 is the largest, heaviest and most powerful aircraft cannon ever built. The A10 is literally two wings, two engines and a cockpit bolted onto it. It fires 30-mm Depleted Uranium armour-piercing shells at a rate of 4,200 rounds per minute, or seventy per second. It is also highly accurate, with the ability to place 80 per cent of its shots within a ten-metre circle from 4,000 feet up. When the gun fired, you could hear its trademark roar and echo five miles away.

It didn't miss the tunnels, either. Some 420 DU shells spanked into the tunnel system in a double sweep up. The soil erupted in flame and dust. It looked like a mini earthquake, the ground doing a Mexican wave. The dust cloud around the tunnels began to clear as the A10 pulled up, throwing off precautionary flares. The DU rounds had exploded with such heat that the earth itself was burning. The rounds lodged up to fifteen metres deep, ploughing up everything in their path.

'That's a Delta Hotel, Tusk. Excellent shooting.'

'My pleasure "mate".' He put on a poor British accent. Tusk had a sense of humour, too.

The tunnels wouldn't have survived that, even if they were lined with concrete. Nobody was walking out of there for a while.

'Okay, Billy, let's go.'

The JTAC took over with an almighty artillery barrage on the village as we departed.

Colonel Magowan's Command Post was located in a wadi six kilometres into the desert, due west of the fort. Vikings, Pinzgauers and the UAV detachment's Scimitar were corralled alongside large canvas tents from which the signallers worked. Everybody else sat around portable desks. Loudspeakers broadcast the mission net traffic. Colonel Magowan put down the radio handset and asked for four volunteers.

His Ops Officer and his JTAC stepped forward immediately, but were indispensable where they were. Captain Dave Rigg, the battlegroup's Royal Engineers adviser, insisted on going. He'd been watching the Nimrod feed for the last ten hours, knew the exact location of Lance Corporal Ford and every inch of the fort.

The colonel called for the Landing Force Command Support Group's regimental sergeant major, WO1 Colin Hearn, the only

member of the command staff who hadn't heard his radio conver-
sation. Nineteen-year-old Zulu Company Marine Chris Fraser-Perry
and Magowan's twenty-six year-old signaller, Marine Gary Robinson,
were also selected.

When the RSM appeared, he was asked to get his weapon, body
armour and helmet, and told he was going on the side of an Apache to
retrieve Lance Corporal Ford. Colin Hearn chuckled to himself and
marched off to pick up his gear. He was well used to the CO's sense of
humour by now.

Magowan's CP was the nearest place we could land out of Taliban
mortar range, which was why it was there. The rolling desert sands
thundering by 1,000 feet beneath us made a pleasant change from
the intensity of battle at the fort.

Tusk may not have been able to hunt and kill the bad guys like
we could, but he could tip in and shoot straight any time. The
Desert Hawk UAV controlled by Magowan's HQ, Predator and
Nimrod were also watching Mathew like hawks. But I still didn't
like leaving Mathew Ford. I just hoped the Taliban didn't catch up
with him while we were away.

I looked at the clock: 10.16am. We'd been over Jugroom for the
last hour and forty-five minutes and every second of it had been
ferocious. I rubbed my eyes. I was starting to get an Apache head-
ache. I hadn't had one in six months.

Carl and Geordie were jabbering away, going over their fuel
states again and double-checking each other's HIDAS self-defence
systems. While they talked, I tried to rehearse my brief to the four
volunteers.

First, I was going to have to show them how to strap themselves
onto the aircraft. I reached involuntarily for the black karabiner

that clipped mine to the front of my survival jacket. Then I was going to have to tell them what to do if they get shot on the wing. What would *we* do if they got shot? Just press on. What if two of them got hit? Badly hit, and before we even reached Ford? We could cope with two.

What happened if we crash-landed on the way down there, or even in the river? What if they were blinded by the dust during the flight and couldn't see shit? What happened if they ran into the Taliban? Could we cover them from the ground? What if they got shot when they were on the ground – or if they turned around and saw their aircraft getting blown up behind them?

There were a million what ifs. I had the answers, but they weren't going to like them one little bit. A three-day planning conference to iron out all the potential mishaps would have been nice. I only had three minutes. Bollocks. I'd just have to wing it.

Carl reared up hard as we closed on Magowan's HQ. Our landing site 150 metres from the vehicles was marked with green smoke. Billy and Geordie came in first, turning 180 degrees to face into the wind and landing hard to limit the dust cloud. Carl put us down between them and the billowing smoke canister, fifty metres to our right.

As the dust cleared, I could make out two figures standing waiting for us, one in full battle rig and helmet, the other just in his shirt sleeves. Behind them were three more marines in full rig. I'd already unbuckled, reached for the door handle and was just about to disconnect my helmet when Carl stopped me dead.

'The mission is off.'

'What do you mean?'

'It's off, Ed. Nick has just been on; he was given a message from Trigger. The Boss couldn't reach us down here so he relayed it. It's been canned.'

'Who by?'

'Zero Alpha.'

Zero Alpha. Our Commanding Officer in Kandahar.

That was it then. It's was totally out of our hands. We couldn't counteract our own CO. We didn't even have comms with him. The regular babble between the marine units crackled away in the background as I sank back into my seat. What the hell had happened?

The disappointment welled up in me so vigorously I could almost taste it. We were out of the game. 3 Flight wouldn't have top cover, so that ruled them out, too. There was no way Zulu Company would make it over and back without more casualties; the Tardis village would make sure of that. It looked like the Last Chance Saloon had called time on Mathew.

I looked out the window at the group of five servicemen standing there expectantly. Nobody had told them it was off. I wasn't going to either. I couldn't get out unless Carl shut down the rotors, a strict Apache rule. Knock the cyclic on your way, and the thing will roll itself straight over and thrash itself to pieces. Billy and I texted each other to minimise the chat on the Apache net.

UNLUCKY 4 FORD … SAD, Billy wrote.

UNLUCKY 4 ZULU … HELL HOLE

AFFIRM

At 10.24am Nick and Charlotte checked in with the JTAC.

'Ugly Five Two and Ugly Five Three, on station.'

That sealed it. We had been relieved.

BREAKFAST TIME … MY LEAD, Billy texted.

But he couldn't hear the mission net. A brand new voice had just come on it – an officer's voice, older than the others, and extremely authoritative. Brigadier Jerry Thomas spoke slowly and clearly, so everybody could hear. And he made sure everybody knew where this order came from.

'All stations, from SUNRAY …

'Option One is a recovery of Lance Corporal Ford by the Apaches. Option Two is a recovery by Zulu Company. Option One has been approved.

'Repeat, Option One is APPROVED. Prosecute ASAP.'

It was an extraordinary message. The phone lines between Lashkar Gah and Kandahar must have been red hot. I didn't care about that now. We'd lost five minutes of precious fuel sitting with our thumbs up our arses. It was going to be tight now. Painfully tight.

'This isn't funny, Ed,' Carl muttered.

'Buddy, do we have enough fuel to do this now?'

Carl had crunched the stats as soon as he'd heard the brigadier's voice.

'No, but yes.'

'Meaning?'

'Legally no, because we've only got 890 lb left. Direct to Bastion from here at endurance speed is twenty-six minutes using up 390 lb of gas. Take off the 400 lb Minimum Landing Allowance we must land with and we have 100 lb of Combat Gas – or just over six minutes' flying time. It will take you longer than that to brief them. I'm prepared to bust the limit and land with 200 lb. That gives us twenty minutes from now and perhaps a minute or two extra when we're on the ground. So, illegally, yes. We'll just get away with it. But you need to be *very, VERY* quick.'

Brief, strap 'em on, fly six klicks, rescue Ford, fly back six klicks … Twenty minutes? Jesus … We'd have to make do.

'You're a genius, Carl. Grab the stick.'

The rotors were turning but I was already halfway out of the cockpit. The rules didn't mean much now. Carl leaned out to pass me his strap.

'Ed, I mean fucking quick. If we're not pulling pitch for home in twenty minutes we'll end up in the desert.'

'Okay, relay the lot to …'

'I have via text, while we were talking. They're up for it. Don't waste a second. Go.'

The first man I reached was Dave Rigg.

'You know what's going on?'

He nodded. 'I've seen the Nimrod feed.'

Good.

He extended his hand. 'Hi, I'm Dave Rigg, I'm the –'

'Sorry, we're mega low on time. Follow me.'

I grabbed Rigg and pulled him up to the right side of the aircraft while I pulled out my strap. The other three followed. I asked for their surnames. The rotors were thumping so hard I had to shout.

'Right …' I held up the strap. 'You've got to strap yourself on because if you get shot while you're on the wing, you need to stay on it. Lots of things might happen out there. I'm not going to go into them all.'

I pointed to the grab bar beside Carl's door.

'This bar here is what you're going to strap onto.'

I demonstrated.

'Okay, with that?'

Three of them nodded, wide-eyed and hanging on my every word. But RSM Hearn didn't appear to be paying much attention. Instead, he just grinned. I hadn't the time to ask what he was finding so funny. I thought that perhaps he was nervous; I would have been, in his position.

'Right, this is what's going to happen …'

I drew a line in the sand with my finger in front of the Apache, and put a small pebble beside it. 'That's the wall, and that's Mathew Ford. Both aircraft will land in the field here, with the wall on our right. As soon as the pilots give you the thumbs up, go. Run to the wall. When you find the big hole in it, Mathew is just to the left. Grab one limb each and go to the nearest aircraft. Strap him onto the foot step in front of the right wheel with one of your straps.

'Get back on the aircraft you got off, in the same place. If you don't have a strap left, just hold on tight. Don't run round the back of the aircraft or the tail rotor will chop your head off. If we go down, stay with the aircraft. The crew will guide you. If the crew are dead, make for the river. The firebase will cover you across it.'

Was there anything I'd forgotten to mention? Yes, loads; but we didn't have the time.

'You.' I pointed to Rigg, the bloke nearest to me. 'You're going to sit on this flat side here, in front of the engine air intake. Wedge your back against the aircraft by jamming your feet against the empty Hellfire rail.'

I took the remaining three round the other side.

'Fraser-Perry, you're going here. Same drill. I'll be back with some straps. You two, follow me.'

We sprinted the 100 metres to the other Apache. Billy and Geordie's canopy doors were open, ready for me.

'Give me your straps, guys.'

Billy threw his down. Geordie just looked embarrassed and put up his hands.

'I haven't got it.'

'What?'

'My jacket's in for servicing. This is a spare, like. Sorry.'

Bloody hell. Geordie was the squadron's Combat Rescue officer. *Of all the people to forget a strap …* He'd be ribbed mercilessly by the lads for this when we got back. Someone would just have to go without.

'Geordie, you lead, we'll follow. Make sure you stay out of the gun line; they'll be firing all the way in to cover us.'

'No problem mate.'

I dished out Carl and Billy's straps to Robinson and RSM Hearn – who was still grinning at me – and ran back to my aircraft.

How the hell do I choose who gets the last strap? Shit – is this going to be a life or death decision? It had to be Rigg. He knew where Mathew was, he was marginally more mission critical. I threw it up to him then went back round to see Fraser-Perry.

'There's no strap for you.'

He looked at me in disbelief.

'Put your arm through the grab bar and then force your hand in under your body armour. That way you won't fall off if you get shot. Do you understand what I am saying?'

He took it well.

'Yes, yes …' He nodded frantically and cracked on.

'Tuck it in.'

The tall marine in shirt sleeves was waiting for me at the front of the aircraft. Now I recognised him. Colonel Magowan. His brow was painfully furrowed, and intense concern was etched over every square inch of his tanned face.

'Good luck,' he said, and we shook hands. It sounded like he meant those words more now than he had in his whole life.

I clambered back inside and plugged in as Carl was completing his last checks.

'Guess who didn't bring his strap.'

'Not the SERE officer was it, by chance?' He grinned. 'Who drew the short straw?'

'Young guy, left-hand side; name's Fraser-Perry. The one on the right's called Rigg.'

I slammed my door, buckled up, pulled down my visor and tried to catch my breath as the air conditioning kicked back in.

'I gave them the fullest brief we had time for. At least they all know exactly what to do when we get there.'

'Good.'

'Okay, Geordie, your lead.'

'My lead,' Geordie replied.

Carl pulled on the collective and we began to lift steadily into our own swirling dust cloud.

Magowan looked up. The loneliness of command was stamped onto his troubled face. I felt for him; whatever the outcome, he would be judged. I wanted to shout, '*Fortune favours the brave!*' but I didn't want to count my chickens yet either.

It was not for some hours that I found out that our four passengers had barely heard a word I'd said.

INTO THE LION'S MOUTH

We flew directly east, and very low – just ten feet off the desert floor. Only the odd opium runner's tyre tracks punctured the sea of sand beneath us.

'We'll be over the ridgeline at 10.38, Ed.'

'Copied, buddy.'

The ridge was our cover. As long as we kept low, the enemy wouldn't see us until the precise moment we crossed it. And by then they'd have other things to think about, if Widow Seven One had done his job. I needed to know that everything was set up right for us.

'What's happening with the fire plan, Carl?'

'The JTAC was sorting it while you were out of the aircraft. We've got a B1 on station now; callsign: Bone One One. He's been tasked to drop a 2,000-pounder bang in the middle of the village at 10.37, just as we approach the berm.'

That was good news. It would give us a far bigger dust cloud to hide behind than the A10's 500-pounder.

'So he's called off the A10.'

'What?'

'Tusk said they had to deconflict. Otherwise the B1 could drop on him. We've got to go with the B1 mate. They say they'll be there.'

'They'd better be.'

The B1s were good but their equipment took an age to get bombs on target.

The rest of the fire plan was simple. Nick and FOG would suppress the enemy to the north of our landing position, the main body of the fort, and Charlotte and Tony would hit them in the east – the treeline that ran down to the river. The A10 Thunderbolt had already strafed the tunnels to the south of us.

That just left the west – and all those lunatics in the village that just wouldn't die. The B1's 2,000-pounder should kill most of them, and stun the rest. More importantly, the mess it made would block the Taliban's view of us just long enough for our smash and grab.

In any fire plan there is always one critical moment. Bone's drop was it for us. And even if he dropped on time, we'd have no more than two minutes on the ground.

I tried to visualise the marines unclipping the straps, hitting the dirt; how quickly they could shift Mathew. Thirty seconds to get to him, a minute to get him back, and thirty seconds to tie him onto the aircraft.

Yes, it was doable – but in two minutes, tops. Any more than that, and the Taliban would be onto us big time, and not just from the west. They'd go ape-shit from every point of the compass.

What about Fraser-Perry?

Shit.

My stomach lurched. I twisted as far as the confines of the cockpit would allow, and craned over my left shoulder. The young marine was exactly where I'd left him, one leg jammed hard against the weapons pylon forward of the wing, the other against the Hellfire rail. I could see his teeth clench and his knuckles white against the grab handle. If he gets hit, he'll fall off; his hand should be tucked into his body armour.

'Just remember to keep it at fifty knots, buddy.'

Carl hadn't forgotten. But I was sure Fraser-Perry would have thanked me for reminding him. Fifty knots was a pain in the arse; this low it made us sitting ducks. Our normal attack run was three times that. But these boys had a job to do when we got to the fort, and they had to be firing on all cylinders if we were to come out alive. The thump of the rotors and whine of the jet engines would already have half deafened them. Any faster and we'd have blinded them as well, with all the dust and shit in the air.

I focused my TV camera on Billy and Geordie's Apache, 500 metres to our left and just ahead, to check on their two marines. They were both there, one perched either side of the cockpit. I wondered if Hearn had lost that grin.

Jesus. Were we really doing this?

I just knew there was going to be something about this tour … All those promises I'd made Emily … I couldn't bear to think about them. I couldn't bear to think about her and the children. My hand moved to my pocket. I could feel my angel under my survival jacket.

It'll be okay. Just as long as the B1 drops on time …

Billy and I had agreed we'd loop south of the firebase so we wouldn't obstruct the marines' arcs onto the fort. We'd duck down over the river and swing up north when we hit the sandbanks on the far side. Then we'd charge the final 200 metres and wheels down right in front of the fort's ten-foot outer wall, where we'd last seen Mathew. I prayed he'd still be there.

'Two minutes to target,' Carl said.

Jugroom Fort was only two-and-a-half klicks away now, still hidden beyond the ridgeline. Double the amount of orange and red tracer now arced high above it before burning out in the bright morning sky. The marines at the firebase had upped it from suppressive to rapid fire, and were giving the Taliban everything they had.

Tony cut in. 'Ugly Five Three has had a long-range missile launch from the south-east.'

'Ugly Five Two has also,' FOG echoed. 'We're chucking out flares too.'

Whatever it was, it was still there. And there was still nothing any of us could do about it. But soon they would have four helicopters to aim at instead of just two. A lazy southern US drawl came on the air net. It sounded familiar.

'All callsigns, this is Bone One One. Bone is running in.'

Excellent news.

'Ugly Five Zero and Ugly Five One; be advised, our coordination for the 2,000-lb strike will take seven minutes. Dropping seven minutes from now.'

Appalling news. We didn't have seven bloody minutes. Bone was the weak link in our master plan and that link had just snapped. We didn't have the fuel to wait. If he wasn't there, we'd just have to go in anyway. Otherwise Ford wasn't coming out. And landing in full view of the west village was unthinkable. We were starting to feel like sitting ducks. Carl was even unhappier than I was.

'Ed, Bone needs to get on this sharpish. Bloody tell him.'

'Negative, Bone. We are inbound with the rescue team now. Repeat: we are running in NOW. You *must* drop at one zero three seven hours.'

That reminded me: time to make ready my own personal weapons. A loaded weapon was the Number One No-No in an Apache cockpit. A round going off would ricochet around the Kevlar until it found me. But the rule book had already been thrown out of the window. If we went down, my SA80 carbine and 9-mm pistol were going to be my only life support systems.

The carbine first, clipped into the bracket on the right of my seat. I fished a full mag of thirty tracer rounds from the ammo bag wedged in next to me, clipped it on, pulled down the cocking handle and clipped it back onto the seat. Red tracer was the emergency signal for downed Apache pilots to get help from the other gunships; you put a burst into where you wanted some suppressing fire, so your mates above could keep you alive until someone picked you up.

The 9-mm Browning next. I unfastened the Velcro straps of the holster on my right leg, pulled back the top slide then let it go with a metallic click and re-holstered it – this time without the Velcro. Both weapons with a round in the chamber, ready to go. Screw the rules; it made me feel better.

'Sixty seconds to target, Ed. Where the hell is Bone?'

Time, fuel. Time, fuel. Carl was doing his nut. We were just 1,100 metres from the fort now, and within enemy range. Better push Bone for a …

An ear-splitting metallic blast on the right side of the aircraft.

'What on earth was that?'

Jesus. Please don't tell me Rigg has been shot …

Our heads shot right and I scoured the airframe for damage. 'Christ knows. Are we hit?'

'Can you see anything?'

There was no damage. Rigg grinned sheepishly, pointed to his

SA80 rifle and gave us the thumbs up.

'Rigg has let one go by mistake!'

'No, it was probably on purpose.' I remembered my conversation with Rigg at the RV. 'He said he hadn't had a chance to test fire his weapon in theatre.'

'He hadn't *what*?'

'Yeah, I know. He wanted to let one off to make sure it worked.'

'Oh, right …'

What a time to check-fire your weapon. But I couldn't blame him.

I looked forward again and started to get my first visuals of the air above the target area. FOG was over the lip of the ridge, at altitude on his first gun run, Nick's cannon already spitting flame. Tony circled on a wheel directly opposite him and kept silent. Charlotte was waiting for us to come in on her eastern flank. She didn't want to do anything to risk giving away our plan of approach. Good girl.

Fresh smoke and dust spiralled up from the last salvo of artillery shells that had exploded on the Taliban village. The three 105s were going like the clappers. They'd stop the second we landed and came in range of their shrapnel.

Again, that's why we needed Bone. For Christ's sake, we were almost on top of the firebase. Widow Seven One just had to sort him out.

'Widow Seven One, this is Ugly Five One. Confirm Bone's time on target.'

Bone didn't even give the JTAC a chance to reply.

'Break, Break … This is Bone. Bomb in the air. Impact in Five Zero seconds, sir.'

Yes. Bone had come up with the goods after all.

'I bet that's the longest gliding bomb he's ever dropped.'

'Thank fuck for that.' Carl's relief was so strong I could touch it.

But we were still going to get there a fraction too soon. The ridge was only 600 metres from the fort and the village, and the Danger Close distance for a 2,000-lb bomb was 590 metres. We didn't want to be anywhere near that thing when it went off.

'Carl, tell Geordie to slow up a little and come right. We're going to be ten seconds too early now.'

'Okay. Ugly Five Zero, Ugly Five One: kick right.'

We banked gradually right. But something was wrong. Geordie hadn't changed course.

'Carl, tell Geordie to come right now.'

'I just have.'

I stamped my left foot on the floor pressel to operate my radio microphone. 'Kick right, Geordie. The bomb's inbound.'

No change. Fuck. The radios were blaring.

I tried a third time to break through. 'Geordie! Break RIGHT!'

Geordie heard us just before they reached the ridgeline and flared their aircraft hard right. Carl slowed up and banked too, keeping in formation. As soon as our wings levelled, the bomb went off. And it was monumental.

To our left, orange fire raged over the ridgeline into the sky. It was enveloped almost immediately by the biggest cloud of black smoke I'd ever seen. It continued to mushroom until it was 200 feet tall, cancelling out the sunshine. There must have been an ammo dump under there. It was our cue. The fear dissipated immediately and I began to fidget in my seat with the anticipation of what was to come.

'Widow Seven One, this is Ugly Five One. Check-fire all weapons except Apaches. Check-fire all weapons except Apaches. Read back.'

All the air and artillery needed to be turned off.

'Widow Seven One is check-firing all weapons except Apaches.'

'Correct. Give me as much fire from ground callsigns as possible to cover us in and out. They know how close they can bring it.'

'Stand by.' There was a five-second pause as the JTAC gave the second order. 'All ground callsigns supporting now.'

'Okay Carl, let's get in there.' I stamped on the pressel again. 'Geordie, we're clear. Go for it.'

The two helicopters veered sharp left and Carl tucked in 150 metres behind Billy and Geordie's tail – far enough apart so we couldn't get shot up in the same burst of fire, but close enough to land ASAP after them. Then we were up and over the ridgeline and hard down towards the glint of the Helmand River.

And there in front of us was Armageddon. It was like nothing I'd ever seen. I caught myself humming *The Ride of the Valkyries*; excitement had replaced anticipation.

The marines were gunning like mad from the ridge with rifles, GPMGs, 50-cals – everything they had. The 30-mm Rarden cannons of the Light Dragoons' Scimitars were also piling in, and Nick and Charlotte were still blatting away with twenty-round bursts from high above us.

This was it; this was the moment. We were really doing it. The metallic taste of adrenalin began to saturate my mouth. The fight or flight instinct had kicked in. As soon as we were over the ridgeline, I slewed my TV camera towards where Mathew should have been and kept it there in the hope of picking him up. I couldn't make out much more than the fort's outer wall through all the shit in the air. The cloud of thick black smoke from the 2,000-pounder was spreading slowly from the village and enveloping the place. Clumps of earth erupted like fountains as our fire poured in, worsening the visibility by the second.

We crossed the river and banked sharp left. Pushing their cyclic levers forward, Carl and Geordie upped the airspeed to eighty knots. It was no place to hang around. To our right was a thick bank of trees – and only Allah knew what joys they concealed.

A quick glance left and right, over my shoulders. Rigg and Fraser-Perry were still hanging on. I looked down at the TV screen, but I still couldn't see anything. Thick black smoke covered the whole fort now. I couldn't even make out its walls, let alone Mathew's body.

Rounds continued to zip backwards and forwards above the fort. The 2,000-pounder had done its job to begin with, but the Taliban were now answering back. We'd entered Tracer Central, and screaming in through the middle of it I felt like Han Solo up against the Imperial Fleet.

We were sausage-side big time, and there was no turning back. My tongue tasted like I'd been licking aluminium and I now needed a piss more than anything in the world. We were 200 metres from the wall. One more turn and we would be over the ploughed poppy field in front of it, wheels down.

'Ten seconds.'

Geordie kicked left and tipped his tail. He began to flare for landing alongside the fort wall. Carl banked and began to flare too, but he had turned in the nick of time.

'Shit, incoming from below right ...'

A muzzle flash, and a long burst of automatic fire from the last of the trees fizzed past Rigg's face as he spreadeagled himself as tight as he could against the Apache's skin. It was game on now. They knew we were here.

'Come on Geordie,' Carl hollered.

Ahead of us, Geordie wasn't landing. He wasn't doing what he was supposed to be doing. Dust from the poppy field had swirled up around his rapidly slowing Apache. The thing had been ploughed so many times the top soil was as thin as talcum powder. We hadn't expected that.

'Jesus, he's about to brown out ...'

A brown-out was the last thing we needed. If we couldn't see them, we couldn't land.

'Don't go into the dust, mate; we'll never make it.'

Carl slowed up hard and pulled on the collective to bring us up. To hover there would be the perfect invite for an RPG to climb right up our arse.

It's going tits up ...

I could feel my heart beat against my chicken plate; things were moving into slow-mo. A huge dust cloud now hung over most of the field, and Billy and Geordie had disappeared inside it. We needed to get wheels down, but neither of us could see shit below. And the Taliban couldn't be more than 200 metres behind us.

Then Geordie's Longbow Radar suddenly materialised, followed by his rotor blades. The tail appeared next, swinging ninety degrees to the left and then lifting. His Apache moved forward, passed directly over the bomb crater and straight through the gap in the wall. Carl was as horrified as I was.

'Where the hell are they going? Through the wall means –'

'Just get us down, buddy.'

Carl thrust our nose forward for a second and then flared the aircraft. Geordie came on.

'There isn't enough space for the two of us in the field. There's no choice; we've got to put down inside the fort.'

I looked right for Billy and Geordie as we went down. All I

caught through the haze was a great burst of flame from the breach of their cannon as it released its steady stream of giant, electrically initiated rounds.

'Engaging!' Billy yelled.

Then the dust enveloped us completely and they were gone.

The urge to say or do something was overwhelming me. I grabbed the handles above my head and shut my mouth tight whilst Carl flew the most dangerous and crucial part of the mission. We'd lost the element of surprise, we'd lost all visibility. We'd even managed to lose each other. And we still had to find Mathew.

He slapped us down hard into the space that Geordie had just vacated. We were totally blind. I breathed again. We'd made it.

'Quick Carl; thumbs up, thumbs up.'

Fraser-Perry whipped past my left window and rounded the aircraft's nose. Rigg shot off from the right, just ahead of him. They ducked under the thumping rotor blades and disappeared into the dust cloud which had begun to merge with the fallout from the 2,000-pounder and now completely blotted out the sun.

If any Taliban were waiting to nick Mathew, now was the time to strike. I strained to catch sight of him, but there was no chance of that; I could hardly see beyond the ends of the rotors. There was nothing Carl or I could do but sit it out.

We weren't used to this. Normally we kept to the skies, with an array of cameras so powerful we could see up people's backsides. Now we were slap in the middle of the enemy's back garden, and we couldn't tell shit from Shinola. Every second felt like an hour.

Then, incredibly slowly, the brown mass began to recede. We could see five metres … then eight … then twelve …

'Where the hell is the wall? Why can't we see the wall of the fort?'

I screwed up my eyes and grasped for the slightest hint of the rescue party. I wanted to see four men running towards us, carrying Mathew Ford between them. *Please, please … Where the fuck are you?*

But they weren't coming. The clock: 10.39 and twenty-five seconds. A whole minute had gone by on the ground. We only had one left. They should be halfway back now.

What was that? A long, horizontal line … The dust cleared further. Could I make out the wall now? Yes … My eyes scanned left, inch by inch. Finally, at least forty-five degrees forward of the aircraft, I could see the hole and the crater. We were a lot further away from it than I had thought. But where the hell were the marines?

I continued scanning left towards the spot I'd last seen Mathew's prone body. One metre, two metres, three metres …

'There!' Carl shouted.

There weren't four of them, only two. Just Rigg and Fraser-Perry. They were a full fifty metres away. Worse, they'd only managed to move Mathew off the raised bank and down into a bloody great ditch. They weren't moving; it was as if they were stuck in quicksand. One of us was going to have to get out and help. Or we'd all be dead by eleven o'clock.

'They're not going to make it.'

'I'm going to jump, Carl.' I started unstrapping my harness.

'No, I'm going. I'm the aircraft captain.'

Neither of us could get out of the thing fast enough, but Carl was the primary pilot and he knew he had to stay. And it was my briefing that was going haywire.

'I'll be back in thirty seconds.' I threw open the canopy door and leaped from my seat without even touching the side of the Apache. I braced myself for the six-foot drop.

Instead of jarring my feet, I plunged eighteen inches beneath the surface of the field. The earth was thinner than talcum powder. God knows how many times it had been ploughed.

Waves of sound burst across my eardrums. The noise was unbelievable. From the air-conditioned silence of the Apache cockpit, it felt like someone had whacked up the volume to max. Rolls of thunderous gunfire ebbed and flowed around the aircraft, punctuated by the pounding of the blades above my head.

I started for the lads at full sprint, but the ground kept disappearing beneath my feet. My boots sank twelve inches with every step before I got any kind of purchase. My legs pumped at warp speed, but I was going nowhere fast. And I felt them getting hot, painfully hot.

As the whine of our Apache engine and the thud of its rotor blades receded, the sound of total war intensified; the constant crack of rifle rounds, bursts of cannon fire from the gunships, and the ground-shaking crump of artillery shells. The reek of cordite was so strong it seared my nostrils.

I heard an unearthly scream and looked up to see a couple of Taliban RPGs blasting their way towards the ridge. Instead of the familiar whoosh, these things were shrieking like banshees.

To my left, the curtain of smoke from the 2,000-pounder still hung thick and high, obscuring the village and dimming the light, but I could now see the treeline clearly to my right. The dust cloud was clearing fast.

By the time I reached the ditch, my lungs were heaving and the blood was pounding through my head. I jumped down alongside Fraser-Perry, sweat streaming from every pore.

They'd given up trying to lift Mathew and were trying to drag him out instead. That wasn't working either. He was now lying, face forward, on the side of the ditch furthest from the wall. His head was level with the field and his legs pushed out to the right. Rigg stood above him, tugging at his webbing, and Fraser-Perry was below, trying to lever him upwards, but the lip of Mathew's helmet was wedged into the earth, anchoring him firmly.

I yelled at them to stop. The guys released him, close to exhaustion.

'Fucking hell, he's heavy …' Fraser-Perry gasped.

Mathew Ford was a giant of a man, well over six foot and solid as rock. We hadn't known that. Maybe if we could turn him over, the three of us might be able to lift him. I shoved my right knee into the ditch wall, grabbed Mathew's shoulder with my left hand and pulled. I slid my right hand beneath his right arm and flipped him around so most of his weight was on my thigh.

As his body turned, Mathew's head flipped backwards and rested momentarily on the bank. That's when I first saw his face. His eyes were closed, his lips slightly parted, and his skin was caked with dust, but he was a handsome giant. He looked like he was fast asleep. The only thing that told me different was the glistening trail of blood that ran from under the lip of his helmet, down his cheek and onto his neck. A few drops had splashed across his shoulder.

Was he still alive? That question had bombarded us the whole morning; the JTAC, his CO on the ground, the Nimrod above us – even the brigadier back at HQ. And I wanted to know myself. If he regained consciousness, I wanted to tell him not to struggle and that everything was going to be okay.

I gripped his right wrist between his cuff and a big watch with my right hand and slammed the fingertips of my left onto his neck. No pulse. I'd trained as a medic in the Paras. If he'd had one, I'd have found it in three seconds.

But it didn't mean he was dead. It just meant his heart had

stopped. It could be started again. Yes; only an hour ago, when we were above him, Billy said he'd seen Mathew move. Five seconds. Still no pulse.

I left my hands where they were a few seconds longer. Still no pulse, but Jesus, his body temperature was just the same as mine. It was five degrees celsius that morning; bitterly cold. He'd been lying out here for over three and a half hours. If he'd died as soon as he'd been hit, his hands would have been as cold as ice by now.

Maybe his heart had only just stopped. That would mean we'd have four minutes before his brain followed suit. *We could still save him.*

I grabbed hold of Mathew's webbing with both hands. 'Right, let's go …'

Rigg grabbed hold of his shoulder straps, Fraser-Perry lifted his legs, and we pushed and heaved and hauled him out of the ditch onto the field. I leapt up onto the bank. My forearms felt like lead. As Fraser-Perry followed, another RPG whooshed over our heads from the fort in the direction of the marines' firebase.

Christ, the enemy … How close were they now?

To our south, the tunnel system had been chewed up and blocked by the A10s. Thanks to the lingering pall of black smoke, nothing was going to come out of the western village for a while. Billy and Geordie would cover us from the north. Or would they? The truth was I hadn't a clue where they were. I hadn't seen *any* of them yet, but they hadn't blown up and they hadn't lifted. So I presumed that's where they were until told otherwise.

But the east … That's where the Taliban would come for us, running round the corner of the wall fifty metres away like men possessed. We wouldn't know about it until they were right on top of us. We had to move fast.

'Okay, we can't lift him up, so we'll just have to drag him. Fraser-Perry, you cover us.'

Fraser-Perry thrust his rifle into his shoulder and gripped it hard. He glanced left and right, left and right, his eyes out on sticks. He wasn't much more than a kid, and couldn't see shit through the smoke.

Rigg and I grabbed Mathew under the shoulder straps of his body armour. It was now a straight forty-five metre line to the aircraft, but through all of that appallingly soft earth. We raised his torso and backside to create as little resistance as possible and took up the strain. His neck and chin sank into his body armour. He really was heavy. Jesus, at least twenty stone with all his kit on.

Another roar of 30-mm cannon; at least five hard bursts and a hundred rounds. Tony flew low over my left shoulder whilst Charlotte slapped it all straight into the treeline barely 200 metres to our north east. It was the closest support fire they'd needed to put down yet.

Keep pulling that trigger, Charlotte …

I looked up to see Carl, still in the Apache's back seat, finish saying something into the radio mike. He gave me a thumbs down, then a scooping gesture with a curved hand. He repeated it, quicker, and then pointed vigorously behind him.

Army sign language: thumbs down means the enemy, and scooping means flanking. The enemy was flanking to the east of us. That's who Charlotte and Tony must have been hosing down. The east; I knew it. And they were obviously closing fast.

'Guys, the Taliban are trying to get through the trees over there. We've got to step on it.'

Rigg and I lurched forwards in unison. I realised how hard it was going to be. We couldn't run with him; we couldn't even walk with him. To get any movement at all, we had to lean hard into each step, and yank Mathew alongside us. As we did so, our leading feet sank deep into the earth, pivoting us off balance. We stopped, took another step and pulled, pulled, pulled again.

The deeper we sank, the higher we had to hold Mathew to stop him from disappearing into the bloody stuff too. We were holding him practically at chest height, but couldn't keep him there for long because our arms were burning. He slipped back down at the end of every lurching stride. It was totally ball breaking.

I snatched another glance at the aircraft. Carl was pumping his fist up and down, a manic expression on his face. I knew exactly how he felt. We'd moved, but not far, and at this rate it was going to take us all fucking day. It was also getting lighter; the dust was starting to clear. Bad news. We needed all the cover we could get.

We had no choice but to press on. After five more metres or so of chaos, Rigg and I established some semblance of a rhythm. Up, lean, take a step, heave, down. Up, lean, take a step, heave, down. Rivulets of sweat gathered beneath the brow pad of my helmet and rolled down into my eyes. My nostrils stung with the cordite. My arms felt like lead and there were daggers in my thighs. But we were doing it. We had twenty metres to go.

Then I realised the supporting fire into the treeline to our left had stopped. The noise had shifted behind us.

'There's AK fire the other side of the wall …' Fraser-Perry strained to see whatever was going on in there. 'Sounds real close …'

A few seconds later, an Apache's 30-mm opened up again 100 metres away, high and to our north. Billy and Geordie. They were obviously in serious trouble; Charlotte must have switched her fire to support them. It left us without any cover, but there was no point in sitting around thinking about it.

I used the momentary pause to change my grip; my arms weighed a ton and my hands were shaking. I rammed one under Mathew's body armour and out the other side by his collar, then grabbed my own wrist to form a tight noose.

Despair was starting to flood through me. For the first time I thought we might not be able to do it. I didn't know where I was going to summon the energy for the last few metres.

The Apache's rotor blades battered the air close by. I needed some Para aggression to get me through this. '*Right*,' I roared. '*Come on!*'

At that moment, plumes of soil and sand erupted like a series of mini volcanoes about a dozen metres to the left of us. I stared at them, momentarily transfixed, unable to work out what the hell was going on.

Then I caught sight of at least six bright orange flashes 150 metres away, perfect star shapes spread out along the treeline. Muzzle flashes. Automatic fire.

The earth continued to erupt only two or three metres away now and the air crackled as bullets whipped above our heads. A huge weight pulled on my right side. Mathew's whole body mass pressed down on my pistol holster, dragging me onto the ground, and then my heel was trapped under his torso and I collapsed back on top of him. Rigg had let go of him entirely. As my head turned, I saw him go down, face first.

I was now pinned to the dirt by Mathew, momentarily powerless to do anything but watch the muzzle flashes approaching through the haze.

And Rigg's hit. Oh fuck. This wasn't how I wanted us to die …

I ripped my right arm out of Mathew's body armour and scrabbled for my pistol. But it was no longer there.

THE WRONG WALL

Three minutes and twenty-eight seconds earlier …

*Timing the manoeuvre with his usual perfection, Geordie had heaved
back hard on his cyclic stick to bring Ugly Five Zero in to land alongside Mathew's body. Dust billowed ahead of them and rose 100 feet
into the air before being sucked back down by his rotors, entirely
smothering the Apache. Geordie had flown over 2,000 helicopter hours
in his ten years as a pilot and this was the worst brown-out he'd ever
been in.*

'I can't put down in this shit Billy. Ed and Carl won't see us; they'll
come in straight on top of us.'

'Well anywhere then. Just get us down.'

'I'm going into the fort.'

'You sure?'

'Just over the wall. It's another big field; there's nothing in it.'

'Copied mate. Do it.'

A quick jerk on the collective and Geordie's Apache was ascending
again. Some left-foot pedal twisted the gunship ninety degrees to the
right, then a push on the cyclic and they were over the wall and into

the adjacent field; a rectangle, 100 metres long and 200 wide. A line of trees to their right divided it into two squares.

Geordie pressed on a further fifty metres so his next dust cloud wouldn't blind Ed and Carl. Billy slewed the TADS to the northern end of the field and lined up his crosshairs on the fort's outer wall.

'Engaging.'

He squeezed the trigger and the cannon threw twenty rounds into the remnants of the watchtower on the far right. Then he raked another twenty along the top of the wall. Rock splinters and shrapnel span off it in all directions as the rounds exploded. If anyone was near the wall, they weren't going to put their heads above it in a hurry now. It bought Billy and Geordie thirty extra seconds.

Nick was watching their insertion from 2,000 feet above. He hosed down the entire western wall and the canal path alongside it with consecutive twenty round bursts, to discourage anyone trying to flank round and ambush his friends in Ugly Five Zero.

Geordie landed hard at a forty-degree angle to Jugroom's main building. Hearn and Robinson jumped off and ran to the wall, as they'd been told to do. The wrong wall.

Geordie watched them disappear into the brown-out and immediately began to worry. 'Do you think they know where we are now, Billy?'

'Probably not. They wouldn't have seen anything on the wing. We could barely see ourselves.'

It took forty seconds for Billy and Geordie to get back their visibility. Hearn and Robinson had groped up and down the northern wall, looking in vain for Mathew, and were now jogging back to the Apache. Robinson was leading, hands and rifle raised as a signal to the pilots of their bewilderment. Geordie spotted them first from the back seat.

'They've got no idea we're in a different field. I'm going to have to show them where to go.'

Billy was the captain and Geordie was the primary pilot, but they didn't have time to argue the toss about who should leave the aircraft. Geordie was out of his seat and gone, safety-locking the collective lever as he jumped but not stopping to unclip his carbine.

He charged over to Robinson and shouted: 'Follow me, he's this way.'

Changing course ninety degrees, Geordie made for the hole in the wall eighty metres to his left. That's where Mathew was, Geordie thought – around the crater and immediately to the right.

The brown-out had disorientated Geordie too. His mental compass was off by ninety degrees. He led the marines at full tilt to a bomb crater in the field's west wall instead. Geordie rounded the corner and turned sharp right. The marines dutifully followed – heading north, ever deeper into enemy territory.

Visibility was down to ten metres. Geordie, Hearn and Robinson were in the midst of the 2,000-pounder's smokescreen. The stench of explosives and burning was overpowering.

'Come on lads, the others will be up here somewhere,' Geordie yelled over his shoulder as he pressed on up the canal path. Robinson was ten metres behind him, and Hearn brought up the rear.

One hundred metres along, Geordie still hadn't found anybody. He knew Ford was just by the wall; he'd seen him from above. Had he regained consciousness and started to crawl away? Down to the river perhaps? Geordie pressed on.

After another eighty metres the black cloud began to dissipate. He was almost at the end of the wall now. The corner had taken a direct hit, strewing rubble across the path. Geordie didn't remember the wall being hit here. When he'd last seen it, it was still standing. Perhaps

Nick or Charlotte had smacked it while the rescue Apaches were at Magowan's HQ.

He could see round the corner now. Fruit trees loomed over the piles of stone. He didn't remember fruit trees either.

Geordie slowed to a walk. This wasn't right. The canal should have been ahead of him. Where the hell was it? It started to materialise through the dust to his left …

So what was in front of him? Just fields, and …

Geordie jolted to a halt. Not more than fifteen metres in front of him, under the spreading branches of a tree, were three men with turbans and beards. One had a PK machine gun slung across his back, the second rested the butt of his AK47 in the dirt, and the third crouched with an RPG in each hand. They were in animated conversation, keeping in the shadow so the Apaches circling above couldn't see them. Taliban …

They stopped talking when they saw Geordie. They looked at him. He looked at them. Each was frozen to the spot; each as shocked as the other.

That's when he realised … We're in the wrong place. This is the north side of the fort, not the west. Jesus fucking Christ.

The Taliban fighters knew that if the British soldiers came for them, they wouldn't come alone. There would be a hundred at least, like the last attack. They hesitated, giving Geordie a few crucial seconds. He spun around and took off back in the direction he'd come, pumping his thigh muscles as hard as he could.

'Go-go-go … Wrong-way-wrong-way …' he jabbered.

Robinson heard the next word very clearly. 'TALIBAN!'

He spun round too and sprinted for all he was worth.

Seeing the red face of his approaching RSM, Robinson screamed: 'Run sir. Run the other way, the other way …'

The Taliban opened fire, and bullets began to kick into the dirt around their feet. Geordie did an impression of the Roadrunner on speed. He overtook Robinson within a few metres. Seconds later he overtook Hearn, too. Then the wall erupted.

Billy had no choice but to sit tight.

His job was to keep the front of the aircraft clear for their return. It was easier said than done; he could only fire the cannon at point-blank range in front of him and up to ninety degrees to his right. If the Taliban came through the hole in the wall, he wouldn't be able to touch them.

The world's most devastating fighting machine was now a sitting duck. Apaches weren't built to be shot at on the ground. From below, fine. Same level, you had a problem.

The Kevlar plating stopped at his waist, and they could hit him in the chest with a pop gun now. An RPG through the window and he was history. Even a brick into the tail rotor would have put the aircraft out of action. How long would it take for the Taliban to know he was there?

Billy soon got his answer. Just over twenty seconds after Geordie and the marines exited the field, two AK47s appeared at the top of the wall, 100 degrees to the right of him, and began blatting away blindly on fully automatic. Billy stamped on his floor pressel.

'Ugly Five Zero has got Taliban doing a Beirut unload from the wall sixty metres to my right. Put some fire down now.'

Nick responded instantly. 'Ugly Five Two copies. Stand by …'

FOG was flying Nick low on a northerly axis over the treeline to the east, scanning the fort for any movement.

'My gun.' FOG slaved the cannon with a flick of his right thumb, aligned the crosshair and loosed off a twenty-round burst.

'Engaging with cannon, Billy,' he bellowed. 'Watch my strikes.'

Great chunks of adobe flew off a long building in the centre of the compound. FOG moved his eyeball swiftly left and shifted the impact zone. A second wave ploughed into the neighbouring courtyard, shredding paving stones and slicing along the wall Billy was being engaged from.

FOG spotted movement inside the far end of it. 'Talibs escaping; firing.' His third burst blasted away the section of wall alongside where Geordie was overtaking RSM Hearn ...

Geordie was blown a metre sideways by the pressure wave four feet above his head.

More explosions, some on the other side of the wall, others on the canal bank to the right of him. Red-hot shrapnel whipped across the path, centimetres behind him, through a waist-high, metre-long shell hole. Geordie's ears rang and his mouth filled with grit.

Jesus, what the hell was that? An RPG? Ten RPGs?

Sound travels at 343 metres per second. So it took Geordie just over three seconds to hear the pounding of the Apache cannon a kilometre away. Shit, the guys are firing on us.

'What the fuck is that?' screamed Hearn.

'Just fucking run,' Geordie shouted.

Geordie didn't know it was possible to run faster than they already were. But he did it then.

'Delta Hotel, FOG, Delta Hotel,' Billy said. 'Good shooting mate. Keep it up.'

Billy was doing mental cartwheels. He checked the clock: 10:40 and fifty-five seconds. Jesus, almost two-and-a-half minutes on the ground. Time up. They needed to get out of there now. The next Beirut unload from God knew which direction couldn't be far off. The

Taliban would have given their eye teeth to get their hands on one of the feared mosquitoes. And now they had two of them, gift wrapped, and delivered to their door.

Where the hell was Geordie? He should have got back by now. He'd been out there for a minute and forty seconds. Maybe they needed a hand. Maybe he should lift and start putting some fire down … But if he moved, he'd brown the place out again, and Geordie and the marines wouldn't be able to see where he was. He couldn't leave them behind, no matter what.

What if they've been hit, and can't get back? They hadn't discussed Actions On for that. Billy tried to flush the disaster scenario from his mind. Of course they were coming back.

Lifting and firing was going to be his last resort if ten Taliban came running round the corner. He wrapped his hand around the collective's grip. It was locked. Geordie must have done it on his way out. He could only take off in an emergency and fly by wire. Shit. Please don't let anyone come round the corner. At least Carl and Ed were in the right place. He stamped on the pressel again.

'Ed, it's taking too long. What's going on? Is Ford strapped onto you yet?'

'Billy, it's Carl. Ed's outside. They're having a really tough job moving him.'

'There are four of them …'

'No there aren't.'

'What's Ed doing out of the aircraft?'

'That's what I'm trying to tell you. There aren't four of them; just our two marines and Ed. Where are your marines?'

'Can't you see them?'

'Negative.'

'What about Geordie? Is Geordie not there either?'

'He's with you, isn't he?'

'Negative.'

Silence.

'Fuck.'

Geordie swept past the entrance to the field where his Apache was as their third minute on the ground began. He turned to check Robinson and Hearn were still following him and snatched a quick glance at the aircraft, eighty metres away through the haze. He couldn't make out his co-pilot. He hoped to God he hadn't been hit.

Geordie was in pain now. He'd run more than 500 metres at a full sprint and his lungs were full of smoke. His throat rasped as he tried to suck in more oxygen. The battle still raged around him, but at least nobody was shooting directly at him now.

The southern end of the west wall was just ten metres away. A left turn and he'd hook up with Mathew and the two other marines. Then they could all get the hell out of there.

Geordie rounded the corner to see Ed and Rigg heaving Ford towards the Apache and Fraser-Perry in position to give covering fire. Muzzle flashes sparked up at the far end of the field. Bullets tore up the furrows, their points of impact careering ever closer.

Rigg and Mathew went down like a sack of shit. Ed went down right after him. Geordie had got there too late.

ESCAPING JUGROOM FORT

The bastards are not getting me alive. I need my pistol.

I glanced back across the field, and there was Geordie, thirty metres away. The Taliban bullets cracked through the air around us.

'*Geordie, put some rounds down!*' Then I saw he didn't have his carbine with him either.

Got to move Mathew out of the fire. Get him behind the aircraft … The fuselage was only seven metres away; we were very near the blades. My eyes dipped as I grasped Mathew more firmly and tugged my foot free. My pistol poked out from underneath him. I grabbed the grip and spun round on my knees, preparing to return fire towards the muzzle flashes. As I did so, the sound of the Apache's rotor pitch changed. *Oh no …*

Carl started to pull power. Dust and grit smacked me in the face as I turned to see the aircraft begin to wobble. The blades coned upwards. I got straight to my feet. I could just make out Carl speaking fast into his microphone and monitoring our every move. He didn't want to hit us when he took off.

'*No Carl, get down!*'

He couldn't hear me. The suspension struts lightened as he

began to lift. I threw both arms out and flapped them vigorously downwards. He finally got the message and powered down. I didn't know whether he was leaving or just turning to engage the treeline, but I wasn't having any of it.

The dust cloud he'd thrown up was so thick I couldn't see my own hands. I stumbled about, trying to regain my bearings.

With an ear-piercing screech, a Hellfire came in to the east of us and exploded with a mighty flash. A quarter of a second later, the pressure wave passed through my clothing. Ten seconds later I heard two deep booms, then the sound of branches splitting and plummeting to the ground. HEISAP rockets. Charlotte and Nick were taking care of the treeline. *Thank fuck, they're onto them.* Carl must have called them in.

The brown-out was still all-consuming. But it was now rippling slowly away from the aircraft in concentric rings, leaving us with a few metres of visibility inside it. The enemy gunfire from the eastern treeline had now dwindled. If we couldn't see the Taliban, they couldn't see us. Carl's brown-out and the pounding from Ugly Five Two and Three had bought us a few crucial seconds. *Got to move right now.* I turned to check how badly hit Rigg was. To my amazement, he was crouching over Mathew and preparing to lift him again. Geordie was with him now.

'Rigg, you okay?'

'Yeah. Just tripped. Sorry.'

'You're not hit?'

'Don't think so. Can't feel anything.'

I was astonished. They'd missed all of us.

I holstered my pistol and lunged for Mathew too. I grabbed hold of his webbing, Geordie latched onto his right leg, and summoning every last scrap of energy we headed for the aircraft.

Fraser-Perry and Robinson suddenly materialised too; one grasped a sleeve and one Mathew's other leg. Last to break through the dust cloud was Hearn, his face red as a beetroot.

We were three minutes behind schedule and had been on the ground for over four. Yet suddenly – and I had no idea how – the plan was working.

'Where the fuck have you lot been?' I hollered above the engine's whine.

'Sorry, bonny lad,' Geordie yelled. 'Detour.'

As gently as we could, we lowered Mathew beneath the aircraft, placing his head below the step in front of the right wheel.

'Anyone got a strap?'

Robinson's immediately appeared in my hand.

'Okay, back to your aircraft guys. We can manage from here.' I turned to Fraser-Perry. 'You get on, too.'

The marines sprinted off, but Geordie hung around. He needed to see it through.

'Honestly, Geordie mate, we're almost there. Last one back to Bastion is Piss Boy, eh?'

'That'll be you then.' He smiled and set off.

Rigg lifted Mathew's shoulders while I wrapped the strap around his back, under his arms, through his body armour and out by the top of his chest. *Bollocks*. It wouldn't quite reach the step. We heaved him forward another six inches. But the strap was as taut as a bowstring and I was worried we would garrotte him in mid-flight.

'Give me yours.'

I repeated the process with Rigg's strap and fastened it to the step above his helmet. Now at least he would hang steady and straight.

'Okay, mate, jump on. And hold tight.'

'Roger …'

Robinson and Rigg were going to have to follow Fraser-Perry's example and just cling on. Rigg leapt back onto his Hellfire rail and hauled himself onto the wing as I clambered back into the cockpit.

I moved my harness buckle away from the cyclic so Carl could lift safely. A quick check on Rigg and Fraser-Perry, then I raised both thumbs and screamed above the din: '*Go, go, go ...*'

We'd well overstayed our welcome at Jugroom Fort, and Mathew desperately needed a crash team: 10.43 and forty-five seconds. *Fuck me, five minutes and ten seconds on the ground. It had seemed like five years ...*

Carl pulled power and the canal disappeared from in front of us as we whipped the dust into a frenzy. He was flying blind, with only the symbology in his monocle: heading, height, torque and velocity. The hardest flying in the world. We began to wobble.

I fastened my harness, clipped the monocle to my helmet and connected my microphone lead. 'Five One lifting. Give us cover.'

I took a firm hold of the two grab handles either side of the cockpit roof. Not to brace myself for a crash – it was the only way to suppress the screaming urge to take hold of the flying controls at a time like this. I wished I was in the back. *Trust your symbology, buddy.*

I felt the Apache move through the seat of my pants, but God only knew where. My monocle told me that we'd swung ninety degrees left, pointing the nose back towards the river. The whine of the engines increased as he pulled more pitch. I checked our height, thirty feet, and torque, 85 per cent. Carl was giving it some serious welly. I checked the airspeed: we were moving forward at five knots. Another five seconds and I looked at the height again, still only thirty feet, same speed and the torque was up to 90 per cent. We'd stopped lifting, and were still not clear of the brown-out. We should have been well away by now. There was a problem.

'Ed, the power is much higher than it should be. Is Mathew tied to the bloody ground?'

'Maybe it's recirculation from the wall ...'

'No way. We should have bags of power. I'm topping out.'

The wobble became an uncomfortable sway. Jesus, we had a fifty-three knot tailwind. *That's* what was destroying Carl's lift. It was blowing away his purchase on clean air.

'Can't be right,' Carl said. 'It's been five knots all morning.'

It was up and down like a yoyo. We had a squall on our hands. It could last for minutes. Afghanistan was full of them, but we'd never faced one on takeoff before. At this height the emergency drill was to turn into it, down the aircraft immediately and wait for the squall to pass. We didn't have that option. Our truckload of luck had finally run out. Our height began to drop.

'Twenty-five feet, and forty-two knots downwind ...'

Carl called up more power, taking the torque to 95 per cent. He was doing all he could to get some translational lift. Increase the speed and you increased the airflow over the blades; then you were up. But we were downwind, so it wasn't happening.

'Twenty-one feet and thirty-seven knots downwind ...'

We were sinking. Carl pushed the torque all the way to 100 per cent. He had nothing left to pull. The velocity vector was off the scale so we were moving forward fast, but still reversing into the wind. Any more and we'd be in serious danger of trashing our escape plan.

'Nineteen feet and thirty knots downwind. Watch your torque, Carl. We're dropping.'

Come on, fly, you bastard. I still couldn't see a thing.

'Fifteen feet, twenty-six knots downwind. Mathew's too close to the ground, mate.'

Carl was going to have to turn back towards the fort to get forward airspeed or we'd ditch in the Helmand River.

'I'm going over 100 ...'

With a mighty heave on the collective, he pulled the torque to 115 per cent. It was our last chance. Six seconds at that level and he'd twist the transmission permanently out of shape. The aircraft would be toast.

Fucking come on. Do it NOW ...

I felt a small waver in the tail.

'Eighteen feet, nine knots downwind. The squall's dropping. Twenty-two feet, eight knots *forward.*'

'Got it! *Sylvia's flying!*' Carl dropped the torque to 90 per cent. We were away.

'Top flying, mate. Thank God for that.'

My guardian angel was looking after my lilywhite arse that morning ...

Height and airspeed continued to climb for five more seconds and the torque remained constant.

Then we burst out of the dust, straight into blinding sunshine and a crystal blue sky. It was a beautiful day; I'd forgotten after so long in the Jugroom underworld. It was mind-blowing, unlike anything I'd seen before, or will see again.

As we soared towards the berm, a myriad red and orange light pulses streaked past the cockpit windows. It felt like Han Solo taking the Millennium Falcon into hyperspace. The marines at the firebase had seen our dust cloud, and were giving the Taliban every last bullet they had to cover us out. Thousands and thousands of rounds winged past us. Some of them were frighteningly close, but the marines knew exactly where they were shooting. It was an awesome display of firepower.

Charlotte and Tony's Apache flew right in front of us, 200 feet above the firebase. The moment we emerged, two Hellfires shot off her rails with their arses on fire and buried themselves deep into the eastern treeline.

Nick and FOG had kept their best till last. I caught a glimpse of them in our two o'clock, running into the village from the desert. Then they let rip instantaneously with every single one of the sixteen Flechettes they had left in their launchers . They came out in pairs, the left ahead of the right – left, right, left, right, left, right, left, right – each leaving a vivid jet of flame in their wake. It was the biggest rocket launch I'd ever seen, and at the end of it, angry clouds of propellant vapour shrouded their entire aircraft.

A fraction of a second later, 1,280 Tungsten darts tore into each and every one of the huts, barns and compounds within a 100-metre radius – turning the village into a giant pin cushion.

Geordie lifted thirty seconds behind us. It was perfect timing. With two final cannon bursts he and Billy broke west and then sharp south down the canal. Tony unleashed all his and Charlotte's Flechettes into the fort and as he pulled hard out of a low-level dive, Nick squeezed off four HEISAPs into the treeline.

I was mesmerised by the sheer ferocity of the attacks. Anyone waiting to ambush us on our way out had been rewarded with a very nasty surprise.

We were over the middle of the river. My excitement vanished and my stomach churned. The straps holding Mathew had never been tested. I looked out for him, but the fuselage blocked my view.

'Mate, I hope Mathew's still on. Just keep it nice and slow.'

'Forty knots. Look right, Ed.'

I looked down through the Perspex and there on the mirrored surface of the water beneath us was the shadow of an Apache helicopter gunship with a man hanging beneath it. A feeling close to euphoria began to pulse through my veins. I felt the tension ease from my shoulder muscles.

'I can't believe it, Carl. We've made it …'

'Don't,' he grunted as we reached the far bank of the river. 'We've 100 metres to go …'

The hillside rose steeply ahead of us. Five seconds later we crossed the ridge, and the Royal Marines' firebase was spread out below us. We'd saved ourselves. Now we had to save Mathew.

'Mate, let's take him into the desert, to the Casevac LS.'

'We don't have the fuel, Ed.'

'We must have; it's only a couple of miles.'

'Trust me, we don't have the fuel.' Carl was adamant. 'We're putting him down right here.'

He'd already begun to bank right and turn the aircraft 180 degrees into the wind to land. He picked a spot just behind the Light Dragoons' Scimitars where he could see Viking vehicles and a red cross. There would be medics and basic life support equipment to keep Mathew going until the Chinook arrived. Carl went into a hover as dozens of marines rushed to our impromptu landing site.

'Keep bringing it left, mate …'

If Carl went down hard, seven tonnes of aircraft was going to squash Mathew flat.

I opened up my door to get a better view; Rigg was already leaning off the side of the aircraft signalling to Carl with his hand. With extraordinary deftness, Carl lowered Mathew gently to the ground, feet first. Next, he eased the aircraft left until Mathew was in a sitting position, and then very gradually laid him down. As his helmet touched the ground, Carl pulled the aircraft back a fraction to ensure that his now prone body was well clear of the wheel as he gently touched down.

'Right, get him off quick, Ed.'

Rigg and I didn't need a second invitation. Carl had done a neat job. Mathew was lying on his back, in exactly the position I had left him. I knelt down and pulled hard on the straps to relieve the pressure on the karabiners. As I spun the locking gate, his dust-caked face was a foot from mine. The blood on his right cheek was still damp; perhaps his heart had started to pump again. The slight crow's feet at the side of eyes made him look as though he was smiling.

I unlocked the second karabiner, then we stepped back and let the marines and medics take over. My hand didn't feel quite like my own as I offered it to Rigg. We shook quickly and turned to watch Mathew being rushed to the waiting armoured ambulance.

'Ed, get in,' Carl shouted. He was flipping a track about the fuel now.

I looked quickly along Sylvia's bottom to see if she was leaking; she had no holes that I could see. Rigg and I found ourselves still facing each other.

'Thank you.'

'No, thank *you.*'

I jumped back in and the second my door closed Carl pulled power and took off, sand-blasting everyone below us.

'Check the fuel burn rate,' Carl snapped, as we left the dust cloud behind. Billy and Geordie had been holding for us over the desert. Now they moved alongside and Carl and Geordie main-lined it back to Camp Bastion by the straightest possible route.

I looked through my monocle. We had 515 lb of fuel and sixty-two miles to fly. Not good. The minimum legal fuel allowance for landing an Apache was 400 lb. Below that, heavy manoeuvring could cause fuel starvation to the engine and a shut down. Below 200 lb, there was just whatever was left in the pipes and pump; the two fuel tanks were empty. At 100 lb the engines cut out altogether.

Carl was keeping the aircraft at 117 knots, the most economical fuel burn speed, and just thirty-five feet off the desert floor. Any higher and the wind from the north-west would have slowed us down. Every second counted.

I pulled up the engine page on the MPD and tasted acid in my throat. We were burning 900 lb an hour, 15 lb a minute – and it was going to take us twenty-seven minutes to get home. I punched *15*27* into the keyboard, then *Enter* ... *405 lb* ... We'd have 110 lb of fuel left when we landed. *Bloody hell.* I gave us 50 / 50 at best.

'Buddy, if we're not going to make it, we're best just putting down at the gun line aren't we? We can get a CH47 to fly down the boys with some fuel bollocks.'

'We can do it.'

'Sure?'

'Of course I'm sure.'

'We could go to Lash ...'

'We're not going to Lash; it's too small. We can make it.'

I realised I was more worried about the embarrassment of requesting fuel if we landed in the middle of the desert than I was of the Taliban.

If anyone knew the Apache AH Mk1, it was Carl. He loved the aircraft so much he even hung out with it in his free time. They almost went on dates together. If he said we'd get back, we'd get back. But it was going to be desperately close. A change in the wind, or any kind of malfunction and we'd shit it.

Billy and Geordie were 400 metres off to our right, and flying just as low. We didn't want to discuss our fuel state over the net. It would only spook them at Bastion; every man and his dog would get on the net and feed us the sort of advice that we could do without. Best to keep schtum. We texted instead.

Billy began: *SEND FUEL STATE*

I replied with ours, and he responded: *490*

'Shit, Carl, they're even lower than us.'

A beep alert signalled another text from Billy. *LASH V BSN?*

He must have been reading my mind.

EWOK HAPPY BSN … YOUR CALL

BSN IT IS

Even Billy the chief pilot doffed his cap to Carl the Aircraft King.

SEND AMMO

That was going to be interesting. We had eight Flechette and eight HEISAP rockets still in the tubes, but we were out of Hellfire and only had eighty remaining cannon rounds.

40*30MM, 0*HEISAP, 8*FLECH, 0*HELLF

Wow. Billy was almost out of everything.

Having stayed on station to cover in the Chinook picking up Mathew, 3 Flight were a few minutes behind us. They didn't need asking.

Beep. 'Text from Five Two, Ed.'

20*30MM, 4*HEISAP, 0*FLECH, 2*HELLF

But Charlotte and Tony won the prize. Their text just read: *WINCHESTER.*

'Winchester' was the air net code for exhausting all your weaponry: bombs, missiles, cannon rounds, rockets – whatever you had. It dated from World War One: when the string-bag pilots had nothing left to fire, they reached for their trusty Repeater. Going Winchester was heavily frowned on. Ammunition was our lifeblood and had to be carefully rationed; use it all up in one go and you had nothing left to fight with. But there were no other troops in contact at Jugroom; just us. And they'd run dry in the very last seconds of our extraction. They'd executed their fire plan to perfection.

CONGRATS, I replied.

Nobody had gone Winchester before – Charlotte and Tony had just made British Apache history.

Billy sent our ammo requirements to Kev Blundell in Bastion so he could have our uploads ready. Carl punched some numbers into the keyboard.

'Check this out. We've used a total of £1,499,000 of ordnance protecting Mathew Ford.'

And that didn't count Nick and Charlotte's earlier mission.

'Not bad for a couple of hours' work.'

Seven minutes and thirty-six seconds from the firebase our fuel level dropped below the 400 lb landing limit. I'd lost count of the number of rules we'd broken that morning. Every few minutes, I recalculated the fuel state in case I'd made a mistake. The answer came back just the same – 110 lb on landing.

'Village twelve o'clock. One klick.'

'Don't change course, Carl. We're too low for them to see us coming.'

Normally we'd keep out of their way. But that meant wasting more fuel we didn't have. A flash of light shot straight across the windscreen, missing us by no more than a few feet. Carl threw the aircraft into an evasive bank, climb and jink.

'What the fuck was that? Have we been engaged?'

I shot a glance out my window, spotting for an RPG smoke trail. Instead, I saw a solitary bright yellow kite flying above the village compound.

'It was a kite, mate …'

It made me think of Khaled Hosseini's novel, *The Kite Runner*, which Emily had made me read on holiday in Egypt before the tour. The Taliban had banned kite flying. Among other things, we were here to defend the Afghan people's right to fly kites if they wanted to. But this one had scared the hell out of us. Maybe the Taliban had a point.

I felt for Emily's angel, but the survival jacket was too tight. It must have shifted position when we were moving Mathew. I desperately wanted to know whether he was alive. There had been no time to check his condition before we left the firebase, and we'd heard nothing over the net. A crash team could have got his heart beating again in an instant, surely …

On another day Carl and I might have put a call into the Ops Room, but they had enough on their plate without our unnecessary questions. We'd find out soon enough.

Ten miles out of Bastion, Billy texted again. *SEND FUEL AT BASTION*

110. YOU?

90. WE LAND 1ST

Twenty pounds of fuel was eighty seconds more flying time. We didn't quibble. Unless Geordie kept his aircraft 100 per cent upright, they were now in real danger of crashing. In a few minutes' time, they'd drop below 100 lb and then the engines could give out on them any second.

We approached the camp side by side. Carl eased off on the power.

'Don't slow down too much, buddy!'

'I'll formate that close to them you'll be able to smell Geordie's arse. Stand by.'

Carl went onto the net. 'Geordie, land long down the runway, so I can land short at the same time.' He wasn't wasting a second more than he had to.

The two pilots kept the same speed all the way in, with us one rotor blade's distance behind Geordie. As we crossed the tip of the runway, Carl flared the aircraft suddenly and hammered the back wheel down onto the lip, catapulting the front wheels forward and down hard too; it wasn't the most graceful landing I'd ever experienced, but it was the most grateful. Geordie did the same.

ENG1 FUEL BAR, Geordie texted as we taxied to the refuelling point.

That fuel bar was an emergency warning that pressure was dropping in the port engine and it would cut out automatically in less than five seconds. Geordie shut down the engine then and there on the runway to avoid having to file a lengthier incident signal.

Geordie and Billy took the right fuel point and we took the left, maintaining radio silence. If we were quick about this, we might be able to get away with nobody officially noting our return fuel states. That would save an ear-chewing by a pencil-neck somewhere along the line.

I opened up my canopy and shouted at the boys: 'Get the fuel in, quick.'

Simon, the Arming and Loading Point Commander, popped his head inside the cockpit as his boys went to work.

'All right, there, Mr M? How close have you cut it today then, eh? – 400 on the nose, I'll bet. Sounds like it was quite a morning … *fucking HELL* …' His eyes almost popped out when he saw the digital reading: 80 lb.

The next stop was the arming bay. The one and only Kev Blundell was waiting for us, hands on hips, with his usual sardonic expression.

He took a stroll around the aircraft. And for the first time I could remember, he didn't say a single word. He took his time with the inspection, peering into every rocket hole and having a thoroughly good look at the 30-mm feed chain running to the cannon. He glanced up at Carl or me periodically, then looked right back down again.

Eventually he was finished. He nodded lugubriously as he leaned his gargantuan weight against the aircraft's wing and plugged in.

'Not bad lads. I've got to admit it, not at all bad.' He broke into a smile. 'I hear you were put to shame by a bird, though.'

I caught sight of the Boss, walking straight towards us. *Thank God we'd got the fuel in …*

A Chinook thumped past over his left shoulder, on its way to the hospital landing site. Must have been Mathew. It was odd that the Boss had come down to the flight line to see us, even today. He was too busy for that. His brow was heavily furrowed and he looked like he had the weight of an elephant on each shoulder.

I gave him a smile, but I didn't get one back. When he saw my hands he stopped short and stared at them. I looked down too and realised they were still stained with Mathew's blood.

He nodded at them. 'You all right?'

'Yeah, it's not mine.' I gave him a big thumbs up as reassurance.

Trigger's expression still didn't change. His clear blue eyes burned with a peculiar intensity. 'Look, I just want you to know that I'm backing all four of you – no matter what happens next.'

There was a silence. I was bewildered. 'What do you mean?'

'The CO has just got in from Kandahar on a Lynx,' he said. 'I'll see you up top.'

He turned and walked away.

IN COMMAND: THE VERDICT

Carl signed in the aircraft while I went to wash Mathew's blood off my hands.

I sat on the lid of a missile box in the bright sun and poured water from a jerrycan. I couldn't bring myself to use the Portaloo handscrub.

I tried to fathom what the hell was going on. It couldn't have been about our fuel levels – Trigger would have understood, given the circumstances. I had never seen him that bothered before. And we weren't expecting the CO in Bastion today ...

I joined Carl inside the Groundies' hangar. We'd been delayed on the flight line while a technician examined my broken FLIR camera, so the others had gone ahead. We were both locked in thought. Okay, we'd broken a few rules that day. But anything we'd done wrong had been whilst trying to do something right. Our problem was that the road to hell was paved with good intentions.

The downside of the rescue didn't bear thinking about. If both Apaches had gone down on the way out of the fort, we'd have been close to double figures dead. The very thought of that would have seriously scared a lot of important people, and the four of us had pushed hardest for the mission throughout. After twenty-two years in the army I knew only too well that a little hindsight could be a very dangerous thing. The more I thought about it, the more I understood what Trigger must have meant. Our actions were now going to be judged in the cold light of day, and it could go either way.

I swung open the door of my locker. The word 'angel' was still scrawled across the inside of it in black marker as a reminder not to leave home without her. Carl was absorbed in his own little ritual: he pulled a letter from his wife out of a drawer and gave it a kiss. My angel deserved one too, after this morning. I tore open the Velcro seal of my right breast pocket and dug in my hand. I could only feel my war ID card.

'Mate, take a look in here and see if you can find my angel, will you?'

He peered in and shook his head. We scanned the smooth concrete floor beneath our feet, but there was no sign of her there either. My throat went dry. How would I tell Emily? She'd think it was an omen; that I'd die on my very next flight.

'This is no joking matter,' Carl said. 'We might need her when the CO gets hold of us …'

He put a hand on my shoulder. His expression told me that he knew this was no time to piss about. 'Shoot a basket for the brews?'

I hesitated for a moment, re-checking my pocket. Still nothing.

'Let's do it,' I replied.

It was another of our sacred post-mission rituals, and nobody was going to stop us doing it. Carl won.

He drove us up to the JHF Ops tent in the Land Rover he had parked by the hangar five hours earlier. Billy and Geordie were already there, and neither could bring themselves to meet my eye. So they'd picked up the vibe too. Nobody in the room was saying much.

Trigger walked in. The look on his face was completely impenetrable. I had a bad feeling about this. 'Can you four go through to the back, please? I'll be in with the CO shortly.'

We made our way out of the tent and into the secure Tactical Planning Facility.

'Make us that brew, Piss Boy,' Carl said, in a bid to break the tension.

'Yeah, make that a double, Piss Boy,' Geordie chipped in. 'You were also last back from the fort.'

But that was the end of the banter. I made four coffees in silence. Trigger reappeared as I handed them round, followed by the Commanding Officer. Trigger closed the door behind them. It was the first time I'd seen Colonel Sexton since his arrival in Afghanistan two weeks earlier.

'Welcome to Bastion, sir.'

The temperature in the room dropped by ten degrees.

'It's the *second* time I've been here.'

The four of us sat in a row on the comfy seats. Trigger pulled up a couple of hard plastic chairs and he and Colonel Sexton took their places opposite us. As always, the Colonel looked freshly scrubbed. His dark, perfectly parted hair gleamed under the neon lights.

'Right, gentlemen …'

He paused to eyeball each of us individually. I suddenly knew how those poor bloody apprentices must feel when Sir Alan Sugar was about to tell them: 'You're fired …'

'What the *FUCK* were you doing?'

We stared at him in stunned silence.

'You have advertised to the wider army a capability we do not have. People are now going to *expect* that this is a service we offer …'

He slowed right down, making every word sound like a threat.

'I'm not sure that you are aware of the gravity of your actions. People are going to come down on us from a great height. The JHC and the Directorate are going to want some answers.'

Hindsight was kicking in. *Shit.* It was going to go against us.

'You decided that you would break the RTS, which clearly states what you can and can't do. Tell me, where in the RTS does it say that untrained troops can use this procedure? It is an emergency procedure, for aircrew only.'

This went against every principle I have ever stood for. How could we have one rule for us, and one for everyone else?

'You decided that you would ignore the RTS. Who here has done this for real? Who here has *trained* for this? Those marines were not trained for this. They were just hanging off the side.'

Billy was the first to tiptoe across this minefield. 'They were strapped on sir. Well, they were o –'

'*HOW* were they strapped on?'

I kept my voice as even as possible. 'I showed each one of them the correct method, sir.'

He ignored me.

'So, without any training and with a total disregard for the RTS, you decided to strap men to an aircraft. What would have happened if one of them had fallen off?'

His dark, slightly hooded eyes flashed dangerously. No one answered. We were starting to realise that there would be no 'well done'.

'You flew into an enemy stronghold! What would have happened if one of your aircraft had been shot down? Do you realise the implications of the Taliban parading round with an Apache?'

You could have cut the silence that followed with a knife. But the Colonel still hadn't finished.

'I simply cannot believe you put two £40-million helicopters in harm's way, in a vain attempt to save someone that was already dead.'

I felt as though I'd been poleaxed. We all did.

'We didn't know, Colonel,' Billy said quietly. 'We didn't know he was dead.'

My mouth fell open. So, it had all been for nothing. A wave of sadness washed over me. The expression on the Colonel's face changed from steely determination to surprise. He obviously had no idea that we hadn't already been told.

'Excuse me, sir.' Billy got to his feet and walked out of the room.

Good on you Billy. You're not going to sit here and take this.

There was another silence as the CO waited for Billy to return.

If only ... If only we'd got to him faster, we might have saved him. If only we'd been quicker getting out of the fort. If only, if only, if only ...

Hope had made me believe in the impossible. Now the book was closed. We had failed, and were getting a good kicking for daring not to. What a shit day.

But it wasn't anger that had propelled Billy from the room. After a few seconds, the silence was interrupted by the sound of him throwing up outside. He came back in, white but expressionless, and dropped a tissue into the bin. We all knew how he felt. The CO gave us a few more seconds for the news to sink in. Our reaction had clearly thrown him.

'Why didn't you wait for the Chinook IRT plan?'

My eyes narrowed. Carl looked as dumbstruck as I was. Geordie shrugged his shoulders. Billy was staring at the CO throughout, trying to make head or tail of what he was saying.

'The IRT plan was to take effect twenty minutes later with a Chinook.'

'As far as we knew sir, there was no Chinook IRT plan,' Billy said.

The Colonel fell silent again. We didn't know about his plan. He rested his hands on his thighs as if he was about to stand up, then changed his mind and turned to Trigger.

'We are going to need to decide how we report this.' He paused. 'We must ensure that we were in the decision process and knew what was happening at all times. At the moment it looks as though four NCOs have gone and done whatever they pleased, without our authority.'

So that was it. *Stay calm, Macy; stay very calm.*

'Sir …'

He looked at me.

Stay calm, Macy.

'I'm not an NCO,' I said through gritted teeth. 'I am a fucking Warrant Officer.'

Well done, Macy … *really* calm …

He glared at me.

Which was preferable: the Taliban videoing a downed Apache or a British soldier skinned alive on Al Jazeera? Who was going to be more upset, the Chancellor losing forty million quid or a family not being able to sleep at night? His mother wouldn't even have been able to bury him.

A long time ago the red mist would have arrived good and proper at that point; the red mist that got me into fights as a kid and in the Paras. It wasn't there now, but I was deep down fucking angry. I knew

I should probably just sit on my hands, but I couldn't help myself.

'I haven't said anything yet, sir.' I leaned forward. 'But I'd like to make three points.'

I looked him straight in the eye.

'First, I don't care how much a helicopter costs; it was a calculated decision.'

'It's not just the helicopters, Mr Macy,' the Colonel replied. 'It's the four marines with you. The risk to them –'

'We asked for volunteers, sir,' I said. 'We asked for volunteers, and I described the plan in detail to Colonel Magowan.'

The CO just looked at me.

'Second, I don't, can't and won't ever see the difference between any British soldier, aircrew or otherwise. And finally ...' I paused, because I really wanted him to hear this loud and clear, '... do you *really* believe for one moment, sir, that we thought you were not in the decision-making loop?'

He looked completely blank.

'I expected both you and Major James to be in the loop, and to have followed the whole thing on a Nimrod feed. You could have turned this off any time. Sir ...'

'I tried to, Mr Macy. And the brigadier went against me.'

That explained the shenanigans over the radio when we arrived at Magowan's command post.

'I didn't know that, sir.'

He now understood that we hadn't a clue about the Chinook IRT; that we had not disobeyed any direct orders, and believed that he knew of – and endorsed – the rescue.

But he also knew that we had thrown the rulebook out the window. The crucial question was: did he think the result was worth the risk?

It was decision time. A decision that would affect the careers of everyone in the room – not least his. Was he going to take a punt and institute a disciplinary investigation against us, or play it safe and wait for someone else to? Would he back us, or throw us to the dogs?

The CO turned to Trigger and took a deep breath.

'Chris, if you were in the flight down there, what would you have done?'

It was a hospital pass if ever I'd seen one. As one of his squadron commanders, the Boss answered to Colonel Sexton; he was duty bound to back him up. Trigger had been given the casting vote. He didn't hesitate for a second.

'Given the same circumstances, Colonel, I would have done exactly the same as my men.'

Fucking good man.

The Colonel's mouth opened and closed, and he looked around the room, as if for inspiration.

Finally, he said, 'We need to talk, Chris.' And with that they got up and walked swiftly to the door.

Billy, Geordie, Carl and I looked at each other.

'Fuck me,' Geordie said. 'I wasn't expecting that.'

'Me neither,' Carl said. 'You okay, Billy?'

'Yeah.' Billy was still reeling.

I fished my notebook out of my trouser pocket.

'Okay, boys, I'm getting all of that down verbatim. We'll need it for the board of inquiry. Right, can you remember who said what?'

Geordie stood up.

'Great idea, Ed, but can we do it outside? I'm in serious need of some fresh air.'

We spent the next hour grouped around a bench in the sun. I

jotted down every word while Geordie and Carl bitched like hell. For once, Carl had a genuine reason to do so, and we weren't going to deny him.

Writing it down helped us revisit our actions and the thought processes behind them. It also took the lid off the pressure cooker after the incredible tension of the morning.

Billy rubbed the palm of his hand slowly over his stubble as we finished. Of all of us, Billy had taken it the worst. He was the mission commander. It wasn't just the shock of Mathew's death that had made him puke. Flying meant everything to him; it was his life. He was going for an officer's commission. The least he could expect if we got done was to lose his wings. As the Sky Police, Billy knew that better than anyone. He was looking over the abyss.

Billy wasn't alone. Geordie was the Rescue Police, Carl the Electronic Warfare Police, and I was the Weapons Police. We kept the rulebook: the same book that was about to be thrown at us – and probably all the harder because it was ours. Billy looked at each of us in turn.

'We did the right thing.'

We all agreed with him. And then the four of us shook hands. All for one, and one for all. It was lunchtime, but only Carl and Geordie were hungry. Billy and I wandered back into the Ops Room to get on with the day's work.

FOG wandered over and told us about the Colonel's IRT plan. It was to re-role a Chinook at Bastion and carry twenty odd marines into the fort to pick up Mathew. Trigger had asked FOG to pass it on to us when we'd hit our radio black spot at Magowan's HQ. He'd forgotten.

It changed nothing. The Chinook was twenty minutes behind us, minimum, and Mathew didn't have twenty minutes. And anyway, it was total lunacy. A big old bird like a Chinook would have been shot to shit at Jugroom. If it had gone down in the air there would have been twenty-five-plus dead. The brigadier clearly had no interest in it either; he'd only mentioned two options during his orders broadcast on the net.

FOG also forgot to tell us that Trigger was sending a second Chinook down to the gun line with extra gas. Now that would have been nice to know. Ironically, the fuel drama was the one thing the CO still didn't know about yet.

HQ Flight was taken off the IRT / HRF task with immediate effect. As with all fatalities, there was a mountain of admin to climb over. A couple of MPs from the Red Caps' Special Investigations Branch turned up to take lengthy statements from all the pilots – Nick, Charlotte, FOG and Darwin included. Under the law, we were all witnesses to a death, and until it was solved, it was treated as suspicious.

Trigger came back after lunch to lead the routine mission debrief. Standing up for us in the face of the CO was a brave thing to do, but he didn't see it like that. As far as he was concerned, he'd just told the truth as he always did. If an officer lied, he had no integrity. Without integrity, how could he lead his men?

He admitted that this was a defining moment in his career, though – because he most probably wouldn't have one now. I told him I'd never forget what he'd done, and I never will. We didn't bother discussing our situation any further. It was out of all our hands now – Trigger's included.

The eight pilots, the guy from Intelligence, the Ops Officer and the Boss filed back into the Tactical Planning Facility and watched the gun tapes on the five-foot-square screen. It taught us some pretty interesting things about the morning.

There were RPGs everywhere. We'd missed most of them because our screens were small and we were obsessed with Mathew. More than 100 were fired at or past HQ Flight while we were on station; the majority in volley-fire from the south-east – the bottom of the treeline and the village.

We checked out Billy's FLIR tape and saw just how hot Mathew had been throughout the mission. He was glowing, and his temperature never dissipated, despite the cold. It meant he had circulation. His heart was beating throughout. I didn't know whether that made things better or worse.

Billy's tape made it clear that Mathew had never moved. We replayed it three times at the point Billy thought he had – then realised his shadow had moved as the sun rose.

Alarmingly, 3 Flight's tapes revealed just how many Taliban had been piling down the eastern side of the fort in their attempt to encircle us: literally dozens of them, using a kilometre-long drainage ditch as cover. Almost everything Charlotte and Tony fired had been to suppress that lot. No wonder they went Winchester.

Overall, we estimated that there had been between around 100 of them to the north and east of the fort. It was impossible to tell how many more lay in wait in the village, the fort's buildings and the tunnel systems, but we reckoned on at least twice as many again. They must have been coming in from miles away; they'd had enough warning.

As the tapes played themselves out, it became ever more obvious how small Zulu Company's chances were of crossing the river again. Once the Taliban had reinforced, even a battalion of 600 infantry couldn't have taken the place.

Last, we watched 3 Flight's coverage of their orgy of fire as we flew out of the fort. The extraction took a total of fifty-five seconds

– during which they'd put down a total of £324,000 of rockets and missiles – £5,890 every second. Nobody in the forty-nine-year history of the Army Air Corps had ever fired half as much ordnance so quickly from one aircraft, and we doubted anyone would again.

At the end of the brief, there was a knock on the TPF door and the Chief Technician popped his head round.

'Boss, got your aircraft damage report here.'

Trigger groaned.

'Go on. How bad is it then?'

'Not a bullet hole anywhere.'

'Really? You sure?'

'Not one. I couldn't believe it myself. I got the lads to look at them twice. It's gen. Not a single round hit any of the four of them down there.'

That spooked us. Tony the bullet magnet had been hit on three separate occasions in Afghanistan. No hits seemed impossible.

The Ops Officer concluded the brief. 'There were no Rules of Engagement issues, the weight of fire was proportionate to the task and we have no damages to report this time. Do we, Darwin?'

Tony grinned. 'No, sir.'

'Well, Geordie, how do you think you did on your six-monthly handling check?' Billy delivered his assessment without waiting for an answer to his question. 'You failed. You broke every rule in the book – and you can refly in the morning at o-six hundred.'

'I'm *never* getting in an Apache with *you* again,' Geordie muttered. 'Not ever.'

It was getting dark by the time we left the facility. Billy told me he was going up to the hospital to have a quiet word with the doctors. If Mathew's death was going to prey on our minds, we needed to understand it better. We needed to know what else we could have done for him.

The Royal Navy Surgeon Commander in charge of the hospital told him that Mathew had been hit by a round in the upper right temple. The injury was fatal; he would have died from his injuries even if he had been shot on the hospital's front doorstep. His body may have lived on for a few more hours, but the damage to his brain was unsurvivable, no matter what anyone did. Mathew was effectively dead the moment the bullet hit him.

Billy and I were silent as we walked to cookhouse for dinner. It was a desperate end to an appalling day.

An older Royal Marine wearing a WO1's rank slide stepped out in front of us. 'Excuse me gents, did you two fly at Jugroom Fort today, by any chance?'

We nodded.

'I'm the RSM of 42 Commando.' He grabbed both our hands and gave them a bone-crunching shake. 'What you boys did there was outstanding. Thank you for bringing him back. We always tell them this, but you showed all my young lads for real that we never leave anyone behind.'

We were gobsmacked by the strength of his emotion.

'If there is anything I can ever do for you, or any of the other Apache guys, just tell me.'

As we queued for our food, we could hear the chefs talking about the rescue as they ladled out lasagne to the blokes ahead of us. We got a few more words of praise or gratitude from other marines when we sat down. Word was obviously spreading fast.

The next time we saw the CO was at the JHF evening brief in the Ops Room. By then, we were resigned to whatever was coming our way. If the gallows were under construction, so be it. The Colonel said nothing to us as individuals. Trigger invited him to address the room at the beginning of the brief as the new commanding officer.

'Thank you, Chris. What a day. Some extremely unconventional events occurred out there today. These were audacious in the extreme – but not something that I would want repeated.'

He paused for the message to sink in.

'I will do my best, but the Joint Helicopter Command may need convincing …'

Billy and I shared a knowing glance. Carl shook his head in disgust. The Ops Officer then read out the full list of stats collated by the brigade from Op Glacier 2 so far. The Apaches weren't the only ones to dish it out on Jugroom Fort's defenders that day.

The three 105-mm artillery pieces fired a total of 430 high explosive shells, and twenty salvoes of Illume. The B1B bombers dropped six 500-lb bombs and eight 2,000-pounders. The A10s fired 1,500 rounds of 30-mm DU, seven CRV rockets, three 540-lb airburst bombs and two precision-guided 500-pounders. As for the Apaches: 1,543 rounds of 30-mm HEDP, fifteen HEISAP rockets, forty-seven Flechettes and eighteen Hellfires. Nobody had bothered to count the small arms rounds yet, but they were believed to be in the tens of thousands.

There was one friendly forces KIA, and four wounded. The enemy had forty confirmed KIA. The final tally was very likely to have been double that, possibly even more. It had been a hell of a ding dong. But I'd be a liar if I said we weren't all very pleased to hear we'd given far better than we'd taken.

'Also be aware,' the Ops Officer added, 'that an SA80 Mark 2 rifle fitted with a SUSAT sight is now missing.'

It was Dave Rigg's. He'd left it at the fort because he couldn't carry Mathew and the rifle at the same time.

Despite our complaints, the Boss put Billy, Geordie, Carl and me on enforced rest and gave the same order to 3 Flight. They'd sat in their Kevlar bathtubs for over eleven hours and had been on the go for twenty so far. He knew a break from combat would do us no harm at all.

It also meant the four of us were back in our usual tents that night. Geordie came in for a chat, wearing just his skiddies and a T-shirt, and we played out the whole rescue over again for hours, piecing together the bits that some of us had missed or hadn't understood. Geordie recounted his escapade at the fort in full.

We crashed out just before 3am. I was totally ball-bagged but I couldn't really sleep. From the amount of turning and creaking coming from Billy and Carl's cots, I guessed they couldn't either. There was still too much to think about, to churn through.

For some reason we all felt a lot better the next morning.

Billy and I played the air temperature game on our walk to the morning brief as usual. Billy won. Despite the bright sunshine, it was plus-one degree celsius and he'd got it bang on. I made the coffees, hot and strong. Carl and Geordie joined us from breakfast as we kicked our feet outside, enjoying the fresh air.

Carl, Billy and I were all going to Kandahar that day to air test the aircraft in maintenance. Two of us could go in the Apache with the broken FLIR camera because that needed to be fixed, too, leaving one to be consigned to the Hercules shuttle. None of us ever wanted to go on the Hercules. Why get flown when you can fly yourself?

Billy and I tried pulling rank on Carl, but he wasn't having any of it. So we agreed to spoof for who got the Apache seats. Billy lost and was furious. I enjoyed that and told him so. 'We'll be in Timmy

Horton's on our second round of doughnuts by the time you arrive, Face.'

'Go do the coffees, Piss Boy.'

'Morning gents.' Trigger swept past us on his way into the tent. 'And what a lovely morning it is.'

The Boss obviously also felt better for a night's sleep. We followed him in. He took his usual spot in front of the map table, facing the room. Billy and I perched on ours, behind his right shoulder.

Trigger turned to us just as he was about to begin. I could see mischief in his eyes. 'Just got a message from the brigadier,' he whispered. 'Thought you might like to hear it. The brigadier wants your citations for Jugroom Fort on his desk first thing tomorrow morning.'

He turned back to face the rest of the room.

'Right, good morning everyone ...'

Billy and I weren't listening. A giant grin crept across our faces and a very warm feeling spread from our stomachs. By hook or by crook, the system had spoken. The official verdict had been passed. The noose had been cut down in front of our very eyes. We were in the clear.

EPILOGUE

The AAC hierarchy felt quite rightly that Mathew's family should be allowed time to grieve before the story of Jugroom Fort was made public. Colonel Sexton decreed that until then the whole rescue should remain under wraps.

The MoD asked for some gun tape clips to release to the media in due course – but a still from my footage of Hearn on Geordie's wing as they flew into the fort was leaked in advance. Within twenty-four hours it was on every British TV news channel and in every national newspaper. The following day it was being broadcast across the world. We were astonished.

Luckily for me Op Minimise was on and we couldn't phone home for two days. It was no easy task explaining it all to Emily.

There were no official probes into our actions at the fort. Nothing more was ever said about disciplinary proceedings. We did hear that the MoD had asked some pretty serious questions when they saw the official reports. Word filtered out that they were unhappy about the Release to Service stuff, but again, nothing was ever said to us.

There was no second attempt by 3 Commando Brigade to enter

Jugroom Fort – which left Geordie with the dubious title of being the British serviceman who'd got furthest inside the place. From what I hear, he still holds it.

In the days that followed, a whole lot of stuff emerged about that extraordinary day. The Taliban's losses had been considerable. A GCHQ intercept revealed that a senior commander was killed in the fighting. The attack had so enraged them that they hit the Garmsir DC for three whole days and nights in reprisal.

Our CO was summoned to Lashkar Gah for a good old-fashioned interview without coffee with Brigadier Jerry Thomas. It turned out he had rung the brigadier from Kandahar at the height of the crisis to tell him there would be no Apache rescue attempt. It had not gone down well. The brigadier reminded him in no uncertain terms who was in command in Helmand, on the day and again during the interview.

I felt sorry for the CO; he'd been fed incorrect information about what was happening at the fort by his headquarters in Kandahar. He'd stuck his neck out, trying to help, and got bollocked for it in the process. I didn't care much that he'd bollocked us without asking what had happened first. We had felt betrayed by him, but in the end he'd let himself down, not us. But I struggle to forgive him for his treatment of Major Christopher James, the Boss.

We also discovered that Zulu Company's commander, a Royal Marine major, had been relieved of his command by Colonel Magowan moments before the rescue began. He'd let the men of Zulu Company down badly. After being given a direct order to prepare the assault many hours before, he'd failed to brief his men and didn't get the Viking vehicles prepped to cross the Helmand River.

A British company commander had not been dismissed from his

post in the field for many years. Understand-ably, it prompted a huge amount of very painful soul-searching among the marines – whose officers' leadership was traditionally second to none.

Back in the UK, a board of inquiry was established by the Royal Navy Headquarters to find out what went wrong, and why Mathew Ford died. It went into everything: the mission, the initial orders, the Zulu Company assault, why five marines were instantly shot, the sacking, and how Mathew was left behind. It took a year and seven months to complete. Its conclusions were equally painful – and staggeringly honest.

First, it found that Mathew Ford and the four other marines wounded at the fort wall could have been all shot by a Royal Marine machine-gunner on one of the rear Vikings in the Zulu Company attack column, just after 7am. The gunner heard bangs coming from through the wall, and opened fire on the gap, thinking he was doing the right thing. Contrary to what everyone thought, it wasn't the seething masses of Taliban in the tunnels, the village or the fort that had got any of them after all; it was one lethal burst of friendly fire. The devastated young marine admitted what he'd done immediately and was sent straight home, his nerves shot to pieces.

Mathew Ford was left behind because of confusion over two Fords – Lance Corporal Mathew Ford, and Marine Ford, who was already safe by this point. That confusion existed primarily because Zulu Company were withdrawing under fire and the Sergeant Major didn't use zap numbers – the special few letters and numbers each serviceman has that are unique to them – to report his casualties.

It also revealed the full extent of Mathew's injuries. A total of three bullets had entered Mathew's body; he took a round in the bicep and a round in the chest, as well as the round in the head. When we picked him up, I had only seen the head wound.

The bicep wound wasn't serious. The pathologist ruled that the chest wound was very serious, but there was a chance that Mathew could have survived it had he received immediate medical help. The chest wound was almost certainly caused by the machine-gunner – the round was analysed and found to be 7.62-mm NATO issue. The pathologist also said the head wound would have killed Mathew 'almost instantaneously'. It was impossible to ascertain whether that bullet had been fired by friendly or enemy forces, as it had fragmented on entry.

Who fired that third bullet, the head wound bullet and *when* it was fired are the crucial questions. This is what is most sad of all: if the head bullet had been fired by the marine machine-gunner, what I don't understand is how Mathew could still have been warm on the thermal camera throughout our guarding him, and then still warm more than three and a half hours later when I got to him at 10.40am. There was a ground temperature of five degrees Celsius at the fort that morning – low enough to turn a body cold pretty quickly. He burned white hot on Billy's FLIR screen lying there all the time.

It's an anomaly that suggests that Mathew's head wound could have been caused by a (possibly) ricochet Taliban bullet fired later – perhaps a lot later. If Zulu Company had picked Mathew up before they withdrew, or if we'd got to him earlier, could any of us have saved his life? The answer, none of us will ever know.

That wasn't all the board revealed. Remarkably, it quite clearly also established that, despite their series of serious errors, the chaos at the fort was to a substantial extent not Zulu Company's fault. It was found that the company hadn't been trained back in the UK for war fighting in Afghanistan. Their sacked commander hadn't done the company commander's course, and was only put in charge of them four weeks before they left for Afghanistan. And the sub-unit hadn't even conducted live firing training together – the most basic of all company tasks.

Zulu Company were given the relatively benign job of security patrolling in Kabul for the tour and even this was asking too much from a unit that had not prepared for war fighting in Afghanistan.

Knowing that, it's little wonder that the rookie machine-gunner accidentally shot his own men, that the sergeant major didn't use zap numbers during this attack, and that the company commander couldn't give the leadership needed. I feel very sorry for all three of those men; they carry round a terrible weight, unfairly.

At the start of the tour, Brigadier Thomas had asked the MoD for an extra manoeuvre battlegroup to carry out everything that was expected of 3 Commando Brigade in Helmand – especially securing Garmsir and carrying out Operation Glacier. Despite countless promises from the Prime Minister about commanders in Afghanistan getting everything they asked for, his request was flatly refused. Instead, the brigadier was told to make do with what he already had, and generate any extra attack forces from his existing establishment. In other words, if Garmsir was to be held he had little choice but to send undertrained men into the most ferocious battle.

Knowing all of that, it's hard not to form a pretty depressing conclusion about Jugroom Fort: Mathew Ford probably died because the government gave the guys on the ground far too little and asked of them far too much.

Operation Glacier continued, with the three further planned attacks passing off as intended.

Glacier 3 set out to smash a relay post – the Cruciform – for enemy fighters five kilometres south of Garmsir. But the attacking force arrived to find it had already been vacated; there were not enough men in the area to man it and fight the DC – strong evidence that the enemy's command chain was already in tatters.

Glacier 4 and 5 were both ground assaults launched from the DC southwards. The Taliban remnants marshalled into the killing fields, exactly where Colonel Magowan wanted them – all he had to do was come and get them. Hundreds of marines and Afghan National Army soldiers, backed by Apaches and fast air, swept through two kilometres of abandoned farmland, destroying everything in their way. With nowhere to run to, the Taliban were routed.

The Garmsir DC was never retaken by the Taliban. The enemy's southern MSR was totally severed, and many hundreds of them were killed. Most important of all, Glacier had bought the marines the time they so desperately needed to consolidate. Yet its benefits could only ever be temporary. With the Task Force never being afforded enough troops to hold any of the ground the marines had fought so hard to win, the Taliban eventually reorganised and regrouped in the south – as Colonel Magowan predicted.

Jugroom Fort was reinfiltrated, and at the time of writing, the Taliban are still there. By the spring, sporadic fighting had returned to Garmsir; killing two of the Grenadier Guardsmen who inherited the DC when the marines left in April. By late summer the hard fighting had resumed. After the guardsmen, it was the Household Cavalry Regiment's turn – and that's where Prince Harry earned his military spurs. He was a JTAC in Garmsir for two months, operating under the callsign Widow Six Seven. The publicity shots showed him firing a .5 calibre machine gun off JTAC Hill, which meant that by Christmas 2007 – after ten months of regrouping – the Taliban, yet again, weren't far from the DC's gates.

656 Squadron went home at the end of February 2007, the day of my departure coinciding exactly with Glacier's finale. But I couldn't leave without having to sit down for one final ammo tally with Kev Blundell. The Boss and the CO wanted the statistical data for 9 Regiment Army Air Corps' final tour of Afghanistan before handing over to 3 Regiment. Only by working out the cost of particular operations and how much the individuals fire, can we plan for future operations.

Kev told me I'd personally fired more ammunition on this tour than the entire squadron had in the whole of the previous summer – some £2.5 million worth of weaponry. To be precise: twenty-six Hellfire missiles, fifty-four Flechette rockets and 4,120 cannon rounds.

The Koshtay raid proved to be (and still is) the most expensive single British Apache sortie in history. In our thirty-two minutes over the target area, we expended £1,060,794.20 of ammunition; or £33,149.82 every minute.

The fastest rate of fire award rightfully went to Charlotte and Tony. They put down £426,353.36 worth in six minutes over Jugroom, protecting us in and then out of the fort with Mathew Ford. They still hold that record today, and I can't see it ever being beaten.

When we got home, I had to confess to Emily that I had returned from the fort with my life but no angel. Emily likes to think she served her purpose and wasn't needed any more. My daughter insists she guided Mathew on his way. I'm a realist, so know what I believe: she remains MIA.

We got a chance to look at the newspaper coverage our families had kept for us. We found out more about Mathew and what sort of a guy he was. I think I would have really liked him.

He was the oldest of three brothers and known to everyone as an outgoing but gentle giant. Mathew's mother Joan initially talked him out of his lifelong ambition to join the forces; she persuaded him to become a car mechanic instead. After seven years in the local garage, he decided to sign up anyway, telling Joan: 'I've done what you wanted; now it's my turn.' Joan gave him her complete support, and told Mathew she was hugely proud of him when he earned his green beret. Joan didn't want him to go to Afghanistan, his first combat tour. Mathew reassured her, telling her he'd be all right.

He was buried on 1 February – seven days after he was due to fly home from Afghanistan – with full military honours in St Andrew's Church in Immingham, north-east Lincolnshire, the town where he'd grown up. He was thirty years old.

On a still, cold morning beneath a blue sky, his hearse was driven through Immingham at walking pace so the hundreds of mourners who lined the route could see him as he passed. His coffin was draped in a Union Flag and decorated with flower arrangements: 'Son', 'Brother' and 'Maff'.

A bearer party from 45 Commando carried Mathew into the church, with Joan, Dad, Bootsy Lewis and his fiancée Ina Reid following behind.

Mathew and Ina lived together in Dundee, where Ina was studying for her degree. They had met three years before – shortly after Mathew was posted to 45 Commando, based at RM Condor in nearby Arbroath – and instantly fallen in love. After almost six years of service, Mathew was planning on getting out of the Marines to settle down and have a family with her. He wanted to be a fireman or a policeman, but most of all he wanted to be a daddy.

The church was so full that many had to stand outside where loudspeakers relayed the service. The priest read out a message from Ina.

> *Another day is gone and I am still all alone.*
> *We never said good-bye.*
> *Someone tell me why.*
> *You were my guiding light, without you it is dark and I am lost.*
> *We were supposed to be for ever and thanks to you I know how*
> *it feels to be loved.*
> *Stay close beside me. I miss you so much.*
> *There is no one in the world that could ever replace you.*
> *I dream of the day we will meet again, and for ever can begin.*
> *I hope you have the same dreams too.*
> *I love you Mathew.*
> *X X X X*

Mathew is buried in the new section of the graveyard and a bench has been placed opposite his grave for the many visitors that come and pay their respects for a man that made the ultimate sacrifice for us all.

Bootsy lovingly tends the grave, a ten-minute walk from the family's home. Joan visits it daily, and Ina comes down from Dundee every few weeks. Delivering a red rose, she often lies down beside Mathew, and tells him about her life.

Back at Dishforth three months after our return, Billy, Geordie, Nick and I were asked to go down to 3 Commando Brigade's HQ, Stonehouse Barracks in Plymouth, to meet Prince Philip. As

Captain-General of the Royal Marines, he wanted to hear about their Helmand tour. We were told they wanted to thank us for our contribution at Jugroom Fort.

We were met at the landing site by two staff cars and whisked off to the officers' mess, where a plethora of majors and colonels were waiting in a line.

'What's going on here?' Billy whispered, as confused as I was. This kind of welcoming committee was mighty unusual for a few ageing warrant officers and a junior captain.

I shook Colonel Magowan's hand. He just grinned at me.

'Let me explain why you're really here,' said the brigade's chief of staff. 'Which one of you is which?' He turned to me.

'What's your name?'

'WO1 Macy, Sir.'

'No, you're WO1 Macy MC. Congratulations.' He shook my hand. He turned to Geordie.

'Staff Casey, sir.'

'Now it's Staff Sgt Casey MC.'

The chief of staff repeated the performance for Billy and Nick, who were both awarded the Distinguished Flying Cross. Billy's DFC had arrived after all, and when he was least expecting it.

They explained that Geordie and I had got our awards for what we did on the ground at Jugroom, while Billy and Nick got theirs for bravery in the air. Military Crosses had never been given to Army Air Corps personnel before; we weren't supposed to fight on the ground. The champagne came out from behind the bar and flowed in true Royal Marine style.

Finally we were ushered into a large hall along with nearly a hundred marines to meet Prince Philip. He'd come down to Stonehouse to congratulate everyone on the Operational Honours List due for publication the following day.

'And these are the pilots who flew into the Jugroom Fort to rescue Lance Corporal Ford,' the 3 Commando Brigade commander told the Prince when our turn came. The old Duke surveyed the four of us with a furrowed brow and issued his trademark grunt.

'Yes …' he said. 'Are you all mad?'

A week later, Emily gave birth to a healthy baby boy.

In December, I was asked to Buckingham Palace, along with Geordie, Billy, Nick and Dave Rigg.

I was only allowed three guests but managed to take Emily, my son and daughter – and the baby strapped to the nearest grab handle. It was the first time in my entire military career I'd worn ceremonial Blues. It would also be my last – I was getting out of the army in a few weeks and I was already on resettlement leave.

We stood near the end of a very long investiture line in the palace's giant ballroom, exchanging discreet banter. Dave Rigg got the biggest ribbing for leaving his rifle at the fort.

As we shuffled forward, waiting for our turn to come, I realised I'd never stand in uniform beside Billy, Geordie and Nick again. I knew then what I'd miss about the army. Not the pomp and ceremony, nor the laurels if you did something right (and definitely not the bollockings when we went too far). I'd miss serving alongside my friends.

Dave Rigg went first. Then it was my turn to approach the dark red dais. I wasn't at all nervous, and to the disdain of the equerry I gave my family a wave before setting off.

'And you must be the pilot,' Her Majesty said, as I took the final step towards her. She was handed my Military Cross. 'Were you very scared?' This was a real honour. She hadn't said more than two words to most of the folk before us.

'Not really ma'am, it was all so fast …'

She wanted to know what happened, so I told her. I tried to keep it as concise as possible as she hung the cross on my left breast pocket. The Queen patted it flat for me and stepped back slightly, lifting her eyebrows as I spoke and nodding gently. After twenty seconds I realised I was rabbiting on a bit, so I ended my story quickly.

'You must have been very proud of what you tried to do,' she said.

'Today is my proudest day ever ma'am,' I responded.

'Not because I'm meeting you …' *No I didn't mean that …* 'because I've been given the chance to bring *my* family to meet *my* Queen.'

Her polite smile widened into a grin and then in to a delightful chuckle. *I must stop chatting …*

'This is my last day in uniform ever ma'am. It's the greatest day of my life.' I knew I was losing it, and she did too.

The Queen started to laugh and thankfully placed her hand in mine for the final shake. It was soft but firm and before I knew what was happening she'd thrust it forward, forcing me to take a step back – a well-practised manoeuvre to signal that the audience was over, and it was Geordie's turn in the limelight. As I walked backwards away from her, the Queen continued to chuckle.

Billy, Geordie, Nick and I and our families went to a hotel round the corner to celebrate.

There was no hiding what had happened from the kids. Mine wanted to know why the Queen only spoke to the four of us and, more importantly, what I had said to make her laugh. My daughter guessed it straight away. 'I bet she asked you a question and then regretted it. She did, didn't she, Dad?'

I officially left the British Army in January 2008 after twenty-three years' service and 3,930 helicopter flying hours, 645 of them in an Apache. I was a born soldier and fighting from the cockpit of an Apache helicopter on operations was the pinnacle of my career.

It was also the last straw. As much as I love the army, the machine and the amazing years it gave me, sooner or later, being away from your family and the worry they go through gets to us all.

The squadron looks very different now; I wasn't the only one to leave after that tour. Now, eighteen months on from the second tour, none of the original Apache pilots are serving with 656 Squadron.

Very shortly, Trigger and two of the four that joined us at the end of 2006 will take thirteen new pilots back out to Camp Bastion for the squadron's third tour of southern Afghanistan. They are lucky people: no pilot could ask for a better leader in the field than the Boss.

Charlotte is his Ops Officer, but plans to leave the army after one final tour of the Helmand to 'make some money'. She will.

Nick went over to 664 Squadron as their Ops Officer and did a third Helmand tour in the summer of 2008. He plans to stay in and I hope he goes as far as we all predicted; the Army Air Corps needs heroes.

FOG left the army at the same time as I did, to fly MD Explorers for the Police.

Darwin, Geordie and Carl were promoted to WO2; Darwin completed his instructional courses and now teaches students to fly

Apaches at Middle Wallop; and Geordie was posted to a specialist military unit to fly civilian helicopters. The two are still incorrigible whenever they are together.

Promotion came too late for Carl and we lost him to the Australian Army. He emigrated to fly the Tiger attack helicopter for the Australian Defence Force and the shrewd Aussies promoted him to captain too.

Billy took a commission and is now a captain, serving as the Assistant Regimental QHI of another Army Air Corps regiment. It's one more step closer to his ultimate dream – to be the most senior pilot in the Corps. He deserves that too.

Because of what we did in Afghanistan, we were told there would always be a threat to us back home in the UK. The more we do, the more the Taliban and their sympathisers hate us; it's the price of success. It's why the MoD affords Apache pilots the same protection as Special Forces; our real names or photographs are never publicly released without our signed permission.

I take sensible but not overly paranoid precautions to protect myself and my family. All my post goes to a special PO Box, I don't vote, and I don't have any contracts. My name doesn't appear on any register or bill and I don't even own my own home – I'm pretty much invisible. To anyone who wants to find me, I'm untraceable. Which does make getting a residents' parking permit a pain in the arse.

But I'm not the sort of person to spend the rest of my life looking over my shoulder or worrying if some radical extremist will wake me up in the middle of the night with a 9-mm silenced pistol. Truth be told, I rarely give it a second thought. The one thing my service taught me is that life's too short to worry.

LCpl Mathew Ford, RM

GLOSSARY OF TERMS

105s: 105mm Light Gun – Towed Artillery used by the Paras and the Marines

2i/c: Second in Command

30 Mike Mike: Military slang for 30 millimetre or the Apache's Cannon rounds

50 Cal: British Forces L1A1 Heavy Machine Gun – 12.7 mm (.50 inch) calibre tripod-mounted or vehicle-mounted automatic

A10: US Forces ground attack warplane nicknamed the Thunderbolt or Warthog

AA: Anti-Aircraft – known as 'Double A'. A large calibre gun used against low-flying aircraft

AAA: Anti-Aircraft Artillery – known as 'Triple A'. Very large calibre artillery pieces used to engage aircraft at higher altitudes than AA

AAC: Army Air Corps – corps of the British Army that operates helicopters and fixed wing aircraft

ADF: Automatic Direction Finder – Radio Navigation System

Affirm: Affirmative – air speak for Yes

Aircrew: People that crew the aircraft: pilots, navigators, door gunners and loadmasters

AH64: AH64A Apache – US Army Apache Attack Helicopter with no Radar, AH64D Longbow Apache – US Army Apache Attack Helicopter with Radar

AK47: Soviet assault rifle – 7.62 mm automatic

Altitude: Height above sea level, rather than ground level

ANA: Afghan National Army

ANP: Afghan National Police

Apache: Apache AH Mk1 – the British Army Apache Attack Helicopter – Built by AgustaWestland and all fitted with the Longbow Radar

APC: Armoured Personnel Carrier

APU: Auxiliary Power Unit – an engine used to power-up the main engines or to provide power to an aircraft on the ground

Armed Helicopter: A helicopter that has had a weapon system fitted but was primarily designed as a weapons platform

ASE: Aircraft Survivability Equipment – the HIDAS

ATO: Ammunition Technical Officer

Attack Helicopter: A helicopter that is designed around being a complete weapon system, rather than a weapon system designed to fit a helicopter

B1: B1 Lancer bomber – US Air Force high altitude long range supersonic strategic bomber

Bag, the: A blacked-out cockpit used to teach Apache pilots how to fly at night with sole reference from the monocle

Battlegroup: A battalion-sized fighting force

BDA: Battle Damage Assessment

Beirut unload: A rough and ready way of firing at something without risking the life of the firer. The firer stands behind cover and places the weapon over or around a wall and fires a full magazine of ammunition in the rough direction of the intended target – name derived from the methods of firing used in Beirut

Bergen: Army slang for a rucksack

Berm: A man-made ridge of earth, designed as an obstacle

Bingo: A nominated fuel amount that allows the Apache patrol commander enough warning to call for a RIP or to inform the ground troops that they have limited Apache time remaining

Bitching Betty: The Apache's female cockpit voice warning system

Black Brain: The black kneeboard Apache pilots fly with on their thigh that contains everything that can't be committed to memory and may be needed instantly in flight

Bone: The callsign for the US Air Force B1 Lancer bomber

BRF: Brigade Recce Force – recce troops for 3 Commando Brigade

Brigade: 3 or 4 regiments of troops with all supporting troops

Buster: Fly at the fastest speed possible

C130: Hercules – a 4 propped military fixed wing transport plane used by most countries to move troops and equipment

C17: Boeing C17 Globemaster III – large US Air Force Strategic/Tactical Transport Plane

Calibre: The inside diameter of the barrel of a weapon

Carbine: Short barrelled SA80 with a pistol grip at the front – used by Apache pilots and tank crews – 5.56 mm automatic

Casevac: Casualty Evacuation

Cdo: Commando

CDS: Chief of the Defence Staff

CGS: Chief of the General Staff

CH47: Chinook – a large wide-bodied helicopter with two rotors on the top. Used by many countries for carrying troops – may also carry equipment inside or underslung below

Chicken Fuel: Just enough fuel to make it back direct line and land with the minimum fuel allowance

Chinook: See CH47

CIA: Central Intelligence Agency – US Government Intelligence

CMSL: CPG (Apache Gunner) has actioned the missile system – CPG's Missiles

CO: Commanding Officer – Lieutenant Colonel in charge of a regiment, battalion or the JHF

Coalition: National Military Forces working together as one force

Collective Lever: The flying control to the left-hand side of the pilot's seat; held in the left hand; when raised the Apache climbs and when lowered it descends

Combat Gas: Fuel that can be used at the target – this does not include transit fuel

Co-op: Co-operative rocket shoot – both of the Apaches' crew working together to fire the rockets at the target

Cow: Taliban slang for the Chinook helicopter

CPG: Co-pilot Gunner – Front seat pilot in the Apache, known as 'The Gunner'

Crow: Derogatory military slang for a very junior paratrooper

CRKT: CPG (Apache Gunner) has actioned the rocket system – CPG's Rockets

CRV7: Canadian Rocket Vehicle 7 – the Apache's rockets

Crypto: Cryptographic – Encoded information

Cyclic Stick: The flying control between the pilot's legs, held by the right hand and used to speed up, slow down, dive and turn the Apache

Danger Close: The proximity to a weapon's effect that is considered the last safe point when wearing body armour and combat helmets

Dasht-e-Margo: Desert of Death

DC: District Centre – the commercial/political/military centre of a particular area. Usually a building that once held power

Deep Raid: Striking the enemy deep within their own held territory without taking ground

Delta Hotel: Phonetic Alphabet for DH – air speak for Direct Hit – call made when a weapon system hits its intended target accurately

Desert Hawk: Small British UAV

DFC: Distinguished Flying Cross – awarded in recognition of exemplary gallantry during active operations against the enemy in the air

DGSE: Direction Générale de la Sécurité – General Directorate for External Security – French Intelligence Agency

Dishdash: Loose kaftan-style outfit worn by many Afghan men
Doorman: Callsign for the British casevac Chinook
DPM: Disruptive Pattern Material – camouflaged print used on clothing and equipment
DTV: Day Television Camera – black and white TV image generated from the day camera in the TADS
DU: Depleted Uranium – kinetic bullets used by the A10
Dushka: Nickname of the DShK – Soviet built Anti-Aircraft Machine Gun – 12.7 mm (.50 cal)
Engine Power Levers: The throttles used for starting the Apache's engines
ETA: Estimated Time of Arrival
EWO: Electronic Warfare Officer
F18: US Navy strike warplane called the Hornet – very similar cockpit to the Apache but less busy
Fast Air: Offensive military jet aircraft
FCR: Fire Control Radar – the Apache's Longbow Radar
Firebase: Friendly Forces firing position used to cover an assault
Flanking: From the side
Flares: Hot flares fired to attract heat-seeking missiles, luring them away from the Apache
Flechette: Eighty-five-inch tungsten darts fired from a rocket travelling above Mach 2
FLIR: Forward Looking Infrared. Sights that generate a thermal picture – an image produced by an object's heat source
Fly-by-wire: Flying the helicopter using sensors from the controls like a PlayStation control works. A Back Up flight Control System (BUCS) used when control runs are shot through
FM Radio: A Frequency Modulated secure radio in the Apache
Force 84: British Special Forces operating in Afghanistan
Formate: Aviation term for formation flying
Frag: Fragments of hot metal that break away from a shell when it explodes
Fragged: As published in the orders
Frago: Fragmented Orders – extracted part of a full set of orders
Fuselage: Main body of an aircraft
GAFA: Great Afghan Fuck All – Dasht-e-Margo – the Desert of Death
GAU8: Gatling gun fitted to an A10 ground attack aircraft
GBU: Guided Bomb Unit – smart bombs
GCHQ: British Government Communications Headquarters – Intelligence and Security Organisation
GPMG: British Forces General Purpose Machine Gun – 7.62 mm bipod machine gun

GPS: Global Positioning System – satellite navigation equipment

GR7: Harrier GR7 – Royal Air Force warplane capable of Vertical Take Off and Landing (VTOL)

Green Zone: Lush habitation of irrigated fields, hedgerows, trees and small woods on either side of the Helmand River, bordered by arid deserts

Groundcrew: People who work with aircraft when they are on the ground, not technicians

Ground school: Academic lessons on flying and all to do with flying; met, law, engines, etc.

Gunship: An aircraft that has the capability of firing its cannon/s from the side instead of having to strafe head-on

Gun tape: The video tape put into an Apache that records what the selected sight sees

Harrier: See GR7

H Hour: The moment offensive action begins – first bullet, bomb or the moment troops walk towards their intended target to attack

HEDP: High Explosive Dual Purpose – 30 mm cannon rounds

Height: The height above the ground

HEISAP: High Explosive Incendiary Semi-Armour Piercing – kinetic rocket fired by the Apache

Hellfire: AGM-114K SAL (Semi-Active Laser) Hellfire II is a laser-guided Hellfire missile fitted to the Apache and Predator

Hercules: See C130

Hesco Bastion: Square metal meshed cubes lined with Hessian and filled with rubble and/or sand. Used as defensive ramparts to protect bases and platoon houses from fire

HIDAS: Helicopter Integrated Defensive Aid System – protection from SAMs

HIG: Hezb-I Islami Gulbuddin – major group of the old Mujahideen with ties to Osama bin Laden referred to in this book as Taliban

HLS: Helicopter Landing Site

Hot: Air speak for clearance or acknowledgment that live bombs can be dropped

HQ: Headquarters – The nerve centre for planning and execution of operations

HRF: Helmand Reaction Force – 2 Apaches and a Chinook full of soldiers on standby at Bastion used to bolster any troops on the ground quickly

HumInt: Human Intelligence – intelligence provided by human sources; spies, snitches, etc.

I Bar: See Steering Cursor

ID: Identification

IED: Improvised Explosive Device – homemade bombs or multiple mines strapped together

IRA: Irish Republican Army – Northern Irish Para-military group

IRT: Incident Response Team – Apaches, Chinooks, doctors, medics and ATO responsible for the immediate recovery of personnel in danger or injured

ISAF: International Security Assistance Force – multi-national military force in Afghanistan

ISI: Directorate for Inter-Services Intelligence – Pakistan's Intelligence Agency

ISTAR: Intelligence, Surveillance, Target Acquisition and Reconnaissance

IX Battlegroup: The Information Exploitation Battlegroup – Magowan's troops

JDAM: Joint Direct Attack Munition Inertial Navigation and GPS guidance system bolted onto a 500 to 2000lb bomb to make it an accurate all-weather weapon

Joint Helicopter Command: The UK-based command headquarters and operating authority for all British military helicopters in the UK and abroad

JHF: JHF (A) – Joint Helicopter Force in Afghanistan – 'Main' at Kandahar and 'Forward' at Camp Bastion – the Afghanistan helicopter headquarters operating under authority for the JHC

JOC: Joint Operations Cell – the functioning control centre of operations in the Helmand province

JTAC: Joint Terminal Attack Controller – soldier responsible to his commander for the deliverance of air ordnance from combat aircraft onto a target. The airspace controller above a battle, normally callsigns Widow or Knight Rider

Klicks: Military slang for kilometres

KIA: Killed in action

Knight Rider: Callsign for the BRF JTAC's

Lance Bombardier: Artillery Rank – the second rung on the ladder after private/marine

LCpl: Lance Corporal – rank – the second rung on the ladder after private/marine

Leakers: Taliban that are attempting to escape (leak) from a target area

Lima Charlie: Phonetic alphabet for LC – air speak for Loud and Clear

Loadie: Loadmaster responsible for passengers and equipment in military troop-carrying helicopters or transport aircraft

Longbow: The Longbow Radar is the Apache's Fire Control Radar. It looks like a large Swiss cheese and sits on top of the main rotor system

LS: Landing Site

LSJ: Life Support Jacket – survival waistcoat

Lynx: British Army Light Battlefield Helicopter – used for movement of small teams

M230: The cannon on the underside of the Apache; 30mm chain fed

ManPADS: Man Portable Aid Defence System – shoulder-launched heat-seeking missile

MC: Military Cross – awarded in recognition of exemplary gallantry during active operations against the enemy on land.

MI6: Military Intelligence Section 6 – nickname for the British Government's Secret Intelligence Service

MIA: Missing in action

MiD: Mentioned in Despatches – award for gallantry or otherwise commendable service

MIRC: Military Internet Relay Chat

MoD: Ministry of Defence

Monocle: The pink see-through glass mirror over an Apache pilot's right eye that displays green symbology and images from the onboard computers and sights

Mosquito: Taliban slang for the Apache

MPD: Multi-Purpose Display – 5-inch screen on the console in the Apache

MSR: Main Supply Route – route for equipment and personnel

Mujahideen: Afghan opposition groups – fought the Soviets during the Soviet invasion and each other in the Afghan Civil War – plural for the word mujahid meaning 'struggler'

NAAFI: Navy, Army and Air Forces Institute – a British military shop and café

NATO: North Atlantic Treaty Organisation – multi-national military force

Negative: Air speak for No

Nimrod MR2: Royal Air Force large-bodied jet that is used as a spy plane

NSA: National Security Agency – US Government's communications intelligence (same as GCHQ)

NVG: Night Vision Goggles – night sights that magnify light by 40,000 times

OC: Officer Commanding – Major in charge of a Squadron or Company group

Ops: Operations – as in Ops tent, Ops room, Ops Officer or literally an operation

ORT: Optical Relay Tube – the large console in the front seat with PlayStation type grips on either side

P Company: Gruelling fitness tests used by the Parachute Regiment to test suitable candidates for parachute training and airborne forces

Para: Nickname for a soldier from the Parachute Regiment or the Regiment itself

Paveway: Laser Guided Bomb (LGB) – the laser guidance system bolted onto 500–2000 lb bombs

Pepper-Potting: One patrol goes firm. The other passes it and goes firm. Then the original patrol passes and goes firm. On and on – one foot on the ground at all times advancing forward or backwards

Pinzgauer: Small 4x4 All Terrain Utility Truck

Piss Boy: The loser of a game who has to make the tea and coffee

PJHQ: Permanent Joint Headquarters – located at Northwood; Commands overseas joint and combined military operations and provides military advice to the Ministry of Defence.

PK: Soviet designed General Purpose Machine Gun – 7.62mm bipod machine gun

PNVS: Pilot's Night Vision System – the thermal camera that sits above the TADS on the Apache's nose

Pongo: Derogatory slang used by the Royal Navy and Royal Air Force for Army soldiers

Port: Left-hand side of an aircraft or vessel

Predator: Large US UAV that contains sophisticated sights and radios similar to those on the Apache. It can be armed with Hellfire

PX: Post Exchange – huge US Military shop that sells almost anything

QHI: Qualified Helicopter Instructor – flying instructor

R and R: Rest and Recuperation – break from combat

RAF: Royal Air Force

Rearm: Reload the Apache with ammunition

REME: Royal Electrical and Mechanical Engineers

RIP: Relief in Place – Apache Flights handing over the battle between each other maintaining support to the ground troops

RM: Royal Marine/s

RMP: Royal Military Police – British Military Police

ROE: Rules of Engagement – law set by a country's Government laying down the rules as to which arms may be brought to bear

Rocco: Rocco Siffredi – Italian actor, director and producer of pornographic movies

RPG: Soviet designed Rocket Propelled Grenade – shoulder launched rocket with a powerful grenade warhead on the front

RSM: Regimental Sergeant Major – WO1 and the senior soldier in a Regiment

RTB: Return To Base

RTA: Road Traffic Accident

RTS: Release to Service – the document that details what can and can't be done with the Apache regarding flight, firing, etc.

RV: Rendezvous – designated meeting place

SA7/14: Soviet-designed Surface to Air Missiles – ManPADS

SA80: British Forces Rifle – 5.56mm automatic

SAM: Surface to Air Missile

Sappers: Military engineers – slang for the Royal Engineers

SAS: Special Air Service – an independent British Special Forces Unit of the British Army

Sausage Side: A term for enemy territory dating back to the World Wars. The sausage loving Germans' side of the battlefield

SBS: Special Boat Service – an independent British Special Forces Unit of the Royal Navy's Royal Marines

Scimitar: British Army Armoured Recce Vehicle

SERE: Survive, Evade, Resist and Extract

SF: Special Forces – e.g. SAS and SBS

SIB: Special Investigation Branch – detectives of the RMP

SigInt: Signal Intelligence – intelligence gained from radio, telephone, texts and email intercepts

Small Arms: Infantry light weapons – pistols, rifles and machine guns – weapons capable of being fired by a foot soldier on the move

Snatch: Lightly armoured military Land Rover

Spoof: Game played with coins to decide who has to do a task

Spooks: Nickname for spies

SRR: Special Reconnaissance Regiment – an independent British Special Forces Unit of the British Army, specialising in close target reconnaissance

Stack: Fast Air that is queued up and held before being passed on to whoever is in need of its offensive capability

Standby Standby: Warning call to watch out for something

Starboard: Right-hand side of an aircraft or vessel

Steering Cursor: The rocket symbol used to line up the Apache so the rockets land on the target, also known as the 'I' Bar

Stingers: US-designed Surface to Air ManPADs (Man Portable Air Defence system) missile. Taliban slang for any shoulder-launched surface to air missile

Sunray: Callsign for a commander

SUSAT: Sight Unit Small Arms, Trilux – the 4-times magnification day/night sight that sits on top of an SA80 rifle or SA80 carbine

Symbology: Flying and targeting information beamed onto the monocle

T1: Triage Casualty Code 1 – needs to be in an operating theatre within an hour to save life

T2: Triage Casualty Code 2 – needs to be in an operating theatre quickly before they become T1

T3: Triage Casualty Code 3 – injured and needs medical help

T4: Triage Casualty Code 4 – dead

TADS: Target Acquisition and Designation Sight system – the 'bucket' on the nose of the Apache that houses the Apache's cameras

Taliban: Collective term used in this book for Taliban, Al Qaeda and Hezb-I Islami Gulbuddin (HIG)

Theatre: Country or area in which troops are conducting operations

Thermobaric: Enhanced blast Hellfire – thermobaric means heat and pressure

Topman: Callsign for the British Harrier

Tornado: Royal Air Force multi-role strike warplane

TOC: Tactical Operations Cell

TOT: Time On Target – the time until an aircraft is due over or weapon is due at the target

TOW: Tube-launched Optically-tracked Wire-guided anti-tank missile – fired from the British Army Lynx helicopter

TPF: Tactical Planning Facility – mobile planning room

TPM: Terrain Profile Mode – the Longbow's terrain mapping mode

Tracer: Bullets that burn with a red, orange or green glow from 110m to 1100m so they can be seen

Tusk: Callsign for the A10 Thunderbolt aircraft

UAV: Unmanned Aerial Vehicle

UFD: Up Front Display – an LED instrument that displays critical information to the Apache crews

Ugly: The callsign chosen by 656 Sqn for the British Apaches – 'Ugly Five Zero to Ugly Five Seven'

USAF: United States Air Force

Viking: Armoured amphibious tracked vehicle

VIP: Very Important Person

VU Radio: A VHF and UHF capable secure radio in the Apache

Widow: Callsign for normal JTACs in Afghanistan

Wingman: The other aircraft in any pair of aircraft

Wizard: Callsign for the Nimrod MR2

WMIK: Weapons Mounted Installation Kit – an odd-looking Land Rover with bars all over it to which weapons can be attached

WO1: A soldier who holds a Royal Warrant is known as Warrant Officer – a WO1; Class one is the highest non-commissioned rank in the British Army

Wombat: Weapon Of Magnesium Battalion Anti-Tank – a huge wheeled or mounted rifle barrel

Zulu Company: A company of marines detached from 45 Commando to the Information Exploitation (IX) Battlegroup for this tour of Afghanistan

ZPU: Soviet Anti-Aircraft Gun – 14.5mm – ZPU 1 is single-barrelled, ZPU 2 has twin barrels and the ZPU 4 has quadruple barrels

ACKNOWLEDGEMENTS

Thank you, Emily, my soul mate, for the love and the freedom to catch my dream and for supporting me in my choice. Thank you also for finding and for pushing me in the direction of my friend and agent Mark Lucas.

Thank you, Mark, for believing that my stories were good enough to tell, and for priceless guidance and advice. Thanks also to Mindy for putting up with my calls at every conceivable hour, and to Alice for keeping me in check.

My sincere gratitude to Tom Newton Dunn for tireless dedication in helping me to tell my story, and to Dominie and Rebekah Wade for putting up with Tom's absences. And huge thanks to wee Arthur for keeping Tom sane.

The groundcrew and technicians are the unsung heroes of the Apache squadrons and the JHF (A). Thank you for your unswerving professionalism.

Chris, Billy, Geordie, Carl and my fellow Apache aviators in 656 Squadron – my door is always open and for once words fail me.

Thanks to Colonel Rob Magowan MBE RM for taking the time to explain the bigger picture and, more importantly, for having the confidence to allow us to return Mathew to his family.

I owe a special thank you to the old DAAvn, Brigadier Thomson, for his support in the aftermath of the Fort, to the new DAAvn, Brigadier Short, and to Colonel Turner for supporting me in the writing of this book.

Arabella Pike, John Bond and everyone at HarperPress, I can't thank you enough for your support, enthusiasm and sheer hard work.

To everyone in Mathew's family, especially Joan, Bootsy and Ina, thank you for allowing me to tell my story.

I am eternally grateful to my wonderful Dad and the British Army for making me who I am today.

To my children, my little AAC: you are my world.

Thank you to my family and friends who have supported me throughout.

INDEX